People Under Hitler

by WALLACE R. DEUEL

NEW YORK

HARCOURT, BRACE AND COMPANY

THIS BOOK IS FOR MARY

Jl '42

Note

This book is the story of the human beings involved in the greatest tragedy of modern times—the nazi revolution, culminating in the Second World War. The human beings most intimately involved in this tragedy are the Germans, and this book is, accordingly, mostly about them. But every other people in the world is involved in the tragedy too, and so this book is about all the others as well.

What was there in the lives of the German people, and all the others, that made the nazi revolution and the Second War possible? What are the revolution and the war, in turn, doing to the human beings upon whom they impinge? This book tries to answer these questions. It tries to answer them with special reference to the Germans: to tell why the Germans turned to national socialism in the first place, and what national socialism has done to their lives, and how the Germans feel about what has happened to their lives.

The nazis proclaim that they are establishing a New World Order. This book tells what that New Order, that Brave New World, is like, and it tells who the men are who are trying to establish it, and how they are going about it and why and how they have been able to come so near to succeeding.

In the immediate sense, this book is about Europe. The crimes and blunders it reports are in the first instance crimes and blunders committed by Europeans. But it would be naive and pharisaical, indeed dangerous now that we are at war, to suppose that this report gives Americans or anybody else grounds for complacence. In this appalling tragedy and this appalling danger, nobody has any grounds for complacence because nobody is innocent of crimes and blunders of his own which, unless they are remedied in time, can cause the same sorts of catastrophes in America that they have already caused in Europe.

Most of those who have helped the most to make the writing of this book possible cannot be thanked by name. Neither their identities nor the nature and extent of their help can even be hinted at. A deep sense of indebtedness and gratitude for their help can at least be avowed in these general terms, however, and the hope expressed that it may some time be possible to acknowledge the debt more openly.

At least one major debt of gratitude may, however, be acknowledged: The Chicago *Daily News* has generously permitted the use of material which first appeared in its columns.

W. R. D.

Saugatuck, Conn.

Contents

People Under Hitler

Prelude: Apocalypse

. . . the beast that was, and is not, and yet is.

REVELATION XVII, 8.

A PALE, DAEMONIC MAN with a comedian's mustache, wearing a field-gray tunic and black trousers, stood in the speaker's rostrum of the Kroll Opera House in Berlin and told the world that there was war again.

It was hot in the Opera House that morning of September 1 —very hot, and humid. The dark-red walls and maroon carpets and the great, bright, lighted eagle rampant on the silver backdrop there behind the man made it seem even hotter, even more humid. Perspiration stood out on the faces of the severally uniformed deputies who filled the main floor seats, men thick and savage and intent, like wild boars just before a kill. There was perspiration on the faces of the cabinet ministers and their aides, all of them uniformed, too, on the benches that flanked the man on either side; on the face of Field Marshal Goering, baleful in the president's place above and behind the man, and on the faces of the diplomats and guests in the boxes and balconies. But the heavy, humid air ached with the tension of the most terrible of all tragedies. Few thought to wipe the perspiration off.

"Since 5:45 o'clock this morning," Hitler said, "the fire has been returned. . . ."

This, then, was Apocalypse. This was war. No matter what else might come, the world would never be quite the same again after those words had been spoken, this deed done. The world

3

of 1939 was gone, just as the world of 1914, too, had gone, and all the other worlds that wars had destroyed.

The deputies and the guests and diplomats listened—listened for their lives.

There had been reports in the outside world that Hitler was "weakening." These reports, too, were part of the nightmare. There had always been such reports in every crisis. This time they were even more false than they always had been before. Weakening? The man had plunged the whole world into war. It was a strange kind of weakness.

In what Hitler said, too, were the repetitiousness and unreality of the nightmare. He began, as he had begun a thousand times before, by denouncing the Treaty of Versailles. The ideas were the same, the words were the same, the voice was the same. Then he denounced the clauses of the Treaty dealing with Danzig and the Polish Corridor in particular. He had made proposals to Poland for the revision of these clauses, he said. The Poles had rejected his proposals. He had warned the Poles. The Poles had defied him. Defied by Poles! Outrage blared in the man's voice. The Poles had attacked Germans, had attacked the Reich itself, the man said, just as he had said the Czechs had done— the Czechs and the others, each in their turn. And so, the man said, "I therefore determined to speak to the Poles in the same language as that in which they had been speaking to us for months!"

He had no claims to make of Western Europe, Hitler said: "I have given formal assurances, and I repeat, that we demand nothing from the Western Powers and that we shall never demand anything."

Again the air of nightmare repetitiousness and nightmare unreality. How many times had assurances like these been heard before by these same dark-red walls, by this same great, bright eagle, by these same listeners?

Then a muted echo of 1914; once again the Italian ally stood aside. "I should like above all, here," the Chancellor said, "to thank Italy, which has supported us throughout this entire time. You will understand, however," he said, "that I do not wish to appeal for foreign help for the conduct of this struggle."

Gamelin had said, "Let Italy join the Germans this time. It will take five French divisions to beat her if she is against us, ten to watch her if she stays neutral, and fifteen to save her if she is on our side."

It was to be as Gamelin had said. This time it would be the Germans who would have to save the Italians. Most Germans sensed that this was so. It would not matter much, whatever the Italians did. But meanwhile Italy stood aside again, just as it had in 1914. It was appropriate that Italy should do the same thing now that it had done before. That, too, was part of the nightmare.

The pale, daemonic man went on. It was more than a declaration of war, this speech, this avowal, he was making. It was a declaration of personal faith, of self-immolation. Seldom can a world disaster have been more completely and more openly identified with its principal author by that same author himself.

"If I have called upon the armed forces and if I require sacrifices of the German people and, if necessary, the ultimate sacrifice, then I have a right to do so," Hitler said. "For I myself am just as ready today as I once was before to make every personal sacrifice. I require of no German anything other than what I myself was prepared to do voluntarily for more than four years.

"There shall be no privation in Germany which I myself do not also accept," Hitler said. "My whole life belongs to my people from now on in a new sense. I wish nothing other than to be the first soldier of the German Reich. I have therefore put on that tunic which once before was the dearest and most sacred to me, and I shall take it off only after victory has been won— or I shall not live to experience the end."

He meant it all, this strange, daemonic man. That made it worse. It was morbid and tormented and agonized, this open flaying of nerves, this public, exhibitionist orgasm of a soul.

There was something incredible about it, too. There stood the pale man in the field-gray tunic, calling down the lightning of war, and directly opposite him in the diplomatic gallery sat the representatives of the powers in the West (the Pole was already gone from the gallery) on which he called it down.

From that moment, these men were consecrated to each other's destruction. This was war. There was no way out. Yet the proprieties were sacred, were inviolate: the lightning would strike, but it would strike later. It was not time for it yet.

Hitler spoke for 34 minutes. It seems to have been the shortest recorded speech he ever delivered to a Reichstag.

THE CITY AT THE BOTTOM OF A SEA

That night, the lights went out. "The lamps are going out all over Europe," Sir Edward Grey had said in 1914; "we shall not see them lit again in our lifetime." It had been a figure of speech then; now it was a statement of literal fact, too.

Busses ran with only single, ghoulish blue lights. Street cars had faint illumination on their route numbers, but inside all the lights were shrouded in black cloth hoods. Automobile head lights were blackened except for narrow slits. A faint square of paleness glowed here and there through darkening material that was not quite opaque on a window. Street arc lamps showed only minute green flames on amber mantles. The only bright sparks in the blackness were the fiery red tail lights of the cars and the blinding blue flashes from an occasional trolley.

Otherwise the city lay in darkness, a capital of 4,000,000 people, almost completely dark and, so it seemed, almost completely still, like a lost city at the bottom of a sea. Pedestrians and traffic moved more slowly, hesitating at corners and at crossings. People spoke quietly. The infrequent bark of a dog startled sharply in the hush.

Only the Recording Angel knows what was in the minds of the 4,000,000 human beings wrapped in that darkness and that hush. But any mere mortal could tell what was in the minds of lovers. Whatever Mars was about in the darkness, there was no mystery as to what Venus was about. The darkness was kind to love, and the fact of war quickened and enlivened it and lovers made the most of their opportunities. Whether it was murmurings or gigglings that came from the park benches, or pulsing silence, there was life in the midst of the darkness ordained to fend off death.

LORD'S DAY

When France and England declared war two days later, it was almost a relief. People had not liked the waiting.

It was at twenty-nine and one-half minutes after 1 o'clock on a still, hot, sunny Sunday afternoon that the Germans finally learned that they were at war with England again. They learned it from the radio. Played by the Hamburg station orchestra, a program of classical music was being broadcast on a national network. At 1:22 o'clock, midway through Liszt's "First Hungarian Rhapsody," the music faded out. A man's voice said, urgently: "Attention! Attention! In a few minutes we shall make an important announcement." The voice stopped, and the music faded in again. The orchestra finished the "Rhapsody." Then came the announcement:

"The British government, in a note to the Reich government, has made the demand that the German troops which have advanced into Polish territory be withdrawn to their original positions," the voice said. "At 9 o'clock this morning the British Ambassador in Berlin informed the Reich government in a provocative note that if a satisfactory answer was not received by 11 o'clock, England would consider itself in a state of war with Germany. . . ."

Outside, the trees stood still in the sun. The light shimmered on the leaves as though reflected from a quiet stream. A street car clacked through a switch. A bird scolded and a child cried.

Inside, there came from the radio the voice that said war. The ultimatum had expired at 11 o'clock. The Ambassador had called at the Chancellory shortly after 11 to ask for his passports.

It was the Sabbath, the Lord's Day. All the church bells of the city must have been ringing for morning service as the Ambassador went down the Wilhelmstrasse.

Once again it all seemed incredible, unreal. War? It was impossible. It was a dream, a nightmare. It had not happened, it was not happening; it had happened to somebody else, somewhere else, at some other time.

And yet the voice went on. It really was war. There were

the times, the places, the people, the papers. Everything was quite in accordance with protocol. All the proper formalities had been observed. All the proper honors had been rendered. All the proper courtesies had been exchanged.

Only the people in the streets still did not seem to believe it. The sidewalk cafes along Kurfuerstendamm were well filled. There were no more uniforms than usual to be seen. A car with a diplomatic license, piled high inside with clothes and rugs, stopped at an intersection, and a man called out from the sidewalk, "You'd better get out of here!" But nobody paid any attention to either the man or the car. A few feet away a fat, berouged and painfully corseted woman of 50 did not even take her greedy eyes off a new model evening gown in a shop window to see what was happening.

In the Tiergarten, the people in their Sunday clothes walked slowly along the paths pushing their baby buggies and leading their dogs on leashes like any other Sunday crowd. The only gatherings of people in the park were those watching the spindly-tailed red squirrels begging for nuts.

There was a crowd in the Wilhelmstrasse, but it was a quiet, subdued and orderly crowd, moving as slowly as fish in a tank, and with as little sign of feeling, looking with only blank interest, at the big, canary-yellow painted stone British Embassy with the lion and the unicorn on the double doors, and standing silently across from the Chancellory down the street.

In the East, only half an hour away as the bomber flies, the big guns were belching, the machine guns were gibbering and the long lines of tanks and troops were moving up and men were fighting and dying. Yet in Berlin it was all still incredible. For years it had been said that the next war would begin with lightning attacks in full force and without declarations of war, and that, to be sure, had happened in the East. But what was happening in the West? There was war, declared with every conceivable solemnity, and yet there were no hostilities in the West at all, as far as the Berliners knew. Nor was anything said about France. There was war with England. But was there war with France, too? Everybody assumed it was only a question of hours, but nobody really knew anything.

It was only the diplomats, so far, to whom the war was real. Plain clothes and uniformed police were posted outside the British Embassy—although not yet at the French—and communication with the British by telephone was cut and callers were prevented from entering. The American Embassy took formal charge. There were only two instances of momentary disconcertment: The first occurred when the red wax used for sealing premises and papers spluttered, and official fingers were burned. The second occurred when a box was opened which a young British secretary had solemnly confided to the care of an American colleague and the box was found to contain live lobsters.

HUMANITY UPROOTED

There was a hush of waiting and suspense along the Western Front that week end of Apocalypse, too, waiting and suspense for the guns to speak, for the bombers to fly. They did not speak or fly that week end. They were not to speak or fly in real earnest for more than eight long months. But neither Paris nor Berlin knew in advance how long they would be still and silent, and so the civil populations on both sides were evacuated from their homes.

The Germans along the Rhine were allowed to stay, but those in a Red Zone of presumably greater danger in the Saar-Pfalz had to go. More than half a million human beings were moved out on the German side that week end. The sick and infirm, the aged and the children under 10, were evacuated in special trains beginning Friday. All the others between 10 and 60 had to go on foot. Orders for their evacuation were issued at 3 o'clock Sunday afternoon. The people were given two hours to lock up their homes and get to the appointed gathering places, leaving most things as they were. War had been declared, the orders said, and there was no time to lose.

But if war had been declared, then where were the bombers and why were the guns still silent—the bombers that everybody knew were waiting in hundreds at their bases, the guns that everybody had seen in the fields and everybody had guessed were in the new "farm houses" and "barns" the army engineers had built so thickly through the countryside? The guns were silent, the skies empty. Here at the Front, too, the war was unreal.

But the people had to go, anyway. The uprooting of humanity had begun—although only just begun. The peoples were on trek.

It was all organized down to the last detail. Roads and rails were choked with the troops moving up to the Front, but two trains were reserved for the last of those who could not walk, and two highways were kept open a few hours for the escape of those who went on foot.

It was hot and sultry in the Red Zone up to midafternoon that Sunday. Then, just before the time set for departure, the skies dulled and darkened and a cloudburst struck. Bowed under the torrent and the weight of their possessions, drenched, sodden and buffeted by the storm, the half million trudged to their meeting places; they huddled there until their turns came and they set out for the interior: men, women, young people, carrying as much as they could, leaving their homes and fields and setting out on foot into a future none could foresee. Most of them had to walk 10 to 15 miles that afternoon and evening through the storm to reach the points from which they were sent on by bus and train to their temporary homes.

Army engineers had already laid charges of high explosive at the bridges. As the last refugee train was about to leave Merzig, lightning struck one of the charges and blew up the bridge over the Saar.

THE APOCALYPSE THAT WAS AN ANTI-CLIMAX

In Berlin, then, and even in the Red Zone, Apocalypse was an anti-climax. Its horrors had threatened too often. They were too great to be grasped. They did not even happen yet and, besides, the people were too tired. They were tired as few peoples have ever been tired without breaking: worn-out, dazed, numb, despairing and confused. They had been through too much. Too many other terrors had gone before, too many other shocks and strains and disillusionments. There had been the other war and the other blockade. There had been starvation. There had been the other revolution. There had been a bitter peace. There had been inflation and deflation and panic and depression, and party and racial strife and civil war and fighting in the streets. Then there had been the new revolution and the new preparations for war and the new crisis. Now there was the new war itself.

Germany had risen again as a great and threatening power, but the price in wear and tear on the German people, too, as well as on the others, had been appalling. The sale of nerve medicines and sleep-inducing drugs had increased year by year, and so had the sale of alcohol (and not merely because so many people were better off). People were more irritable, more often absent from work, more often ill. The war of nerves was more than a metaphor. It was a literally shocking organic ordeal to those who were its victims.

The individual human organism mobilizes for danger just as the social organism does (or perishes), mobilizes on a total scale, and the process is just as violent and just as costly in the one case as in the other, can be just as disastrous if too often undertaken. It little mattered whether it had been fear or rage that people had felt in the recurrent crises and in the final shock of war. The visceral reactions had been the same, had, in the end, wrought equal havoc. For adrenin is no respecter of persons, no umpire of emotions, and neither are the neurones of the sympathetic nervous system, and these are the vehicles of "the stormy processes of the thalamus" which Hitler had unleashed, the processes by which the organism prepares for the dangers he had so often threatened and had now invoked.

When there is danger, the body's reactions are swift and sweeping; impulses race out along the fibers of the sympathetic system, the tiny glands by the kidneys inject adrenin into the blood. Digestion stops. The heart pounds. The lungs labor. The blood rushes under a new head of pressure to the brain, the lungs, the muscles of the arms and legs. The liver yields up sugar, the spleen, red corpuscles. The blood is quickened to coagulate. The cold sweat the tellers of tales tell about, the hair that stands on end, the flesh that creeps—these are the further symptoms of the body's readiness, a readiness for either fight or flight, in either rage or fear.

"The question which of the two impulses we shall follow," says James, "is usually decided by some one of those collateral circumstances of the particular case, to be moved by which is the mark of superior mental natures."

But the requirements likely to be laid upon the body are the same, no matter what the "collateral circumstances" may decide—and no matter how superior the mental nature. In fight or flight or struggle to escape there will be violent exertion and some likelihood of wounds. The preparations of the body are, accordingly, likewise the same. The quick coagulation of the blood will help check hemorrhage, the laboring muscles will be better energized by sugar, better rid of waste by red corpuscles.

It is a startlingly efficient plan of preparation. It has helped to keep the race alive. But it is also an expensive plan. It takes a heavy toll if tried too often. The toll may be a greater or a lesser one, depending on the person and on circumstance. But the processes of total preparation take some toll of everyone. For in everyone they are reflex, instinctive and involuntary. No cortex can inhibit, no will control them. The most the will can do is repress their outward show, and this, too, has its dangers, for the inner storm still rages.

"If tears or anger are simply suppressed," says James, "whilst the object of grief or rage remains unchanged before the mind, the current which would have invaded the normal channels turns into others, for it must find some outlet of escape. It may then work different and worse effects later on. Thus vengeful brooding may replace a burst of indignation; a dry heat may consume the frame of one who fain would weep, or he may, as Dante says, turn to stone within."

But these were precisely the circumstances of the war of nerves. The shocks to fear and rage were repeatedly given, the "stormy processes of the thalamus" unleashed. Even between the crises, the reminders were constantly there, the ever-present sense of danger. The blare of martial music, the thud of booted feet, the snarl of a voice on the radio, mere recollection, some inner prompting whose outer source was hidden—these things, too, could set the powder train afire. But then, most often, nothing happened. There was nothing that people could do. The object of grief or rage remained unchanged before the mind, but tears and anger were suppressed. Blocked from its normal channels, the current turned to others, for it had to find some outlet of escape. It worked its different but its worse effects thereafter. It was no wonder that the people found Apocalypse an anticlimax. They could not even feel it. Too many of them had turned to stone within.

I

Sons of Chaos

1. The Germans: Are They Human?

If you inquire what the people are like here,
I must answer, "The same as everywhere!"

GOETHE

He thinks too much; such men are dangerous.

SHAKESPEARE

The German people are so strong that they can
even stand a Hitler.

ADOLF HITLER

THERE IS AN OLD SAYING that national character is the last resort of baffled historians, and certainly some of the judgments
of national character in which historians (mostly amateurs) have
indulged, and some of the uses to which these judgments have
been put, seem to justify the reproach.

Thus the French are commonly supposed to be immoral, for
example, the British supercilious, and the Italians excitable and
credulous and childlike, whereas the truth of the matter is that
the French are among the most moral of all peoples, the British
among the shyest, and the Italians among the most skeptical,
not to say cynical, with the skepticism and cynicism of a long
history and, in this sense, of great age, and among the most
difficult of all peoples to move to any real excitement or enthusiasm on any grounds whatever.

Misjudgments of national character like these have befuddled
the study of national history and politics in positively startling
measure. For these and other apocryphal qualities have been

held to explain everything from the French Revolution to the tawdry proceedings at Vichy, from Magna Carta to the Munich Conference, and from the Holy Roman Catholic Apostolic Church to fascism—"which," as the more cautious mathematicians would say, "is absurd."

The consideration of national character abounds in snares and pitfalls for the unwary. It is, in fact, ground where angels fear to tread, and where, accordingly, those others rush in who habitually do into such areas. Because there are apt to be significant variations in character within even the most homogeneous of peoples—differences due to the regions where people live and the climate of these regions, to the several racial stocks from which they come, and even to their classes and occupations—and peoples vary, also, or at least seem to do so, from one era of their histories to another.

The Triestine with a liberal seasoning of Serb, Austrian and Jewish blood can be a notably different creature from the Catanian with a seasoning of Arab, Greek and Turkish blood. The navvy at the India Docks, the barrister's clerk in the City and the Duke of York may appear to differ more than they resemble each other. And if there was any such thing as a "typical Frenchman" in 1915, what had happened to him (or to his son) by 1940?

But the fact that the characters of peoples may seem to change from time to time and from place to place, and that they may vary according to class and racial stock, does not prove that there is no such thing as national character. Nor does the fact that national characters have been misunderstood and that false judgments have been made on the basis of these misunderstandings prove it. The Triestine and the Catanian resemble each other in certain important respects, although they may differ in others, and so do the navvy, the clerk and the Duke of York, and there are undeniable basic resemblances between the "typical Frenchman" of 1915 and his son of 1940. These qualities that men of the same nationality have in common and that they do not share in anything like equal degree with men of other nationalities—not, at least, in the same periods of their histories— these qualities, taken together, constitute national character.

It would be silly to pretend that there is no such thing as national character, understood in this sense. The Americans, who are often cited as a people without a true national character, actually provide, on the contrary, the final, perfect proof of its reality. Anyone who has lived abroad long enough, and thus has had his perception for such things sensitized, knows that even in New York City itself the taxi driver who may have been born in Cracow and his silk-hatted fare whose ancestors may have come over in the *Mayflower* have important qualities in common, that they share these qualities with the stockyards butcher in Chicago and the orchestra leader in Los Angeles, and that no other people on earth has these qualities in anything like the same degree.

"OUR DEAR LITTLE GERMANY"

So it is, too, with the Germans.

The Germans differ widely among themselves according to how they have been conditioned by the parts of the Reich where they live, the mixtures of blood in their veins, their classes, their occupations and their times. The East Prussian nobleman with great landed estates, the small factory owner in Saxony, the game warden in Thuringia and the coal miner in the Ruhr —these differ conspicuously.

The Germans have seemed to change even more than most other peoples, furthermore, in the course of time. The grandfathers of the middle-aged Germans of the Second World War era were accounted admirable and lovable but, above all, impractical men. They were thought of as a nation of poets and dreamers. Queen Victoria once referred to the Reich of her day as "our dear little Germany," and Jean Paul Friedrich Richter observed that "Providence has given to the French the Empire of the land; to the English that of the sea; to the Germans that of—the air!" It is a measure of how much the Germans have changed, or have seemed to change, that it may be necessary to explain that Richter meant that the French were supreme in land armies and the British in sea power, but that the Germans had their heads in the clouds and were of no particular consequence at all in such practical matters as warfare. Time

and the Wright brothers—and Professors Heinkel and Messer-
chmitt—have given Richter's remark a sinister turn as well as
an ironic one.

Let us begin, accordingly, by admitting that the Germans
have differed from one era to another. Let us also concede that
they differ among themselves even in the same era. Let us
grant that it takes all kinds to make a nation, just as it does to
make the world. And let us allow, finally, that most peoples
of all classes and races and nationalities living in essentially
similar civilizations have many and perhaps even most fundamental traits in common; that the differences among peoples
are differences of degree rather than differences of kind, and
that all human beings tend to react similarly to similar experiences.

But let us also affirm that, since Bismarck, at least, the Germans have had certain fundamental qualities as a people in
common; let us consider what these qualities are; and let us
examine how these qualities may help in some measure, even if
it may be only a modest one, to explain some of the things the
Germans have done during this period and some of the things
they have suffered to be done to them.

THE "GROBIANS"

Physically, the Germans are a big, a heavy and a powerful
people. Men and women alike must average ten pounds heavier
in weight than Americans of corresponding heights and ages.

German men carry their weight better than German women
do, especially the younger men. But, even so, too many German
men are apt to be too bulky and too ponderous and to run to
what Ibsen called the "boar's head type," with thick folds of
fat and skin at the back of the neck. And on the distaff side it
is only the young girls in Germany who can compare in any
way, in lines and proportions of figure, to their American cous-
ins. German girls' figures are good, generally speaking, although they tend to be somewhat low-waisted because their
legs are shorter from knee to ankle than American girls' legs
are. But even the best-proportioned German figure is liable to
err on the side of substance and solidity. There is too much of

Juno in German womanhood, Juno and Diana, and not enough of Venus. Not nearly enough.

The Germans' substantial bulk may help explain the strength and the capacities for doing hard work and for enduring privation and pain which also characterize them as a people.

"The Germanic race is among the sturdiest in the world, the most capable of enduring privation, a race of outstanding physical endurance," said Lord D'Abernon. "Their capacity for enduring patiently long hours of monotonous toil certainly exceeds that of Western Europeans. . . .

"The German is [also] exceptionally tolerant of pain," Lord D'Abernon added. "Not only does he bear pain stoically, but he apparently feels it less than men of other races. Medical students who have studied in German hospitals testify that the capacity of the patients to endure suffering is far greater than in England and France. German doctors and surgeons have become so accustomed to this fact that they resort to anesthetics less than their English colleagues do."

The German's bulk and strength are also often associated with a ponderousness and awkwardness of appearance, of manner and of movement alike. Whatever else may be said of the German, and whatever other virtues he may have (and he has many), not even his best friend, if he were honest, would say that the German is ordinarily beautiful or graceful or deft. Still less is the German elegant. A Venetian gondolier cut a better figure than a Berlin Privy Councilor in Nietzsche's time, and he still does (although a Venetian gondolier also cuts a better figure than most other people in the world too, and the comparison may therefore be unfair). The German is liable to be a distinctly unlovely creature, given to bumps and knobs and protuberances and bulges in the most unexpected and least desirable places. He is also liable to be clumsy, maladroit and, above all, undistinguished.

German women are too firm and sturdy, not fragile enough in their femininity, for American tastes. And German men are often coarse and gross. The German male's voice is deep and he is apt to be fond of shouting—preferably shouting orders. His hand is heavy and he is apt to be fond of pounding it on a table.

When the German blows his nose he is apt to sound like a trumpeter of doom. When he eats, he does so with Gargantuan gusto. He prefers heavy food—sausage and spareribs and sauerkraut rather than truffles and caviar, beer rather than wine, and cheeses which, at their ripest, make Camembert and Gorgonzola and Roquefort seem as diffident as camellias in comparison. One popular Bavarian cheese, for example, is known in the countryside as "country mailman's sock"—which is characteristic of German taste in both cheese and humor. German humor, in fact, reeks of the bathroom, not to say the backhouse, to an astonishing degree, and German bedroom humor is of an essentially similar quality.

The Germans themselves have a word for this grossness and coarseness of manner and appearance. They say it is "grob," and they say of people who are conspicuous for this quality that they are "Grobians." The terms are uncomplimentary, and are considered such even by most Germans, but otherwise—or maybe precisely for that reason—they provide as fair a description as any of this quality so common in Germany and of the people who display it.

But these German qualities of strength and endurance and ponderousness and coarseness are not only physical in their nature. They are also mental and spiritual. The distinction can be difficult to draw and may be even fictitious, but in this sense it may, perhaps, be permissible to try to draw it: that the amount of pain and privation you endure and the amount of hard work you do depend partly, at least, on the amount you think it is necessary or desirable to endure and to do. Ease and lightness and grace and delicacy of manner, equally, may be at least as much the outward and visible signs of spiritual and mental ease and lightness and grace and delicacy as they are of a slender, supple figure and superlative muscular co-ordination.

What, then, are the qualities of the German spirit?

HERR DOKTOR JEKYLL UND HERR HYDE

The German's soul is more difficult to discover and describe than his body is. One reason for this difficulty is that the Germans' psychology and manners have generated more heat than they have light in the minds of many of those who have come in contact with them. "The German character is one of the finest but one of the most inconvenient developments of human nature," Harold Nicolson has said, and this judgment is a miracle of restraint compared with those, even, of many Germans on their own people. "All our greatest men have despised us," a German once remarked, and if this is an exaggeration, it is not a wildly excessive one.

Frederick William III of Prussia, who led the German armies to the edge of Paris after the Battle of Waterloo, refused to let his peasant soldiers enter the city, as Joseph C. Harsch has pointed out in a similar connection. For to the Prussian king "Paris represented the center of civilization, and he refused to let his uncouth peasants defile its streets. Before him, Frederick the Great had his favorite palace at Sans Souci [even the name is French] built by French architects in the French manner, spoke only French in his court circles and surrounded himself with men like Voltaire, who represented the supreme achievement of Western civilization." Both Nietzsche and Goethe, too, despised the Germans, and the list of great Germans who shared their feelings could be prolonged to an impressive length.

There is another principal reason, too, why it is difficult to discover and describe the German soul. For it is an extraordinarily complicated soul, and besides enraging the possibly prejudiced it has also baffled some of even the most honest and objective of those upon whom it has impinged. Edgar Ansel Mowrer has summed up as well as anyone the complications, contrasts and apparent inconsistencies of the German soul:

"To the outside world," he writes, "Germany seems the country of organized science. But equally it is the country of rampant superstition. This people is rich in intellect, poor in common sense. It radiates intelligence, yet its several minds are open to the cosmic night. Through the openings drift in thousands of useful inventions and great ideas, fairy tales, philosophies, and, perhaps even more, fads and follies, distorted, bat-like fancies, illusions, madnesses. It is essentially chaotic, illogical and romantic. It is ill-defined in its being, hospitable to novelty, paradoxical. It is a country where men are continually flying to extremes that meet again at the end of some unexpected rainbow."

This quality of contrast and paradox in the German character has struck and startled everyone who has had enough to do with Germans to find out what they are really like. Mowrer himself tells of a German acquaintance of his, a heavy, "boar's head type" of industrialist, who honestly and devoutly believed in gnomes. He had seen many of them, he told Mowrer; he had coaxed them out of German forests with chocolate bars, of which gnomes are extremely fond. This man was perfectly "sane" as the term is ordinarily used; he was just extremely German. So, too, are the S. S. men of the "Death's Head Brigade," who guard the nazi concentration camps and who commit there literally unspeakable crimes against the bodies and souls of their prisoners, but who yet go strolling sentimentally in the parks on Sundays when they have leave, with girls on their arms, positively cooing and gurgling over what they themselves call "the dear, sweet little goslings" and cygnets and baby birds. So is Julius Streicher, the sadist anti-Semite of Franconia, who wept when two pet canaries died. And so is the typical German Hausfrau who entirely approves of Himmler's deliberate assault on the very existence of the Polish people.

These apparent inconsistencies are fundamental to the German character. The German is at one and the same time two entirely different kinds of person. More than any other European, he is Dr. Jekyll and he is also Mr. Hyde. Some of the time he is outwardly Dr. Jekyll, and some of the time he is outwardly Mr. Hyde, but inwardly he is always both. He is the battleground of opposing and furiously contesting qualities. And not only does everybody else with whom he comes in contact suffer from the consequences of this conflict of personality—or personalities—but so, also, does the German himself.

"STURM UND DRANG"

The basic fact about the Germans is that they suffer from a sense of inner insecurity. They are deficient in natural feeling for form and proportion, for balance and control, and they realize that they are, and they are uneasy and unhappy in the realization. The German is essentially unsure of himself. He lacks poise. More, he is chaotic and violent. He is a creature of constant "Sturm und Drang," of storm and stress and striving, of self-consciousness and self-examination. Not unnaturally, therefore, he is, generally speaking, unhappy.

Various explanations have been advanced for the Germans' sense of inner insecurity, for their lack of proportion and poise. This quality (for it is all essentially the same quality) has been attributed to the mixtures of racial stocks which are so striking among the Germans, to the Reich's central position in Europe, and to the fact that Germany's unification and rise to world power occurred late, in a world already largely pre-empted by other peoples who were well-established and therefore self-assured.

The racial explanation is advanced by the nazis themselves, but the fact that the nazis advance it, and that they do so in the bizarre vernacular they employ in these matters, does not necessarily make it untrue. And certainly the Germans are at least as striking a mixture of racial stocks as most other peoples are. In East Prussia, for example, besides every sort of Germanic element, there are strains of Borussian, Polish, Lithuanian, French, Dutch, Swedish, Bohemian, Scottish, Danish, Swiss, Russian, Kassubian, Cossack and Masurian blood. In Wuerttemberg there are traces of Celtic, Roman, Turkish, Wend, French and Piedmontese blood. There are equally mixed strains in most Germans.

Germany's central position in Europe has contributed to these mixtures. Armies from all the quarters of the continent—and sometimes from all the other continents, too—have fought and encamped on German soil, and some of the soldiers have stayed after the wars were over, and even some of those who did not stay sired sons. Frederick the Great deliberately brought in soldiers from almost every people in Europe for his army, and these soldiers were no more celibate than other men. Frederick also imported colonists from other countries, as several other Prussian monarchs did. And once he made an even more spectacular contribution to the strength of the Prussian racial stock; he forcibly "imported" 7,000 Polish girls, each with a cow and a feather bed, and conferred them on the doubtless appreciative males of Pomerania. Migratory workers, too, as well as armies and colonists, have mixed their blood with that of the Germans. The most conspicuous case is that of the Poles, who have made their characteristically fecund way clear across Germany, from the farms of Silesia and East Prussia to the mines and mills of the Rhineland, but there have been hosts of others, too, and still are. And, finally, the alien peoples the Germans have conquered and annexed on every side in recent generations have added their strains, too, to the German blood.

Germany's central position exposes it to spiritual influences from all the quarters of the compass, also, as well as to eugenic ones. "The German mind has never been able to make itself up," Dorothy Thompson writes. "Most importantly, it has never been able to choose, once and for all, between the East and the West. Dominant Prussia undoubtedly pulls it North and East; Bavaria and the Rhinelands pull it South and West; Austria and the new Slavic territories acquired will pull it South and East."

Or is the German sense of inner insecurity and lack of form and balance due, in some measure, to the historical fact that the Germans as a people have been unified and rich and powerful so short a time? Are their uncertainty, their *gaucherie*, their self-assertiveness, their not infrequent coarseness—even, perhaps, their capacity for hard work and privation and pain—are these qualities, so typical of the individual who has just "arrived" also due, partly, at least, to the fact that the Germans as a people have also just "arrived"?

Perhaps Providence knows why the Germans are as they are. Perhaps, too, the Germans' sense of inner insecurity, their qualities of "Sturm und Drang" and chaos, defy "rational" explanations like these, as psychic phenomena sometimes do. In any event, and no matter how the Germans "got that way," that is the way they are.

A RULE FOR EVERYTHING

But, as Mowrer says, "everything you say of such people must promptly be completed by its opposite," and after you have said that the Germans are characteristically uncertain of themselves and chaotic you must promptly also say that the Germans are likewise characteristically passionate believers in and seekers after order and form and system and organization and strong authority; that they are extraordinarily partial to principles and theories and abstractions; and that they have a regard for titles and formalities that is often comical to the non-German, and even exasperating.

The German's respect for authority is proverbial, and whole libraries could be filled with tales like that of H. R. Knickerbocker about the revolutionists who dutifully bought platform tickets before seizing a State railways station and Hugh R. Wilson's about the Spartacist demonstrators who carefully kept off plots of grass where "Verboten" signs were posted.

Serge Chakotin, who for a time before 1933 sought to combat nazi propaganda in Germany by similarly effective methods of his own, tells one of the most striking of such stories. As part of an electoral campaign, he wanted to send out men to chalk up the socialist symbol of three arrows on walls and fences and sidewalks everywhere. But Otto Wels, the leader of the Socialist Party, refused to approve this heterodox proposal. Chakotin begged and pleaded and argued, but Wels was adamant. He said it was outlandish to chalk symbols on sidewalks, it was improper and it was quite probably illegal, and he refused to allow it. He maintained his opposition until Chakotin obtained a special permit from Berlin police headquarters permitting it, an official document drafted by lawyers, signed by the competent authorities and bearing the appropriate stamps and seals. "Amid a people conditioned to obedience," as Mowrer says, "only [the nazis] knew what they wanted and were not afraid to take it."

Rubber stamps, incidentally, are among the most typical and universal properties of system and regularity in Germany. One of the things that most convinced Hitler of the inconsequence

of the German Workers' Party when he first investigated it
for the army was the fact that it did not even have a rubber
stamp.

This respect for authority and discipline arises out of the German passion for order and system and regulation in everything.
For authority, by means of discipline, establishes and maintains
order and system and regulation, and the German must have
these things. "Here, there is a rule for everything," a German
once told an American newly arrived in Berlin. "You always
know exactly where you stand." The American found it distinctly boring always to know exactly where he stood on everything. But most Germans do not find it boring. They find it
comforting. They find it, in fact, absolutely indispensable to
their peace of mind.

ORDER IN DOGPATCH

The German passion for system and regulation manifests itself in ways which, to the foreigner, at least, are sometimes
distinctly bizarre; in the rules that have been laid down for
naming horses, for example.

At last reports the naming of horses belonging to private
citizens in Germany was still left to the discretion of individual
breeders and owners. Not so, however, the naming of police
horses. Nomenclature here is regulated according to a satisfactorily rigid system. Horses born during the year 1931 have to
have names beginning with "A," those born in 1932 names
beginning with "B," and so on. This system was promulgated
in 1938. Hundreds and possibly thousands of horses' names
had to be changed to accord with the new regulations. But what
did either equine or human inconvenience and confusion count
as against the beauties of a scientific system?

There was only one concession to libertarian feelings in the
1938 order; horses born before 1931 could keep the names
they had. It was a shocking, an almost chaotic state of affairs
in horse-naming. One wonders why it was tolerated.

The Germans' fondness for titles, and especially their insistence upon proper respect for their own, are part of this same
passion for system and regulation, too. For a title systematizes

and regularizes a person; it puts him in his proper place and category. And the Germans dearly love to have everything in its proper place—proper, that is, according to the regulations dealing with that subject.

Hitler's own father, who was a petty Austrian customs official, was typical in this respect. He always insisted on being called "Herr Oberoffizial," according to Olden. If anybody called him "Herr Offizial," he considered himself insulted. "Don't you degrade me!" he would say, angrily. "You might as well say 'Herr Hitler' straight out."

Few Germans would be quite as sensitive on such a point as Herr Oberoffizial Hitler was, perhaps—but few, also, relish having their titles ignored or deprecated, and even fewer, in the middle class, at least, relish having no titles at all. They feel as naked without titles as they would without pants.

There is a classic joke in Germany about a woman who left instructions in her will to have herself described on her tombstone as "Frau-Widow-of-Master-Chimney-Sweeper So-and-So." But titles are no laughing matter to most Germans.

There is a scholar in the field of international law in Berlin who has three degrees of doctor of philosophy and who uses them all on his personal cards, thus: "Dr. Dr. Dr. Hans K. E. L. Keller."

The characters in American funny papers, too, were made to feel this German respect for order and titles on at least one occasion. A Foreign Office diplomat who had served in the United States and whose wife (at least he said it was his wife) was fond of American comics, asked an American correspondent in Berlin to send all of them he could to him at his office regularly. The diplomat's rank when he made the request was that of consul, and the comics were, accordingly, addressed to "Herr Konsul X" in the Wilhelmstrasse.

A few weeks later, the diplomat was named a "Vortragender Legationsrat," a rank and title one grade above that of consul. The correspondent did not learn of this blessed event, however. He supposed that X was still a consul, and in all innocence he sent the comics, the week after the apotheosis of the diplomat, to "Herr Konsul X," as usual. He was called to order, and at once. By return mail came a note to the correspondent, on official Foreign Office stationery. "Please send *The Chicago Daily News* comics to *Herr Vortragender Legationsrat X*," it said, and the last wrapper used for mailing the comics, with the offending title of consul, was enclosed to emphasize the reproof.

A rose may smell as sweet by any other name, perhaps, but not a Vortragender Legationsrat. There must be some order, even in Dogpatch, and in the Wilhelmstrasse even Li'l Abner must have respect for the proprieties.

CRITIQUE OF PURE REASON

At its best, or most effective, the German love for order and system does much toward explaining the achievements of mathematical and scientific and philosophical thought for which the Germans are celebrated, and the lethal semi-perfection of German general staff work. It is, in fact, this quality plus zealousness and hard work and an infinite capacity for taking pains that chiefly explains both the frequency of genius in general among the Germans and what the world calls "German efficiency."

The German does not know what efficiency means. There is no such word in the German language. The German gets results, and they are often impressive and not seldom awe-inspiring. But he gets them by perseverance and hard work and thoroughness and skill and method in extraordinary measure, not by what Americans call efficiency. The whole idea of getting maximum results at the cost of a minimum of expenditure in time and effort is apt to strike most Germans as downright immoral. The German is liable to devote three times the time and effort that are necessary to achieve a given result. (Similarly, the Germans, who are often called a patient people, are not patient at all, but perseverant; the distinction is important.)

At its worst, on the other hand, the German's love of order and system is partly responsible for the excessive fondness for theories and abstractions having little or nothing to do with reality, and for the weakness of preferring theory to reality which also characterizes many Germans. It further helps to explain the German's inferiority to men of some other races in dealing with an unforeseen contingency for which he has no theory and no plan, and his liability to revere the letter of the law without regard for its spirit.

Somewhere between these "bests" and "worsts," the German bureaucracy is perhaps the most typical manifestation of the Teutonic passion for systematizing and regulating everything and everybody. "The fact that the civil service stands in the foreground of German life, that the stupendous offices with their endless rows of windows are an object of pride to every true German, is rooted in a thousand years of German history and development, in the German's passion for administration and jurisprudence and, finally, in his want of confidence in his fellow man," Eugen Diesel writes.

"Experts have calculated," he adds, "that until recently no less than 1,000,000 police regulations were in force. The police consider this an exaggeration, but themselves admit to 250,000. For the most part these regulations are insulting in tone."

Diesel's book was published in 1931, under a Republic sometimes referred to as the freest in the world.

The German's passion for order is so ardent that, combined with other qualities, it often makes him an incurable pedant, a giver of advice and orders whether or not he has any right or occasion to give them, an inveterate meddler. Supererogation is one of the German's besetting sins. He is constitutionally incapable of true tolerance, of living and letting live. He is unhappy unless and until everybody else is compelled to live the way he thinks he ought to.

"In my kingdom, everyone can seek salvation in any way he likes," Frederick said. But Frederick, as has already been remarked, was not a typical German. (And even Frederick may not be an entirely reliable witness.) Under a truly German ruler, everybody must seek salvation in strict accordance with the regulations governing such enterprises—which, you may be sure, will be detailed, exhaustive and "insulting in tone."

This is one reason why the German is likely to be an intolerable ruler. He cannot, and never does, leave anything or anybody alone—to what Burke called "a wise and salutary neglect." Neglect "wise and salutary"? To most Germans the very thought is shocking.

Most particularly, the German cannot leave a fact alone. He has to "organize" and systematize it, as he organizes and systematizes everything else; he must have a theory into which it can be fitted. He must have a philosophy for everything. He is prone to think too much about too many things and to have too much respect for the conclusions he reaches by his ratiocination and too little for facts that may not conveniently fit his theories.

The German secretary of an American correspondent in Berlin literally almost starved himself to death once a few years ago because of this quality of mind. The secretary evolved a theory, on the basis of what he took to be impeccable logic, that men would be healthier and stronger on a diet consisting exclusively of fresh fruit and nuts than they are on more conventional foods. Primitive man, the secretary reasoned, was strong. Primitive man lived on fruit and nuts. Therefore if I live on fruit and nuts I will be strong too. There were certain defects in this argument, but these the secretary failed to see. He proceeded to subsist on fruit and nuts.

He grew thinner and thinner and paler and paler, but he turned aside his employers' questions about his health by insisting that nothing was wrong and that he had never felt better in his life. How could anything be wrong? His theory was sound. He *had* to be well and strong.

Finally, though, the secretary fainted dead away one day in the office, and when he was revived he was induced to explain what he had been doing. The correspondent was aghast. He told the secretary to return to a normal diet.

But this, too, proved disastrous. For the secretary responded to the voice of authority with the same uncompromising violence as that with which he had hearkened before to the voice of pure reason; he bolted a meal of pork, cabbage and potato that very day, and spent 6 weeks in a hospital as a result.

THE DRUNKARD AND THE SANITARIUM

But this is only a catalogue of characteristics. It may describe the Germans but it does not explain them. It is all very well to say that the Germans are sentimental and romantic and kind and that they love nature and like comfort and are heavy eaters, and that the Germans are also practical and scientific and cruel and that they are capable of enduring great privation and pain. But this is superficial. It does not greatly help to discover the true inner nature of the Germans. How does it happen that the Germans have these several, apparently so contradictory qualities? What are the Germans really like? Is there some key to the puzzle of the contrasts and paradoxes of the German character?

Mass psychoanalysis of a whole people is manifestly impossible. Other reservations were entered and other self-denying avowals uttered at the beginning of this essay. Subject to these conditions, however, a rule-of-thumb judgment nevertheless seems possible. There is, at least, general agreement among a number of the judgments hazarded by those who have known contemporary Germans best, and no opposing judgment seems to have been pronounced in any equally competent quarter. Without pretending that this judgment is altogether scientific or necessarily eternal, therefore, it may, perhaps, be considered as the most satisfactory to be formed so far.

This judgment, then, is that the contrasts and paradoxes of the German character are due to a conflict between the true inner nature of the German on the one hand and the attempts the German makes, on the other hand, to guard against the weaknesses and excesses of his true inner nature, and to overcome them—attempts that often lead to behavior as excessive in one direction as the original quality is in the opposite. The German character—that is, more than others—is the resultant of the clash of conflicting forces, of which two are the most important: The original and fundamental sense of inner insecurity and formlessness, and the passion for authority and order and system and regimentation that seeks to compensate for the inner insecurity and formlessness.

"The German does not accept discipline because of a neat love for order," Dorothy Thompson writes. "He accepts it the way a drunkard delivers himself into a sanitarium. He wants somebody to impose it on him because he cannot impose it on himself."

"In thought as in politics," says Mowrer, "this people is formless, and therefore craves a form so strong that it cannot be broken."

If the German "behaves offensively," Diesel suggests, "he does so because he is not sure of himself, not from undisguised coarseness and brutality, as in the case of the French and Italian and Slav. . . .

"Even the peacefully disposed German takes a peculiar delight in the order and discipline of the marching columns. The German loves hard discipline and precise commands; he always works best when he is treated in military fashion. . . . The German rejoiced in a system in which blind duty acquired so much prestige that it supplied him with a definite moral code. He looked to the army to provide him with mental poise and the community spirit."

There are other elements and explanations in the German character, of course. German "militarism," for example, is doubtless due partly to the fact that Germany's greatness has been so obviously, not to say ostentatiously, the result of the successes of German arms, and partly to the fact that the Germans are discontented as a nation and still seek power and property that are only obtainable, in the last analysis, by force of arms. But the inner nature of the Germans also helps explain their fondness for soldiering, too, for one of the reasons for this "militarism" is that the army affords the best possible combination of that form, authority, and system which the German so insistently seeks.

There is nothing mysterious or even improbable about this explanation of the German character. The terms in which it is sometimes expressed, the words like "compensation" and "overcompensation," may sound esoteric, but the behavior they seek to describe is one of the most common kinds in the world. It is the behavior of many little men who swagger or bluster or try to make up for the disadvantage of their shortness in some other way. It is the behavior of any man who is almost moved to tears by music or a sentimental play or picture and who tries to conceal the fact by swearing violently in the deepest bass he can muster. It is the behavior of P. L. Crosby's Skippy, who once, on viewing a sunset at the Grand Canyon, said, "It's so gosh darned beautiful I want to kick somebody in the pants."

ARE THEY HUMAN?

These, then, are the Germans: Big, heavy, powerful; with unusual capacities for hard work and for enduring privation and pain; on the whole unlovely; ponderous rather than grace-ful of manner and movement and not seldom gross and even coarse; a people suffering from a sense of inner insecurity and lack of a sense of form and proportion, of balance and control, and constantly striving to compensate for these deficiencies by seeking for authority and discipline to impose order and system.

Are the Germans "human"? The question is not meant too seriously (although it, doubtless, will be taken all too seriously by some Germans who may see it put; the capacity of the Ger-man for being solemn and for taking offense accordingly is extraordinary). Yet it is as convenient a way as any for con-sidering the principal difference between the Germans and most other European peoples, a difference that goes far toward ex-plaining the German capacity for annoying others.

There are at least two different and opposing senses in which most people use the term "human." Strictly speaking, perhaps, "human" means differing from the (other) animals by the more or less successful attempt to regulate conduct by intellect and reason as opposed to instinct and impulse.

In this sense, clearly, the German is likely to be not human at all at one moment and all too human the next. He is likely to be governed by his violent and chaotic instincts and impulses part of the time and by a positively awful (in the strict sense of the word) faith in the processes of ratiocination the rest of the time. And he is, inevitably, equally exasperating in either case and doubly exasperating because of the inconsistency and contrast between the two kinds of conduct and the difficulty of predicting when he will act one way and when the other. When the German surrenders to instinct, he is likely to be subhuman; when he acts on "pure reason" he is likely to be inhumanly human. It is no wonder that he baffles and enrages so many people.

"Inhumanly human"? But this introduces the second sense in which people use the term "human," the less scientific but more popular sense, a sense almost opposite to the first—the quality of being guided to a relatively great degree by the good and friendly and informal (although not, of course, by the evil) natural impulses, a feeling for moderation and balance and proportion and ease, and a skepticism of the rules of conduct worked out by intellect and reason; the sense in which an urchin might say, for example, that Abraham Lincoln was "human."

In this sense, of course, the Germans are among the least human of peoples. They think too much. They have too much respect for thought. They are too earnest, too ill at ease in life. They are too afraid of themselves, not natural enough, not silly enough, not irresponsible enough.

The Germans—are they human? Probably not. They are either too human or not human enough, by any definition of the term.

Any German who takes this diagnosis solemnly will, of course, only prove its correctness.

2. Natural History of a Revolution

Poverty is the parent of revolution and crime.

ARISTOTLE

The real source of fascism lies in the social resentments and the political confusion of lower middle-class life. REINHOLD NIEBUHR

It is absurd, I submit, to attempt to distinguish between nazis and Germans, just as it was absurd to attempt to distinguish between "military circles" and the "German people" as we attempted to do twenty years ago. HUGH R. WILSON

An UPHEAVAL in the life of a human society is much like an upheaval in the life of an individual human being.

There are good, bad and indifferent qualities in every individual. According to which of these qualities dominate the individual's conduct, he is a good, a bad or an indifferent person. But the individual is more complex than this indicates, for there are different sorts of good and bad qualities in every person, if not of indifferent ones. Goodness may take the form of generosity in money matters or physical courage or forgiveness toward an enemy, or any one or any combination of scores of others. And badness may take the form of alcoholism or thievery or murder or any number of others. Even in so-called normal individuals, furthermore, some good qualities and some bad ones, as well as many indifferent ones, are usually found

37

together. Thus one man may have a weakness for alcohol and even petty thievery and yet be extraordinarily brave and forgiving toward his enemies, and another may be a murderer and yet openhandedly generous in money matters.

The question which of these various sorts of good, bad and indifferent qualities dominates the individual's behavior depends on his heredity and his environment. Generally speaking, if his heredity is reasonably sound and his environment reasonably stable and favorable, the average individual behaves "normally." That is, he tends to be governed most of the time by essentially the same combination of the many different qualities of which his character is composed; his conduct is "consistent," it creates no problems in his relations with other human beings which cannot be settled by peaceable, or at least juridical, means—although even under these circumstances human beings are, of course, much more complex and much less predictable in their behavior than they often appear to be.

By the same token, a human society whose members for the most part are reasonably sound hereditarily and whose environments are reasonably stable and favorable will be a "normal" society.

The problem of good and evil as among whole human societies is more complicated than it is as among individuals. For one thing, there is not the measure of agreement as to what constitutes good conduct and evil conduct on the part of whole societies that there is as to what constitutes good and evil conduct on the part of individuals. For another thing, even to the extent that there is such agreement, there are so many different human beings of so many sorts and conditions in any large society that one society is ordinarily neither more virtuous nor more evil than any other, but only virtuous and evil in different respects.

At the same time, the parallel is still valid in large measure, even in this respect. For when the circumstances of life for a nation are reasonably stable and favorable, the society, like the individual under similar circumstances, behaves "normally." It tends, that is, to be governed most of the time by essentially the same combination of the many different elements of which it is composed. Its conduct is consistent, and it creates no problems in its relations with other societies which cannot be solved by peaceable, or at least juridical, means.

But a person of perfectly sound, normal heredity may behave very differently from ordinarily if the circumstances of his life change radically. If he inherits a fortune, or makes a happy marriage, or breaks a world record at the Olympic games, he is apt to behave differently in some ways afterward from the way in which he did before. If he loses his job and his savings or makes an unhappy marriage or is dropped from the Olympic squad for breaking training, he is apt to behave differently in other ways afterward from the way he did before.

He will still be the "same" person. Philip drunk is the "same" human being as Philip sober, and so is Philip down and out the "same" as Philip the president of the bank and pillar of society. The combination of qualities that made up his character before are all still there, and no new ones have been added. But he will also be a "different" person. He will not be "the old Philip we used to know." He will not be "himself." Because some of the qualities of his character that governed his conduct when he was sober and president of the bank will no longer do so when he is drunk and down and out, and some of the qualities that were dormant or suppressed in the one case will be dominant in the other.

So it is in human societies, too, most notably in nations. Changes in their circumstances produce changes in their conduct. When these changes are violent enough, they constitute revolutions.

A nation is the "same" nation during and after a revolution that it was before. It is made up of the same human beings. Even the most violent of revolutions ordinarily occur before any considerable element of the population that was there before has disappeared or any considerable new elements that were not there before have been added, although the appearance or disappearance of key individuals or elements may hasten the coming of a revolution or accompany or follow it. But the nation during and after a revolution is also a "different" nation from the one it was before. It is not "itself." Because during and after the revolution it is governed by elements different from those that governed it before.

The French nation of 1780 was the "same" as the French nation of 1791 and 1815, and the French nation of 1815 was the "same" as that of 1871 and 1915 and 1940. But it was also a "different" nation in each of these eras and phases of its history, because it was governed in these several eras and phases by different elements.

To say that the French themselves were responsible for these changes does not alter the fact of the changes. So, also, is Philip sober responsible for the fact that Philip gets drunk. The fact remains that Philip drunk is a "different" man from Philip sober—and, at the same time, is, of course, also the "same" man.

This understanding of the nature of social upheavals—of revolutions—provides the answer to the puzzle which has most perplexed the world about the nazi revolution, the puzzle of how so "nice" a people as the Germans could have turned to so evil a leadership.

PHILIP DRUNK

Except for the interval of the First World War, most Americans for generations have thought of the Germans as a kindly, friendly, decent, clean, hard-working, trustworthy people. Many if not most of the Germans whom most Americans knew personally are this sort of people. But how is this to be reconciled with the savage cruelties and obscenities of the nazi revolution?

Puzzled by the apparent contradiction, people have sought to explain it in a variety of ways. Some have clung to the "fact" that the Germans are "nice" people and have decided that the accounts of the savagery and obscenity of the nazi revolution are untrue. Others have accepted the accounts of the savagery and obscenity and have decided that the Germans are not "nice." Still others have accepted both the "fact" that the Germans are "nice" and the fact of the savageries and obscenities of the nazi regime and have tried to reconcile them by making a distinction between the German people and the nazis.

The Germans must hate the nazis, these people have said, and must long to be rid of them. The stability of the regime must therefore be precarious, these people have argued; the nazis could be overthrown by such a shock as that which would be caused by war. This is the view that lies—or lay—at the roots of the theory that the Second World War is a war against Hitlerism but not against the German people and that all will be reasonably well if only the nazi regime can be overthrown—which should not be too difficult.

But none of these explanations explains anything at all. It is true that the Germans are "nice." They are as "nice," that is, as any other people. Yet even this statement of the case is misleading. For it is equally true that the Germans also are not "nice." Because all nations are nice and they are not nice and they are both and they are neither, and one is no "nicer" and no less "nice" than another. It is true, furthermore, that the nazis are most extraordinarily evil men. There is no blinking the fact and there is no escaping it, whether by reaction from the "atrocity propaganda" of the First World War or simple, ostrich-like unwillingness to face unpleasant realities or for any other reason. If the nazi revolution is to be understood, both these fundamental facts must be faced and they also must be reconciled.

But the reconciliation that has been most commonly attempted, the explanation that there is a fundamental difference between the German people and the nazis, is a false reconciliation.

For it is just as true of the Germany of the 1930's as it is of any nation at any time that a people gets the government it deserves, and the German people of 1933 and the years that have followed have deserved Hitler's government. They have even wanted it. They have wanted it, that is, in this sense: That a sufficient number of the German people have been in such a state of mind as to enable Hitler to seize power and to keep it and to wield it as he has wielded it.

A fairly large proportion of the Germans actually voted for Hitler before the nazis were able materially to control the balloting or falsify the results. The nazis polled more votes, in

the last free Reichstag election in the Reich, than any other
party had ever polled in Germany.

A majority of the Germans never voted for Hitler in a free
election, it is true. Almost two-thirds of the electorate voted
for other parties even in the ballot in which the nazis reached
the peak of their electoral strength. But these others, who voted
against Hitler, deserved him and his government, too. For most
of them also wanted most of the things that Hitler was promis-
ing, and quarreled (and not too violently) only with his methods, and almost none of them opposed Hitler by the means that
clearly were required to keep him from power. Hitler has been
able to seize power and keep it and wield it as he has because
most of the German people have either actively wanted him to
do so or have not cared strongly enough whether he did or not.

What has made so "nice" a people as the Germans want, or
at least accept, a rule like Hitler's? There are two main parts
to the answer to the question. One part is to be found in the
character of Hitler himself and of the movement he created;
this part will be considered in subsequent chapters. The other
part is to be found in the German people themselves, both the
kind of people they are basically and the state in which they
have been in the years in which Hitler has won power and
kept it.

The German people have accepted Hitler partly because they
are the kind of people they are in general and apart from
circumstances, but largely because of the special circumstances
of the era after the First World War, just as Philip drunk
acts the way he does partly because he is Philip but largely
because he is drunk.

The Germans, too, got drunk. Qualities that had governed
the political conduct of many Germans before ceased to govern
it now, and qualities that had been dormant or suppressed
before became dominant now. There were and still are "nice"
Germans, but they were not and are not as "nice" politically
as they were before, no matter how "nice" they may have continued to be personally. This change has been sufficiently great
among a sufficient number of Germans to constitute a revolu-

tion; to cause the Germans to be prepared to accept a rule like that of Adolf Hitler.

What happened, then, to the Germans, to make them act the way they did? What had made Philip drunk? There were four principal causes: A fundamental crisis of faith by which the whole Western world was stricken, the defeat and disaster of the First World War, the post-war inflation, and the world economic depression.

PRIDE

It was hard to read the signs of the fundamental crisis of faith in Germany the last few years before the First World War. To most Germans there seemed to be simply no grounds for doubts or misgivings.

The authority of the state was firm. It was even Draconian. But the Germans preferred Draconian leadership. And the leadership they had at the turn of the century had achieved prodigies of power and glory.

Militarily, politically, economically and socially the Germans were triumphant in the Western world. Their army was invincible. Their navy challenged that of Britain. The political leadership of a Bismarck had outshone the military leadership of a Moltke—and was not a Moltke now chief of staff again? A great merchant fleet sailed the seven seas, and German goods were famous for their quality in every market in the world. The social problems of the industrial revolution had been better solved in Germany than in any other country.

The Germans were proud. They seemed to have every right to be. They may, perhaps, be forgiven if they implicitly believed in 1914 that a Lutheran and Teutonic God was in his Heaven and that all was right with the world.

Yet a crisis of faith that was latent throughout the Western world was latent in Germany too, in spite of everything. The faiths that men had lived by earlier were dying, if not dead, and no new ones had arisen to take their place. People were hardly aware yet, it may be, of the cancer of doubt that had begun to grow in their hearts, but it was already there: doubt and, with it, a sense of inner insecurity.

This growing doubt and insecurity were unbearable, in the

long run, for most men everywhere; most men everywhere must have faith to live. It would not do to exaggerate the importance of the peculiar character of a single people as a cause of an experience common to many.

Yet this much, at least, is true: The very fact of the Germans' success and assurance and pride would make failure and humiliation doubly bitter and therefore doubly catastrophic in their consequences, and the fact of the German need and therefore respect for strong authority would, if authority should be destroyed and not replaced by another, create a vacuum which the Germans even more than others would find unbearable and to fill which they, even more than others, would be ready to seize at the most desperate means.

DESTRUCTION

In the event, failure and humiliation came, and came with a vengeance, to this proud and, outwardly, at least, self-confident people, and the authority of the state that they so particularly revered and needed was utterly destroyed and they were left without anything which adequately replaced it. The fundamental and almost universal crisis of faith was heightened and intensified by a national crisis which the Germans were peculiarly unfitted to endure.

The First World War would have been a great enough shock, even if the Germans had won it. (It was to those who did win it.) Eleven million men were mobilized. Sixty-five per cent of these were casualties; more than 1,750,000 were killed, more than 4,200,000 wounded, more than 1,150,000 were taken prisoner or disappeared. The property accumulated by generations of men was destroyed.

The defeat and the terms imposed by the victors made matters vastly worse, not only because of the defeat and the terms themselves, but also because of the character of the people to whom these things happened.

Defeat? It was impossible. Germany was invincible. It could not be defeated; therefore, to many Germans, it had not been defeated. And therefore there could be no justification for the peace terms. But if Germany had not been defeated, then what had really happened? The Germans refused to face the facts (a weakness to which they were always susceptible), yet they could not discover a theory that explained the facts away.

And what was this new society, this new state, that emerged from the catastrophe? "The freest republic in the world"? But the Germans admired this kind of freedom less than most Western peoples under any circumstances, and under the circumstances of the defeat and the bitter humiliations that the defeat entailed, they soon came to detest the republic that had been foisted on them by their victorious enemies. This state partook, to Germans, of neither power nor, much less, of glory. It was feeble and uncertain and most conspicuously inglorious. Protect them against, and compensate them for, a sense of individual psychic insecurity now grown to terrifying proportions? This wretched republic was not even itself secure.

And now came a new disaster, the inflation. Chiefly to finance resistance to the occupation of the Ruhr, the government resorted to the printing press. The Reichsbank alone issued 189 trillion marks of paper money. But this was only the beginning. It seemed that almost everyone with access to a printing press was manufacturing money. Local governments printed between 400 and 500 quadrillion marks. The State Railways issued 114 trillion marks' worth more. More than 300 paper factories worked full time to turn out banknote paper for the Reichsbank. The government's own presses could not keep up with the demand, and 133 other printing establishments, with a total of 1,783 presses, were put to work to print still more currency. The exhausted printers went on strike, but the government called in strikebreakers to keep the presses going.

The consequences of this orgy were catastrophic. The Reichsmark fell to one-millionth of one-millionth part of its face value. It took 4.2 trillions of them to buy one single American dollar. Both politically and economically the Reich sank deeper and deeper into a slough of discredit, demoralization, and despair.

The world pulled Germany out of the slough, it is true. The Reich surrendered on the issue of the Ruhr, the mark was stabilized, the Dawes plan went into effect, and Stresemann championed a policy of fulfillment. Foreign capital poured into the country, and there was a measure of both economic and political prosperity. A degree of security and self-respect returned.

Yet this period lasted less than five brief years, and it ended in yet another catastrophe: in the world economic depression, in a deflation that was as disastrous as the earlier inflation had been. The national income sank from 76 billion marks in 1929 to 45.2 billions in 1932, the number of registered employed from 17,870,000 to 12,500,000.

These catastrophes affected all Germans in one way or another and in greater or lesser degree. But they affected some Germans more than they did others, and some Germans differently from others. These differences, too, help to explain the nazi revolution.

CATEGORICAL IMPERATIVE

The defeat in the war and the further disasters that followed struck savagely at two of the most sensitive and most vital spots in all human beings: National pride and economic security. Both blows in turn affected personal self-confidence, individual psychic security.

The war and the defeat filled the Germans with a bitter hatred and with a panic fear. But there was no way to vent this hatred and this fear on those whom most Germans held responsible—the victorious allies. There was no way to rehabilitate the national pride in defiance of the allies and there was no way to rehabilitate the national wealth at their expense. Not yet. Germany was far too weak and they were far too strong. The hate and fear, though, had to be vented somehow. It was a psychological necessity, a categorical imperative.

Some Germans vented their hate on themselves. But hating one's self was a solution of neither the psychological nor the political problem. And so, inevitably, in time the Germans vented their passions on each other—encouraged to do so, furthermore, by the refusal to believe that the Reich had really been defeated, which led increasingly to a search for the causes and agents of the disaster at home.

The disasters of the inflation and depression exacerbated the fear and hatred aroused by the disaster of the war and the defeat.

The more the national income shrank, the more bitter became the struggle for a share of what remained, the more violent the extremes to which men would resort to keep what they had or get what they did not. Those whose interests and inclinations placed them to the left of center moved further and further toward a left extreme. Those on the right moved further and further toward the right extreme. The further away from each other they moved, the more they hated each other and the more desperately each sought means, no matter how heroic or how vile, to destroy the other. Germany was being torn apart.

Superficially, at least, the extreme German left was formidable. Aided and comforted by the Kremlin and by the whole Third Internationale throughout the world, the communist party in the Reich was the largest outside Russia. From 1930 on it was the third biggest party in Germany, inferior only to the nazis and the social democrats. At their high point in the Reichstag elections of November, 1932, the communists polled almost 6,000,000 votes.

Numerically the extreme right was a dwarf party compared to this. The German Nationalists ran consistently a poor fifth in votes in the Reichstag elections, trailing the nazis, the social democrats, the communists and the center party. Their greatest strength at the polls, in anything like a free election (November, 1932) was 2,186,051, only a little over two-fifths of the communist vote in the same balloting.

Yet the right had great advantages which were denied the left. It had its own "internationale," too: the internationale that always exists among property-owning classes everywhere. In Germany itself, furthermore, the upper and middle classes together far outnumbered the proletariat, and it was easier for the upper and middle classes to co-operate politically than it was for either one to co-operate with the proletariat. Also, political activity of any kind needs money, and the right had money, and political activity of a revolutionary—or counterrevolutionary—kind required at least the acquiescence of the army, and the right controlled the army. And, finally, the right also controlled the chief executive, the president, and therefore could make and unmake cabinets.

As the German crisis deepened and the factional bitterness increased, however, it became more and more apparent that the right could not maintain itself in power alone. It had all the constituent elements of political power except one, but that one was indispensable, and there was no prospect of the right's acquiring it—a great mass following. Yet the right was determined to maintain itself in power and to destroy the left, the communists and social democrats alike. Therefore it had to enlist a great mass following in some other quarter. And this could only be the disinherited middle class.

Such a mass following was ready at hand: the nazi party. National socialism grew out of the disinherited of every sort and condition of Germans: rich men and poor men and beggar men and thieves, doctors, lawyers, merchants, chiefs. But its leadership, its program, its greatest numerical strength and its outstanding characteristics were of the middle class, and, most particularly, of the lower middle class.

There were certain affinities between the extreme right and national socialism. Thus the nazis were "safe" both politically and economically, or at least they professed to be. They were pledged to the destruction of Marxism and to the achievement of national greatness. They were also pledged, of course, to the destruction of the extreme right as well. But Hitler protested privately that he did not really mean his promises to the left— while yet meaning every word of what he promised the right— and some of the right believed him. And while others of the right wisely believed none of Hitler's promises, but only all his threats, even these cynics thought that they could use and control Hitler no matter what he wanted and tried to do. This was the broader basis of the Papen-Hitler deal that gave the nazis power.

The lower middle class out of which national socialism grew merits, obviously, a closer consideration.

THE CORPORAL'S CLASS

Sometimes known as "the corporal's class," the German Kleinbuergertum, the lower middle class, is the class of white-collar employees and small shopkeepers and lower civil servants. The term, however, is inexact, and sometimes it is used to include small peasants and handicraft workers too.

The members of this class may earn no more—they may earn less—than many a skilled mechanic. They consider themselves, however, socially and intellectually one with the upper classes. They attach the greatest importance to the distinction between themselves and manual laborers, no matter how skilled and how well-paid the laborers may be, and they feel a peculiarly bitter sense of degradation whenever they are threatened with being pushed down into the ranks of the proletariat.

The typical member of the Kleinbuergertum is ambitious, both for himself and for his children. He spends an unusually high proportion of his earnings on education and often borrows money to help to finance it—although, for the rest, it is ordinarily difficult for him to obtain credit for any purpose. He also goes to considerable pains and expense to dress as well as he can, partly because his employers expect it of him but also partly as a matter of personal pride. This same pride commonly inhibits him from taking advantage of the public and other eleemosynary social health and other services that are available to the proletariat, even when he is eligible for them.

He is "unorganized"; that is, he belongs to no occupational guild or other association for the betterment of his position. His bargaining power is consequently feeble at best. He often has none at all. Owing partly to this fact, his salary is usually low in terms of his standard and cost of living, it is commonly slower than the earnings of both capital and labor to rise and it is quicker than theirs are to decline. The typical representative of this class has little or no social or group insurance. His greatest ambition is to accumulate at least a modest capital, most commonly in the form of an independent business or a home of his own or both.

This man is a conservative and a patriot in politics. In any-

thing like normal, stable times he and his kind provide the bal-
last of the state. They are the staunchest champions of decency
and property and national honor as those terms are conven-
tionally understood. Even in times of upheaval the lower middle
class may be slower to lose its head, and may lose it less
completely, than the extremes of both the right and the left.
But if and when the lower middle class does lose its head, it is
the most likely of all to cause revolutions—partly, no doubt,
because of its sheer numbers and partly because of the very
strength of its national and economic feelings. This is the class
that has been primarily responsible for the most spectacular
social revolutions that have occurred in Europe (as distinct
from Asiatic Russia) during the past 150 years: the French, the
Italian fascist and the German nazi revolutions.

EMANCIPATION OF CONVENIENCE

The German lower middle-class generation that spanned the
turn of the twentieth century grew rapidly to great numerical
strength. Salaried employees and public officials, who totaled
only approximately 1,000,000 in 1882, or 6.4 per cent of all
gainfully employed, totaled more than 5,000,000 in 1925, or
16.5 per cent of all gainfully employed, as Schuman has pointed
out. The number of salaried employees per 1,000 manual workers in industry rose from 82 in 1907 to 154 in 1925, the number
per 1,000 manual workers in quarrying from 41 to 75 and the
number in transportation from 252 to 994.

In spite of its numbers, however, this class was peculiarly
lacking in self-confidence, both collectively and as individuals.
For it had not attained power "by its own revolutionary efforts,"
as Peter Drucker puts it: "Unlike the middle classes in Western
Europe, it was liberated from above. Its emancipation was not
a social end in itself; it was effected for the purpose of national
unification. [It was, that is, an emancipation of convenience.]

"Politically and socially the bourgeoisie therefore never became a ruling class," Drucker writes. "The aristocracy and the
hereditary, though often untitled, nobility of civil servants and
officers remained the social and political master.

"Accordingly, the typical bourgeois professions did not receive full social recognition. Outside of a few small areas like Hamburg and Frankfurt, with their old trading tradition, the business man was not accepted as a social equal."

Thus the German sense of inner insecurity, the German inferiority complex, reaches its most acute form in this German middle and lower middle class. All Germans tend to suffer from a feeling of inferiority and inner insecurity, but the members of the middle class suffer by far the most. And so, accordingly, does the middle class also have a most extraordinary passion for authority to compensate for its inner insecurity by imposing, by means of discipline, the form and order and system and regulation that are lacking within. The middle class, that is, was above all others devoted to and dependent upon a state that is sure of itself and powerful and glorious both at home and abroad.

THE UPPER AND NETHER MILLSTONES

The disasters of the First World War and the era that followed struck with especially cruel effect at this German middle class; they struck it at precisely the points where it was most vulnerable.

The war destroyed the state which had, in a sense, created the middle class and which had constituted and represented the power and glory that were peculiarly essential to it, and replaced that state by one that failed to serve the moral and political needs of this class even more than it failed to serve the needs of the others. And the inflation and the depression cost the middle class, not only a great share of its earnings and savings, but also—and this was vastly worse—they "degraded" hundreds of thousands of its members to the proletariat and threatened to do the same to hundreds of thousands more. Whether or not the inflation and the depression hurt the middle class worse than capital and labor economically, they certainly hurt it more psychologically and this, from the point of view of revolutionary dynamics, was even more important.

After the First World War, as Edgar Ansel Mowrer has pointed out, both the German workers and German capital prospered, at least relatively and at least for a time. Thanks to their unions and to the power of the social democratic party, German workers achieved a higher standard of living than workers in victorious France and Belgium. The upper classes, too, defended their positions well. Big industry was even better organized than the workers, even more aggressive, and at least as well protected by the state. The Junkers, too, were protected: the army insisted that they be subsidized to the extent of billions in order to guarantee a domestic grain supply.

But these successes of capital and labor were achieved to a considerable extent at the expense of the middle class, which was neither organized in its own defense nor protected by anyone else. The German Kleinbuergertum was ground between the upper and nether millstones. It not only was reduced to poverty, to economic desperation, but it also felt itself degraded and was panic-stricken and was therefore driven to mental and moral desperation, too. And the chaos which this class always feared the worst threatened to become a horrible reality now.

THE DEADLY PARALLEL

There is an exact and deadly parallel between the degree of desperation of the German people, and especially of the German middle class, and the fortunes of the nazis.

When times were relatively good and affronts to national pride not too numerous and not too outrageous, the nazis lost ground. If times had been good enough for long enough and if the national pride had been less violently inflamed or could have been sufficiently assuaged, the nazis probably never could have come to power in Germany. (Although even in that event some other regime of similar national and imperial, howbeit probably less revolutionary, aims, would have come to power instead, for nothing short of world power second to none would have satisfied the German people for any length of time as long as they thought there was some chance of winning it.)

But times were good for less than five short years, and only moderately good, even then, and the rest of the time they were most desperately bad. And the worse they got and the longer they stayed that way, the greater the number of Germans who turned to national socialism. Hitler was the incarnation of German bitterness and German desperation.

In the Fall of 1923, the currency inflation was at its height, the Ruhr was occupied, and blatant displays of wealth by a few were flaunted in the faces of the many who were suffering the agonies of a grinding poverty—and Hitler made his first grotesque attempt to seize the state.

The effort failed, it is true, but it failed partly, if not largely, because of Hitler's personal ignorance and inexperience. Bavaria and not only Bavaria, was ripe for revolution. It had already had two revolutions since the war, and might well have had another if the proper men had prepared for it properly. The margin by which Hitler failed was not so great as is commonly imagined.

Even five months later, with Hitler and the other principal leaders incarcerated in a fortress or in exile and with the party under a ban and operating in disguise, the nazis, in an alliance with nationalist and racial elements in North Germany, made impressive showings in both national and local ballotings. They won 32 seats in the Reichstag, 23 in the Bavarian Diet and 8 in the Diet in Wuerttemberg.

But by December of 1924 conditions had improved. The Reichsmark was rehabilitated, the Dawes Plan in effect, the Ruhr evacuated. And in the Reichstag elections of that month, the nazi coalition won only 14 seats.

By the time of the presidential election of 1925, conditions were still better, and the nazis' voting strength had declined still more. Ludendorff, their candidate, polled fewer than 300,-000 votes, only one-seventh of the maximum strength they had shown four years previously and only one-third of what they had shown less than four months before.

The times continued to improve and the nazis continued to lose ground. In the Reichstag elections of May, 1929, the national socialist coalition won only 12 seats. There was a significant feature of the list of candidates elected, however, for all 12 of them were nazis. The allied parties of the coalition had all been frozen out. Hitler was master of only a "splinter" party, but he was master.

But now came the second and final disaster. Stresemann died and his policy of fulfillment was jettisoned. The world crisis came and economic hard times added all their bitterness to the bitterness of a policy of uncompromising nationalism. And less than 17 months after the elections in which Hitler had won 12 seats he won 107, and the nazis became the second largest party in the country. By March of 1932 Hitler polled 11,000,000 votes against Hindenburg himself for the presidency of the Reich. In April in the run-off election Hitler polled 13,000,000. In the Reichstag elections of August 31, the nazis polled 13,700,000. They were the strongest party in Germany.

It is true that in the November elections Hitler lost 2,000,000 votes. It is possible that he might have lost even more votes later, and even that he might never have come to power at all, if it had not been for the plotting of the Papens that gave him his chance.

But there was vastly more in Hitler's appointment as Chancellor than Hitler's own intelligence and ruthlessness and Papen's inadequacies. For not only Papen but any other leader of the right had to have Hitler because Hitler had the mass following that the right had to have, and Hitler had his mass following because the middle class was desperate and because he had succeeded in exploiting their desperation.

The only thing that could have eliminated Hitler would have been an appreciable improvement in both the economic and political position of the Reich and particularly of the German middle class. The parallel between despair and national socialist success was too exact, too deadly, to permit of another view.

It has been said that the middle classes turned to Hitler because they were desperate, and this is clearly true. Yet that is still only part of the story. The middle classes were ripe for somebody like Hitler, for something like national socialism. But why did they turn to this particular Hitler and this particular national socialism, rather than to others of the score or more of men and movements that equally sought to exploit their desperation in those same times? The answer to this question, obviously, must be sought in an examination of Hitler and his party.

3. The Failure

Hitler, Adolf. Son of a petty Austrian official living near the Bavarian border. Fought in the Bavarian army during the war. Rose to notoriety in 1922 shortly before the Mussolini coup d' état by founding the so-called German National Socialist Workers Party. . . . In the Autumn of 1923 he joined with General von Ludendorff in leading the insurrection in Bavaria, but after a temporary escape, was arrested and subsequently tried for high treason, receiving a sentence of five years' fortress. He was finally released after six months and bound over for the rest of his sentence, thereafter fading into oblivion.

EDITOR'S FOOTNOTE TO LORD D'ABERNON'S "THE DIARY OF AN AMBASSADOR: RAPALLO TO DAWES, 1922-1924."

THE FACT that Adolf Hitler has a Charlie Chaplin mustache is one of the most fateful facts of modern times.

Seldom has the hair on the face of a single human being figured so prominently in the affairs of men. For the ridiculous tuft that Hitler bears on his upper lip made it difficult, and, indeed, almost impossible, for millions of people to take him seriously in time. People simply could not believe that this man with the comedian's mustache could be the political genius he really was. They thought he was funny. They laughed at him. And while they were laughing, Hitler destroyed them and their whole world around them. There is nothing funny about

Adolf Hitler, nothing at all. But thanks in large measure to his comedian's mustache, millions of human beings found this out too late.

Hitler's facial hair is so important that its history warrants a brief investigation:

The Chancellor has not always had his Charlie Chaplin mustache. He copied it, as he copied so many other things, from somebody else—although not, as it happens, from Chaplin.

Hitler's hirsute history began when he let his beard simply grow untended when he was a young man in Vienna. The result was a growth of soft, black, fuzzy down that covered his cheeks and chin. It was much like the first beard of any other dark-haired youth, except that it looked much more non-Aryan than most. Why did the young Hitler let his beard grow? Why not? Most youths try it, or wish they had the nerve to try it, at one time or another. And besides, Hitler was desperately poor, which gave him an economic reason, and he considered himself an artist and a bohemian, which gave him an occupational excuse.

But Hitler was as mercurial in the matter of whiskers as he was in so many others, and the soft, black fuzz on his cheeks and chin did not long survive. At about the time he went from Vienna to Munich, in 1913, when he was 24, he shaved off his beard. He kept only a mustache. This was not yet, however, the later Chaplin version. There were to be two intermediate phases and fashions in his facial hair. The pre-war mustache was a good enough specimen of its kind, but it was not remarkable. It was just a typical middle-class German pre-war style, in the large, bushy, walrus or handle-bar manner.

This adornment, too, however, was destined to be but short-lived. Some time during the war came a new transmogrification: Hitler grew whiskers again. He grew another beard, this time a pointed goatee. The goatee had its merits. It was not a bad goatee, as goatees go. But it, too, fell victim relatively soon to the shears (or razor) of the Fates and to Hitler's younger fickleness in matters of hair. For in the latter part of 1919 Hitler met a man who bore a style of mustache that captivated him, the style that was destined, upon Hitler's upper lip, to play so important a role in history. This man was Gottfried Feder.

Feder was an engineer who fancied himself as an economist— a not uncommon idiosyncrasy, and one not confined to Germans. He had concocted a "theory" that there were two kinds of capital in the world: "international, Jewish, exploitive, loan capital," and "national, purely German and productive capital." Many of the world's ills, if not most, were due, said Feder, to the "interest slavery" of the wrong kind of capital, and he preached that salvation was to be attained by breaking the bonds of this enslavement.

Feder also fancied himself as a Beau Brummell, as well as an economist. He took great pains with his personal appearance. And he had a carefully tended Charlie Chaplin mustache. Why did Feder like his ludicrous tuft? Had he ever seen Chaplin in a film? Had Hitler? It seems unlikely, but the record unfortunately does not clarify this point.

All that history reveals is that Hitler was much taken, both with Feder's economic theory and with his mustache, and that he promptly adopted both as his own.

Feder's theory helped Hitler win thousands of votes. Having served its purpose, it was jettisoned as soon as the party seized power. The way to avoid enslavement in the bonds of interest, it was officially explained, was to refrain from borrowing (no matter what the kind of capital) in the first place. It was that simple. Feder himself was appointed to a grandiloquent-sounding but otherwise meaningless office for city planning and he soon dropped out of sight.

But while Hitler abandoned both Feder's theory and Feder personally, he kept the mustache. It was Gottfried Feder's one contribution to world history—and it was not, all things considered, an unimportant one. It certainly was more important than his theory, for it misled even more people—many more— and misled them much more seriously.

A short but tangled growth, in Hitler's case, the dark hairs tinted with auburn, growing in several different directions, now touched with white, it provides the world with yet another proof, this time a singularly tragi-comic one, that appearances are indeed sometimes deceptive.

LITTLE MAN

Hitler's preposterous mustache has been more responsible than any other one single factor for the world's inability to take the man seriously in time. The tuft on the upper lip would have been misleading enough even if Hitler had been an impressive figure otherwise. But Hitler is ludicrous in other ways, as well, judged by the world's conventional standards of expectation for political leadership. The mustache has been important, not only in itself, but also as a sort of epitome and symbol of this man's other unprepossessing qualities, too.

For Hitler is extraordinarily undistinguished in physique, in manner and in movement, in his dress and in his conduct. He even speaks bad German. Decidedly, it was hard to take this man seriously at first.

In appearance, Hitler is mediocre and nondescript. He is exactly like tens of millions of other miscellaneous "little men" in poor physical condition all over the world. He is five feet eight or nine tall, and must weigh approximately 180 pounds. His legs are short for his torso. His arms and legs, as Rauschning expresses it, are "ill-fitting and awkward." He is round shouldered and hollow chested and has a paunch. His legs are slightly bowed. He stands badly and walks badly, tending to toe out.

His dark hair is thick, straight and fine, with an auburn tint when light falls on it, graying now, but not remarkable in any way except for the comical forelock he cultivated for a time, the pomade he used as a younger man but later abandoned, and the excessive dandruff that has always plagued him and of which he has never kept his collar and shoulders as free as a more fastidious man would do.

Hitler's skin is coarse and pebbly, and often pasty and unhealthy in appearance. His eyes he has from his mother: eyes of a gray-blue-green so intense and so changeable with moods and other circumstances that equally careful observers have called them everything from azure to emerald and even "white." The Chancellor's nose is big and strong, his mouth cruel. His teeth are bad, principally, perhaps from lack of care. When he was barely middle-aged his lower front teeth had to be pulled and replaced by a bridge that was not remarkably good. Saliva tends to collect at the corners of his mouth, clouding his diction.

Hitler's diction and his style of German in general, in fact (he has never learned more than a few badly spoken words of any other language) are almost as misleading, to North Germans, at least, as his mustache is. He speaks with a thick, provincial Austrian accent, his choice of words is clumsy and his syntax strained. North Germans laughed at him for years. Take a man seriously who spoke and wrote like that? It was impossible.

Hitler's dress and demeanor also conspired, in the earlier years of his struggle for power, to make him seem ludicrous.

When he set out for the Buergerbraeukeller the night of November 8, 1923, to overthrow the Weimar Republic, Hitler donned a long, black, badly cut frock coat, he carefully parted and slicked his hair, he put a revolver in his pocket, and—unwonted gesture of luxury—he drove to the beer hall in a taxi. "Poor little waiter!" one of the few "gentlemen" present exclaimed when this strange figure jumped up on a table to proclaim that the revolution (yet another one) was at hand. "The affair, whichever way you looked at it, lacked chic," in the view of another "gentleman," as ironically described by Olden.

But worse was yet to come. For in the midst of Hitler's harangue a henchman handed him a jug of beer, and this, inevitably, caused "immense amusement and some relief" among those who heard of the incident, as Olden writes: "After all, it was thought, [it was] simply a private Bavarian affair, and really quite harmless." Hitler "existed chiefly for the comic papers. For them, he was the man who had attempted his ridiculous Putsch with a revolver in one hand and a jug of beer in the other."

At the trial that followed the ignominious failure of the Putsch, Hitler made this same sort of impression on at least one seasoned observer present (who was not, however, misled by the man's appearance). "Was this provincial dandy, with his slick, dark hair, his cutaway coat, his awkward gestures and glib tongue, the terrible rebel?" Edgar Ansel Mowrer asked himself. "He seemed for all the world like a traveling salesman for a clothing firm." (But what clothing firm, even in darkest Saxony, would send out a salesman like that?)

The instances in which even the best-trained students completely misjudged this man, even in later years, could be multiplied almost indefinitely. A single further example must, however, suffice: "When I walked into Adolf Hitler's salon I was convinced that I was meeting the future dictator of Germany," Dorothy Thompson wrote not long before Hitler became precisely that. "In less than 50 seconds I was sure I was not. It took me just that time to measure the startling insignificance of this man who had set the world agog."

UN-GERMAN

The fact that Hitler was and is unprepossessing in manner and appearance to the outside world would not necessarily have been incompatible with his rise to power in Germany. But Hitler was just as preposterous a figure to most Germans at the outset as he was to most people everywhere else.

Charlie Chaplin was almost as well-known in Germany as he was in America during the years of Hitler's struggle for power, and Hitler's mustache seemed just as ludicrous to most Germans as it did to most Americans then.

The nazis banned Chaplin's pictures from the Reich as soon as they had the power to do so. They said the principal reason was that Chaplin was not altogether "Aryan." Even if Chaplin had been as "Aryan" as an Eskimo, however, he would have been banned from the screen in the Reich none the less. His mustache was definitely subversive.

The ban was motivated more by personal feelings, though, than it was by any conviction that Chaplin's mustache could really have impaired the Chancellor's authority. After all, the mustache had been shown on the screen before and during Hitler's rise to power and had seemed to have little effect, if any, on Hitler's career. Why should it suddenly become effective after the Chancellor was established in power?

It was the same with Hitler's other unprepossessing qualities: the lock of hair, the mediocre physique, the whole manner and appearance, were at least as much against him in Germany as they would have been in most other places. And his awkward, clumsy use of his own language, was, of course, a particular disadvantage to him.

In several other respects, too, in matters both great and small, Hitler is actually an even stranger creature to the Germans than he might be to some other peoples, for in these respects he is conspicuously "un-German."

Among a people who tend to be strong and sturdy and even grossly and coarsely masculine, he is womanish. Among a people who attach great importance to hard work, he is, in effect, a loafer. Among a people devoted to discipline and order and tidiness, Hitler is notably slipshod, erratic and without self-control. The Germans are a nation of short-cropped heads; Hitler flaunted for years a theatrical forelock. The Germans are heavy meat-eaters and drinkers of beer and wines; Hitler is almost a complete vegetarian and teetotaler. The Germans are gymnasts and sportsmen and hunters; Hitler never takes any exercise at all, except for brief walks, and abhors the taking of all animal life. The Germans are studious and have great respect for learning; Hitler is untutored and cannot even use German well.

Even more fundamental is the fact that in a nation with at least as much respect for success as any other, Hitler had never succeeded at anything whatever up to the time he went into politics. Let us consider how utter a failure Adolf Hitler was at 30 and even at 40.

MISFIT

Some of the details of Hitler's early life are obscure because Hitler has deliberately shrouded them in obscurity, but the principal relevant facts have been established in spite of this calculated obfuscation: the story of Adolf Hitler's failure in life is clear and unmistakable.

Until he was 8 or 9 years old, Hitler was a normal enough

boy. In his 10th or 11th year, however, he began to display the qualities of bitterness and moroseness that have characterized him more and more markedly ever since. Students of Krafft-Ebing and Freud and Havelock Ellis may be able to guess at an explanation. In any event, from about that same time on, Hitler failed completely in everything he undertook to do and be.

At 12 he failed to get passing grades in his studies and had to be taken out of school. His father sent him to school in another town and Hitler repeated a year, but failed to pass the second time, just as he had the first. That was the end of Adolf Hitler's formal education. He spent the next four and one-half years loafing and living, with his doting mother, on the meager pension that was the family's sole means of support after Hitler's father died.

Hitler himself says in "Mein Kampf" that he suffered at this time from a "severe lung ailment." The most painstaking research has failed to discover any corroboration for this claim, however, and the Hitler family physician has flatly contradicted it. It may well be, therefore, that Hitler lied in this case as he has lied in so many others, and that he invented the "lung ailment" to try to excuse both his failure to pass his studies and his even more discreditable failure to do anything toward helping to support himself, to say nothing of his mother, for several years thereafter. Certainly a readiness with alibis has been one of the most striking qualities of this man throughout his life.

When Hitler's mother died, the pension stopped, and Hitler, at long last, had to work for a living or starve. He went to Vienna—and failed there, too.

He wanted to be a painter, and applied for admission to the art academy. He was told that the work he submitted as part of the entrance examinations was below the minimum standard for acceptance and that his modest talents appeared more suited for architectural studies. Hitler applied for admission to the academy a second time, in spite of this first rebuff; on the second occasion he was not even allowed to take the entrance examinations. And when he sought to enter the architectural school he was rejected because he had never completed his elementary education. Hitler lacked the money necessary to go to school and make up this deficiency then, and quite possibly he lacked the will to do so, too. (It is hard to believe that he lacked the intelligence to pass his studies if he had really wanted to do so.)

He became an odd-job handy man. For a time, he worked as an unskilled laborer in the building trades. He failed at this also. He talked too much. He was lazy and undependable. He considered himself superior to the other workmen, and showed it. It was no wonder, consequently, that he could get along with neither workmen nor employers and never lasted long on any job. Between jobs he shoveled snow, ran errands and did anything else that came to hand to keep body and soul together. He even begged.

For a while Hitler joined forces with an etcher named Reinhold Hanisch, who was also down and out. He proposed that he roast his own oil paintings in an oven until they were "aged" a plausible brown and that Hanisch should then sell these as "old masters," the etcher later said. But Hanisch had too healthy a respect for the police, according to his own account, and refused to be a partner to the fraud. So the two collaborated on less imaginative projects. Hitler painted postcards and advertising signs and pictures that frame-makers used the better to set off their wares, and Hanisch peddled these. Olden reports that one of Hitler's signs could be seen years later in a drug-store window in Vienna, an advertisement for "Teddy's Perspiration Powder."

Apart from fleeting relationships like this, Hitler was a bitterly and desperately lonely man in Vienna. He had few acquaintances and literally no friends. Also, he was a bitterly and desperately unhappy, frustrated man. He considered himself a "gentleman," and wanted to be an artist; not an unknown starveling in a garret, but a successful, prosperous painter—like Lenbach, who, as Olden points out, "had been ennobled, lived in a palace, was overwhelmed with gold, called Bismarck his friend, [and] had married a countess; and he, after all, had been a poor Bavarian cottager's son almost like Adolf himself." But the "gentleman" was a literally verminous bum, an inmate of flop-houses he shared with the dregs of a polyglot empire, and the artist was reduced to painting advertisements for perspiration powder.

In 1913 Hitler gave up trying to make his way in Vienna. He moved to Munich. There he was less bitterly wretched than he had been in Vienna. But he was still a failure, still a frustrated, unhappy man. When the war came in 1914, therefore, it came to him as a release from a civil life and a whole civilization that he hated. Hitler went off to war with positive joy, he says, and here, at least, he can probably be believed.

Yet Adolf Hitler was a virtual failure as a soldier, too. He was a model of discipline and his courage seems to have been adequate. The various nazi accounts of his supposed feats of heroism are so contradictory and otherwise confusing that little sense can be made of them, but Hitler seems to have every right to the Iron Cross, First Class, that he almost invariably wears. Yet Iron Crosses were distributed so freely in that war that the distinction they conferred was but a modest one, and Hitler's verifiable military record was far from extraordinary.

He served throughout as an orderly on a regimental staff, ordinarily neither too dangerous nor too exacting a position. He was never promoted above the rank of lance corporal. ("I'll never make that hysterical fellow an officer," one of his superiors is quoted as saying.) And he got along with the other soldiers no better than he had with the other workmen in Vienna. They found him, in fact, insufferable: obsequious to his superiors and surly to everyone else.

Yet Hitler himself seems to have been not too unhappy in the army, in an almost perverted, masochistic way. And when the beaten empire collapsed and Hitler heard the news he said he wept for the first time since his mother had died. His whole world had come to an end.

This, then, was the failure that Adolf Hitler was at 30: a failure in school, a failure as an artist, a failure as a workman and not far from a failure as a soldier; a man who had never been able to make a decent living and had never been able to get along with others. There he lay on his bed in an army hospital in Pasewalk, blinded by gas, according to his own account, a misfit and a failure by every standard that the world applies to men.

ADOLF, RUDOLF OR ROBERT?

So startling is the contrast between Adolf Hitler's appearance and demeanor and the utter failure that he was in everything he tried to do and be until he was well along in life, on the one hand, and, on the other hand, the almost unparalleled success that he achieved as a national leader later, that serious doubts have been raised on several occasions as to this man's real identity. Could the Adolf Hitler of Braunau-on-the-Inn and Vienna and Munich and the war and the Beer Hall Putsch be the same human being as the Adolf Hitler who became Chancellor of Germany and conquered a whole continent? To many, it seemed incredible.

The true Hitler died before the nazis ever came to power, (or shortly after) some have said; his place was taken by a double—by several doubles.

The original Hitler is still alive, others have said, but doubles often appear for him in public to spare the Chancellor's time and energy and reduce the chances of his being killed.

Adolf Hitler changed places with a brother, still others have said: "In Munich national socialist circles," Konrad Heiden writes, "it was asserted many years ago that Adolf Hitler's real name was Robert and that he had exchanged his [civil identification] papers for those of his brother Adolf in order to avoid Austrian military service. The assertion is extremely questionable and would not deserve mention had not the national socialist Otto Lurker, Hitler's prison warder at Landsberg, stated in his book, 'Hitler Behind Fortress Walls,' 'Another Adolf Hitler —who did not seem to be quite normal—obstinately demanded to see his brother, Rudolph Hitler—known as Adolf Hitler—in order to beg him for financial assistance.' "

Others have accepted the Adolf Hitler who became Chancellor of Germany and commander-in-chief of the armies that conquered all Europe as the same human being as he whose identity has been established as a boy in Braunau-on-the-Inn, but they have said it really does not matter much which Hitler it is, or whether it is Hitler at all, who became Chancellor, because this man is only a figurehead anyway, a puppet of other men who really plan and carry out the enterprises credited to him.

Hitler himself has helped to nourish these legends by surrounding his early life with mystery. His account of it in "Mein Kampf" is fragmentary at best, self-contradictory, and has been proven to be false in several respects. For some time after the First World War, furthermore, he refused to be photographed and forbade the party to publish such few pictures of him as existed—mostly in groups of soldiers taken during the war. And since nobody else had any wish or occasion to publish pictures of Hitler, very few are available of him during this period.

But no convincing evidence has ever been presented to substantiate any of the theories that Adolf Hitler is not Adolf Hitler; still less is there any justification for believing that he is a puppet.

The story that Hitler has doubles who appear or even act for him was widely believed for a time. The nazis themselves disseminated both the story that Hitler was dead and the story that he was alive but that his place was often taken by various doubles. These stories confused opponents and discouraged potential assassins. But the first story certainly is untrue and the second most probably untrue, too. Hitler is his own double in the sense that he is a man of so many phases and facets of personality.

Nor is Hitler anyone's puppet. There have been men in the Reich at various times who thought that they really ruled Germany, and fondly believed that Hitler was "their man," and who said so openly, and Hitler has seen no harm in several cases in allowing these men to cherish their delusions for a time. It has actually helped him by raising false hopes among his adversaries. But the delusions of those who have thought in these terms have almost invariably been short-lived, and the several destinies of these men have been the proof of their mistake. Papen was one of these men. Schacht was another. Minoux was a third. Thyssen was a fourth. There were many others; they all met the same disillusioning fate. No, Adolf Hitler is no figurehead. He is, on the contrary, one of the greatest political geniuses, howbeit a singularly evil one, of all modern times.

And, finally, Adolf seems definitely to be Adolf, and neither Rudolph nor Robert. And even if he were "his own brother" (or anybody else) the problem of explaining him would still remain. Adolf or Rudolph or Robert or Fritz, it is the personality, not the name it goes by, that is all-important.

MYSTERY

To mark one of Hitler's last birthdays before the Second World War, *Das Schwarze Korps*, the official organ of the S. S. and the police, published a special article in the form of a kind of prayer to the Chancellor. The author said, among other things:

"On this day I draw near to your image. It is hard, magnificent and sublime. It is simple, benevolent and warm. It is, in one person, our father, our mother and our brother; it is more still . . . Thus you stand in the basilica of the love of millions of human beings, a basilica whose luminous cupola rises toward Heaven."

Some time before this, another national socialist, a responsible leader in the Labor Front, had expressed this same state of mind in blunter words: "Centuries which come later," he had said, "will judge what is happening in Germany in a fairer light. They will come to the conclusion that Jesus Christ was a great man, but that Adolf Hitler was still greater."

Sickening—and terrifying in their implications for a whole way of life—these are the sorts of things that are frequently said by men who rule the destinies of the most powerful nation on the continent of Europe about a leader who a few short years ago was the most abject and even ludicrous of failures. This fawning, nauseating, Byzantine idolatry is madness, if you like. But this is no answer to the question: How did Adolf Hitler the abject and ludicrous failure become Adolf Hitler the conqueror of Europe and the object of this idolatry? What is there about this man that explains his rise to power?

It is always difficult and even dangerous (because it can be misleading) to try to break down any human character into its component parts. It is especially difficult and dangerous to try it in the case of a character so extraordinary as that of Adolf

Hitler. But failure to make the attempt at all would be infinitely more perilous. The failure of most of Hitler's opponents to make the attempt has, in fact, been responsible to a considerable extent for this daemonic man's stunning achievements. And by the time the Second World War entered its decisive phase, furthermore, it was possible as it never had been before to understand him.

These, then, are the principal aspects of Hitler's character and mind that explain his rise to power:

First, outwardly unprepossessing, even ridiculous, and "un-German" too, Hitler nevertheless is utterly and exquisitely German in his essential character. Second, Hitler devised an "explanation" of his own failure in life that fitted the failures that millions of other Germans were later to experience. Third, Hitler is endowed in extraordinary measure with that passion and faith in himself that are such priceless assets in politics as in other human relationships. And, finally, he is a political genius of the very first order.

4. The Storm of Passion

One in whom persuasion and belief
Had ripened into faith, and faith become
A passionate intuition.   WORDSWORTH

Only a storm of glowing passion can turn the des-
tinies of nations, but this passion can only be roused
by a man who carries it within him.

ADOLF HITLER, "MEIN KAMPF"

ADOLF HITLER was no more prepared than the average human being to admit that the fact that he was a failure in life at 30 was his own fault. It had to be somebody's else fault. There had to be excuses. Hitler looked for excuses and, of course, he found them.

The first excuse that Hitler found was the "severe lung ailment" to which he refers in "Mein Kampf." This he used to justify his failure in school (which, in turn, explained his inability to enter the Vienna school of architecture later) and his failure to do anything toward supporting his mother or even himself for four and a half years thereafter. But Hitler could not use the excuse of the "severe lung ailment" to explain away his subsequent failures. For if he had ever had such an ailment, he had recovered from it by the time he went to Vienna. When he had to work or starve, he worked. He was healthy enough to engage in physical day labor and to serve in the army throughout the entire First World War.

A new excuse had to be found. Whose fault was it that Adolf

Hitler was still a failure although his health was perfectly satisfactory? Why, it must be the fault of the society which permitted such things to happen, which made them happen. And what was this society? What was wrong with it?

Hitler looked about him. He did so, naturally, from the point of view that his early life had given him. Most particularly, he looked at things from the point of view of a strong Pan-Germanism that a schoolteacher had inculcated in him as a boy. Even before he went to Vienna, Hitler was a Pan-German. He admired Bismarck's great Reich and the House of Hohenzollern which seemed to him to have been the artificer of its greatness, and he longed to share, as a German subject, in its power and glory. But what did Hitler see about him in Vienna?

THE PERFECT ALIBI

The Austria-Hungary of before the First World War was a mosaic or, perhaps, better, a crazy quilt, of peoples: of Austrians and Hungarians and Czechs and Slovaks, of Poles, Italians and Ukrainians and of a score of other nationalities. The Austrians and Hungarians held the others in a bondage that was all-too-strait. But it was not strait enough for Hitler. There was much in this pre-war Austria-Hungary, in fact, of which this strange youth from the provinces disapproved, much he bitterly hated.

Hitler became interested in politics. He read the newspapers and he sat in the galleries and watched the proceedings on the floor of Parliament and he listened to what his fellow down-and-outers said. And, of the views he heard, he inevitably believed those that seemed to him to explain his own experience best, especially since these same views also coincided with what his boyhood teacher had taught him to believe and, furthermore, were the generally accepted views of the middle class as a whole in Vienna at that time, the class of which Hitler considered himself rightfully a member, to which he now looked up and to which he aspired to return. What were these views?

What was principally wrong with Austria-Hungary nationally, these views held, was that the "superior" "Nordic" and Germanic Austrians, instead of constituting a worthy component part of the neighboring Reich, as they should have done, ruling,

as such, the "inferior" peoples around them, were instead allowing the "inferior" nationalities to insist upon their own identities
as peoples, to urge their national pretensions and, indeed, to
challenge the rule of their Germanic masters and even threaten
the ruling nation's very existence.

But there were more things wrong with Austria-Hungary
then than this, in dominant middle-class views. What was most
conspicuously wrong, according to these views, was that apart
from the question of nationalities, the international socialist labor
unions and the Jews were entirely too powerful and were using
their power to further their own interests at the expense of the
Germanic master people as a whole.

Such liberalism as existed in Vienna then was also made partly
responsible for the fact that society fell short of Pan-German,
middle-class ideals, because it was this liberalism that gave the
inferior peoples and the Jews and labor unions a chance to make
themselves felt.

Hitler's early background and training predisposed him to
adopt this explanation. His circumstances enforced this predis-
position.

Hitler could not make a living. Was this his own fault?
Impossible. It must be somebody's else. But whose? The workmen said it was the fault of the employers and the middle class
in general. But Hitler hated and depised—and feared—the
workmen. (They were not even patriotic enough to suit him.)
He considered himself the social and intellectual equal of the
upper classes. And the middle and upper classes said that the
fault was that of the international socialist labor unions and the
Jews.

This was a highly convenient explanation, not only for the
middle and upper classes, but for Adolf Hitler too.

This view of the labor unions "explained" the workmen's
"lack of patriotism." It "explained" their disrespect for people
like Adolf Hitler. It "explained" why Hitler could not get
along with them. It "explained" why he could not hold a job.

The explanation that the Jews, too, were responsible for much
of what was wrong was even more convenient and therefore
even more plausible. There is some reason to suppose that Hit-

ler's anti-semitism was partly sexual in origin. He seems either to have had an unhappy love affair with a Jewish girl in Vienna or to have been rejected by a gentile girl who accepted a Jewish rival instead. But the convenience of the Jews as scapegoats was enough in itself to explain Hitler's anti-semitism, even if there was no sexual basis for it.

The Jews were not Germanic. They were therefore necessarily "inferior." Some of them were strange, barbaric creatures, with curls and caftans, from the ghettos in which their "superior" master-people rulers had locked them for generations. Some of them were not ardent believers in German nationalism. And best of all, for the purpose of buttressing Hitler's alibi for his failure, the Jews—said the propaganda of their enemies—played a disproportionate part in the socialist labor unions. This was convenient indeed. The Jews were the perfect scapegoat.

Hitler was only too ready to believe what his betters said of the Jews—just as his betters had calculated he and millions of others like him would be. Hitler embraced the conventional middle-class Pan-German view. His political philosophy was formed. Adopted in the flop-houses of Vienna, it was never to change materially thereafter.

The war only confirmed Hitler in his views. For if the invincible Reich was beaten, it could not be due to any fault of that master people, the Germans, or to any superiority in strength or in any other respect of the British or French or Americans or Russians, or of all of them and all of their allies together. It must be due to the treachery of the same elements that had been the enemies within the gates before: the "inferior" subject peoples who had been disloyal all along, the Czechs and the others who had gone over to the enemy, and the "international Jewish socialists," who had administered the "stab in the back" that had caused defeat.

This was the explanation that Adolf Hitler found for the fact that he, a "superior" person, a member of the middle class and therefore a "gentleman," and a "German," howbeit born in Austria, had sunk to the gutter while obviously less worthy men had succeeded.

Under normal circumstances, neither Hitler's failure nor the excuses that he made for it would have mattered very much to anyone but himself. But the circumstances were to be very far from normal. For millions of other Germans were to fail, too— to fail militarily and politically and economically; to lose the war and lose control of their country and lose their savings and literally to go hungry. And these millions, too, were to refuse to blame themselves. They, too, were to look for an "explanation," an excuse. They, too, were to seek for a scapegoat. And they were to find that Adolf Hitler was ready with a convenient and therefore a plausible explanation, a gratifying excuse and an ideal scapegoat. The alibi that was perfect for Hitler was perfect for them as well.

SYMBOL

There was a close parallel between what had happened to Hitler and what happened to millions of other Germans. Hitler had been forced down from the middle class to the lowest level of the proletariat. So were hundreds of thousands of others, in the post-war inflation and depression. Hitler had served through-out the war in a German army that was invincible but that had nevertheless been beaten. So had millions of others. Hitler had revered the power and glory of the great Germanic Reich, had actually needed its majesty and authority for his own spirit's security. So had millions of other Germans. Hitler had to have an explanation for the catastrophes that had overwhelmed him. So did millions of others. The Germans always have to have an explanation, a theory, a philosophy, for everything, and especially now did they require one.

Hitler had evolved such an explanation. The true German people, like himself, he said, were the greatest of all the peoples of the earth. They were destined to rule the world. But, guile-less and trusting as they were, they had allowed the enemies within the gates to stab them in the back. It was all the fault, in the last analysis, of the Jews.

It is not surprising that millions of others found this view admirable. It explained their failures as conveniently as it ex-plained Hitler's.

"Power came to him," says Schuman, "because he was able

to capitalize upon his own value as a symbol of the mass frustrations and insecurities of the Kleinbuergertum from which he sprang. In finding an emotionally satisfying solution for his own problems, he was to afford a comparable solution for the problems of multitudes who suffered as he had suffered."

So it is that the fact that Adolf Hitler was an abject failure at 30 and even at 40 is one of the very reasons why he was such an amazing success by the time that he was 50.

It is hardly the only reason, obviously, though. It explains why Hitler had a theory to explain and excuse what had happened and why millions of Germans were ready to accept this theory. But hundreds and even thousands of others offered this same explanation. Why did the Germans turn to Hitler rather than to one of these others? The answer to this question must be sought in Hitler's temperament and character and mind, which set him off from the others and enabled him, and not them, to win the power they all coveted.

THE "MADMAN"

The central fact about Adolf Hitler's temperament and character is that he is a man of violent and even terrible passion.

This passion takes now one form and now another. Different observers have been struck by different aspects and expressions of it. Some have noted principally Hitler's faith in himself and in his mission, others his stupendous nervous energy and power of will. Some have chiefly remarked his savage bitterness, his awful frenzies of rage, others his fits of hysterical tears and threats of suicide. To one student Hitler is most conspicuously a lonely and aloof man, to another a sensitive, a subtle and an intuitive one; to still another Hitler's almost mesmeric powers of suggestion are most striking. Or it may be Hitler's utter unscrupulousness in general and, more specifically, his apparently absolute inability to tell the truth when it is contrary to his interests to do so that seem most characteristic of this man.

But these are all only different names for what is essentially the same quality, or, at the most, they are different aspects and expressions of it—the quality of violent emotion, of tempestuous passion: of emotions and passions so fiercely flaming that they

verily compel the man in whom they rage to prodigies of faith
and will and energy, and that also flare up in frenzies of both
bitterness and despair; that set him off from other, more normal,
men; that temper his perceptions to points of refinement and
subtlety unknown to those of colder, blunter temperaments;
that yet seize upon and hold these others by a power of awful
fascination; that blind the man himself to values, to proportions,
to obstacles and to facts and truths that to other men are ineluctable and all-important.

This is the sort of man that Adolf Hitler is, a man daemonic,
a man who is, in the older sense of the word, "possessed."

So violent are Hitler's passions that it has often seemed they
must consume and destroy him utterly. It has, in fact, often
been said that he is mad, and still oftener has he seemed to
hover on the very brink of madness, or at least of complete
collapse of mind and spirit.

In a nature so violent it is, of course, always possible that the
furies of passion will sweep away the last controls of the will
at any time. In the case of a man possessed as Hitler is possessed, the line between sanity and insanity can, in fact, be difficult to draw. Perhaps all great and ruthless conquerors and
oppressors, furthermore, are mad. Hitler is quite probably mad
in the sense that Attila and Genghis Khan were mad. He may
hover even more closely than they may have done on the brink
of what most ordinary mortals would call insanity.

But, these reservations aside, Hitler most certainly is not mad
in the everyday, rule-of-thumb sense in which the world mostly
uses the term—not, at least, as these lines are written. Judged,
in fact, by the capacity to perceive realities and to exploit them
to the utmost, Hitler for several years was the sanest man at the
head of a major power in Europe.

HYSTERIA

But even if none of the forms and expressions of Hitler's passion prove that this daemonic man is mad, and even if not all
of them taken together do so, they have often seemed at the
very least to make him incapable of the effective exercise of

power, even by the most cynical standards of effectiveness and without regard to the morality of either method or purpose.

This is particularly true of Hitler's unscrupulousness and lying, of his hysterical fits of tears, his threats of suicide and his awful rages. Hitler is forever saying that he is going to kill himself, or bursting into storms of tears or indulging in black rages of fury. According to some accounts (one cited by such a careful student as William L. Shirer, for example) Hitler is sometimes so seized by frenzy that he rolls on the floor and chews the carpet. According to other accounts—among them one given by Hermann Rauschning—Hitler not infrequently has attacks of hallucination and delirium.

Facts and allegations like these have inspired more than one critic to ridicule, contempt and scorn. Goering, for example, when once confronted by a difficult situation, is reported to have said, "We can always get Adolf to weep." Others have been even more contemptuous. Noting that Hitler himself said that when news of the armistice reached him in 1918 he wept for the first time since his mother's death, Mowrer writes: "Later his tear glands became more active: in the course of a single interview with Otto Strasser he wept no less than three times." And Olden, in reporting that Hitler threatened to go on a hunger strike when sentenced to detention in fortress after the 1923 Putsch, says scornfully, "He was easily persuaded not to do anything so distressing."

How could this utterly unscrupulous. man, this apparently pathological liar, win the confidence of others that is indispensable for acquiring power, if not for keeping it? How could such a "sickeningly moody" man exert effective power, even if he could acquire it? How could a man unable to control himself be able to rule others? Many did not think he could. (This, too, contributed to the underestimation of Hitler.)

But Hitler could and did acquire and exercise effective power; he could and did rule others. He did so, in fact, partly by means of some of the very qualities that seemed to disqualify him for rule.

It would be agreeable to report, as it would be agreeable to believe, that deceit, unscrupulousness and treachery failed, that crime did not pay. Unhappily, in Hitler's case, and combined with other circumstances, deceit, unscrupulousness and treachery did not fail. They succeeded, and succeeded brilliantly. Crime did pay. It paid, at least, to the extent of helping to bring Adolf Hitler to the threshold of the greatest power ever wielded by a single human being in history.

So it is, too, with Hitler's so-called "hysteria." Because Hitler, like some women, seldom becomes "hysterical," in either a suicidal or a homicidal spirit, when to do so is likely to harm him. On the contrary, his fits of tears and rage and threats to kill himself most often produce exactly the effects that Hitler wants produced: sympathy, fear, acquiescence, obedience. They also rouse and maintain an intensive spirit of combativeness in Hitler himself, and this stimulates him and reinforces the power of suggestion he exercises over others.

Hitler can control himself better than most men, when he chooses to do so. But sometimes he does not choose to do so. Why should he, when "hysteria" pays so well?

SALVATION

The other forms and expressions of Hitler's daemonic passion likewise do little or nothing to harm him, even at their worst, and, at their best, do much to help him.

Hitler, for example, has been notoriously aloof, since his early years of boyhood. He has had little to do with most of his own immediate family, to say nothing of other relatives. He could not get along with the other workmen and down-and-outers in Vienna. During the war he could not get along with the other soldiers; he wrote no letters, he never received a single package from home, and he cared nothing about leave. Only three party henchmen ever seem to have addressed him by the familiar "du": Gregor Strasser, Ernst Roehm and Ernst Hanfstaengl, and the first two of these Hitler ordered murdered June 30, 1934, and the third he allowed, if he did not order, to be driven out of Germany by party enemies three years later. All other party leaders, without exception, including even Goering, Hitler has always addressed formally as "Party Comrade So-and-So," and they have all addressed him as "Mein Fuehrer."

This loneliness and aloofness may have made it harder for Hitler to get along with other men, and harder for others to get along with him. In this sense, the quality may have been a handicap. But, on the other hand, it has also helped to create that illusion of god-like remoteness which is one of his greatest advantages in dealing with most other men. Reduced to its most sickening and most blasphemous form, it has found, in the words of Hans Frank, this expression: "Hitler is lonely. So is God. Hitler is like God."

It is the same with Hitler's savage bitterness and vindictiveness. For the Chancellor makes great use of fear and terrorism and frightfulness as implements of policy, and the knowledge that he is bitter and savage and vindictive contributes to the effectiveness of these implements.

For the rest, Hitler's passion in its other forms and expressions is incalculably advantageous to him. Only the kind of faith in himself and his mission that Adolf Hitler has can conjure up the nervous energy and power of will that Hitler has had to have, and has had and does have, to achieve the results that he has achieved, and his quickness of perception, his subtlety and almost clairvoyant quality of intuitiveness are scarcely less useful to him.

Hitler's passion kindles a feeling of inner kinship in millions of Germans and stirs them deep in their subconscious. There comes this man, prophet-like, preaching a doctrine that assuages the agonies of their bitter fate and tells them of a promised land. Hitler has suffered as they have suffered, he has found salvation and he now offers it to them. The same fires burn in him that burn in them—and burn with a wild fury. The Chaplin mustache, the comical forelock, the awkward manner (they too, are awkward), the mediocre physique and even the clumsy language—these things are forgotten or they have actually served to enhance the spell that this man casts. Prophets are not supposed to be fashion plates. "Un-German"? This man's strange, tormented, daemonic soul is the very quintessence of the souls of millions of Germans.

THE MIRACLE OF FAITH

More than anything else, the Germans were seeking and still seek faith. Their old ideals and beliefs have been shattered and they have found no new ones. Yet they have to have faith to live by. And Hitler offers this, too: faith and a passionate conviction that this faith is true and good. Hitler's appeal is rational enough, in many respects, but much of his power is due to his ability to inspire an utterly irrational faith.

"Those who followed Hitler did not believe, they did not have convictions," Dorothy Thompson writes. "They had faith. They *had* to have some faith."

"In despair the masses turn to the magician who promises to make the impossible possible," says Peter Drucker. "So it is not in spite of but because of its contradictions and its impossibility that the masses turn to fascism. For if you are caught between the flood of the past, through which you cannot retrace your steps, and an apparently unscalable blank wall in front of you, it is only by magic and miracles that you can hope to escape. *Credo quia absurdum*, that cry of a master who had known all the bitterness of deepest and blackest despair, is heard again for the first time in many a century."

THE VIBRATIONS PER SECOND

Hitler's oratory is the most conspicuous expression of his own faith and passion and the principal means by which he inspires faith and passion among the Germans.

"As long as Hitler's vocal cords are unimpaired, he will be the greatest asset of the national socialist party," Emil Lengyel once wrote. "But what would happen if they were impaired?"

Hitler's vocal cords have been impaired on more than one occasion. The principal one of these impairments, in fact, badly frightened Hitler himself. Not merely, though, because he feared for his voice: he feared for his very life, because he thought the impairment was caused by a cancer of the throat. But the trouble was only due to a simple polyp (at least so the operating surgeon said), a relatively harmless affliction to which all singers and public speakers are susceptible, and the only disquiet that it caused was the failure of the patient to rally for more than 14 hours from the effects of the morphine that the surgeon had had administered as an anesthetic.

Even if Hitler should lose his voice, he still would be by far the "greatest asset" that the national socialist party had, to put it mildly. Yet it is certainly also true that Hitler's qualities as an orator are among the most valuable of the many that help to explain his power.

Hitler breaks all the rules of the professors of public speaking. His speeches are interminably long; they often last two hours and even longer. His voice is thick, as though he always had a cold or a bad sinus inflammation. His enunciation is indistinct. The material in his speeches is usually badly organized, his sentences badly constructed, his figures of speech awkward and his choice of words unhappy. His addresses sound just as involved, as tortuous and as infelicitously phrased in the original German and to the Germans to whom they are primarily directed, as they do in the translations in which the rest of the world reads them. They sound even more clumsy, in fact, to most Germans, because of Hitler's provincial Austrian accent and choice of words.

Most of the gestures with which Hitler accompanies and seeks to emphasize his words, furthermore, are as awkward as the words themselves; made only from the elbows and the wrists, they are often actually grotesque.

Hitler usually speaks from full notes or a complete text, and most of the time he keeps his eyes on the manuscript before him and seldom even looks at his audience.

Nor has he any change of style or pace to relieve and enliven his speeches. His humor is infrequent and almost always sardonic and even harsh. He is earnest, stern, scornful, tragic, bitter and savage by turns, but he is almost never anything else.

Yet this orator who breaks all the rules achieves effects that no professor of public speaking who knows every rule and device of oratory has ever dreamed of achieving, effects that few orators of any place or time have ever achieved, effects that are terrifying in their implications. What explains this paradox?

The first element in Hitler's power as a speaker consists, of course, of what he says. For the most part, he tells his listeners things that they passionately, desperately want to be told. But the way in which Hitler says these things is at least as important as what he says, in spite of its apparent faults—and, indeed, precisely because of some of them.

Even the thick, harsh voice that can be so repellent plays its part in the spell that Hitler's oratory creates. Professor M. D. Steer, of Purdue University, has analyzed Hitler's voice and reports that it has a frequency in a typical sentence of 228 vibrations per second, whereas 200 per second is a usual frequency for anger. "It is this high pitch and its accompanying emotion that put the people in a passive state," Professor Steer says. "He stuns them with his words in much the same fashion as we are stunned by an auto horn."

IN TONGUES

But while the frequency of vibrations of Hitler's voice and, doubtless, other qualities in it, may help to explain the hypnotic quality of Hitler's oratory, it is broader qualities of his appeal that are the principal causes for its success.

Hitler almost always speaks in one of only two moods. One is a mood of mystical and semi-religious self-abasement. It is in this mood that he habitually appeals for the confidence and support of the German people. In it, he speaks of faith and destiny and miracles, of regeneration and martyrdom, and of his struggle for the souls of men. Often in this mood he uses purely religious terms: shame, sin and expiation. He is a redeemer, calling upon the people to lay their sins and sufferings on his shoulders.

Hitler's other principal mood is one of bitter, savage violence. He storms, he rages, he abuses, he threatens, he reviles, he attacks again and again. Now he is no more the pleading redeemer; now he is a terrible avenger.

Both of these moods release and rouse the most powerful passions of men: the passion for self-sacrifice, the passion to serve, the passion to protect—and, most notably of all, the passion to fight. And in both moods, Hitler strikes deep into the subconscious of his listeners. This is one of the reasons he speaks at such length. He needs time to develop the theoretical, philosophical basis for his argument that is so essential for Germans. But he also needs time to release and set off the stormy processes of the subconscious, not only among his listeners, but also in himself.

So it is that he usually begins on a relatively unemotional level, sometimes on a note, almost, of indifference, and goes on and on, searching and reaching for the words, the tone, the manner that will break down both his own inhibitions of the conscious will and those of his listeners. Then, sooner or later, as Olden describes it:

"The moment will come when the speaker is overcome by his own inspiration, and with a sobbing, screaming and gurgling, something unknown and indefinable breaks out of him; it is then no longer a question of set sentences or articulate words—in an ecstasy he speaks 'in tongues.' Should a man have remained unmoved up to this stage, now is the time when he becomes aware that before his very eyes there is occurring a manifestation of the unconscious; sense and nonsense have become one, and he finds himself in the presence of an ineffable force of nature. This is the moment when men break out in delirious applause, when women groan and feel the tender, painful ecstasy of passion. From this moment on, the agitator has a transformed public before him. Those he cannot hypnotize go away nauseated and never return. The others are his, body and soul."

Olden here describes a style that Hitler has invoked increasingly rarely in public since becoming Chancellor. Even in his most formal public speeches, however, the essential nature of his oratory has always remained the same, and in Hitler's private outbursts of passion it is precisely this quality that produces the effects on his listeners that are so important a part of this man's daemonic power over others.

5. The Power of Evil

Every deed has its place, even crime.

ADOLF HITLER

ADOLF HITLER's heredity, so far as it can be traced, his environment, his manner and appearance and the story of his early life, all seem to indicate that he must be a typically mediocre member of a mediocre class, remarkable, if at all, only for being an even less effective human being than most others of his type. Yet he is one of the great—and one of the most evil—political geniuses of modern times.

The circumstances favored Hitler. The universal crisis of faith, the German defeat in the First World War and the inflation and depression that followed were what made it possible for a man like him to rise to such unprecedented power. The flaming passion which is the outstanding quality of Hitler's character is the second element in his success. But these by themselves explain neither the man nor his career. The circumstances favored others almost or just as much as they did him, and Hitler's extraordinary character might have harmed more than helped his rise to power if it had not been leashed to an even more extraordinary brain. It is Hitler's brain that is the most important thing about him. In politics (although not in other things) Hitler is a genius. And this genius is fettered by literally no scruples of any kind whatever.

Hitler's evil genius manifested itself first in the fact that he perceived the weaknesses (without, however, perceiving the strengths) of the men and systems arrayed against him, both in

83

the Reich itself and in the rest of the world, the men and systems that seemed so formidable to most others. Hitler has always mistaken the nature and causes of these weaknesses. He has thought they were due to democracy and to Marxism, which they most certainly are not. They are due to quite other and much deeper causes. If Hitler should win the war, it would be in spite of his having made this mistake. If he loses, it will be primarily because of it. But even if Hitler has mistaken the nature and causes of the weaknesses, it is a part of his genius that he has seen so clearly from the first that the weaknesses were there. And while others perceived the weaknesses, too, Hitler did much more: he exploited them, and he did so on such a scale and with such success as to threaten a whole civilization and a whole way of life.

"TREASONS, STRATAGEMS AND SPOILS"

As a politician, Hitler excels first as a mob psychologist, and most particularly as an orator; and, second, as a tactician.

Among the most important respects in which Hitler surpassed almost all his earlier adversaries (and his collaborators) were the pains and skill with which he prepared his plans before he acted. Other things being anything like equal, the man who knows what he wants and who has a well thought out plan for getting it will almost inevitably win against the man who is not sure what he wants or, even if he is sure, has no plan of action for obtaining it. Hitler has almost always known exactly what he has wanted, and he has almost always had a plan for getting it. His great, strategic, all-inclusive plan he laid down in "Mein Kampf," and this in itself has given him a great advantage over most of those who have been arrayed against him, because they have had no comparable plan of their own and have depended on improvisation. But Hitler also usually has a detailed and tactical plan for each of the measures he takes for the accomplishing of his final purpose. Rudolf Olden has best summed up this aspect of Hitler's brilliance as a politician:

"He will work out the tactics of his behavior for days, indeed weeks, beforehand, planning attack and counterattack, advance and retreat, step by step. He will weld together his band of sympathizers, neutralize opposition by counter-opposition, prepare arguments, charge himself with tense excitement—and before the discussion begins the decision has fallen. . . . Admiring fellow workers like young Esser sometimes boast of the quickness of his decisions. But they are people who cannot imagine anyone's lying awake all night to spring a decision upon a committee in the morning."

Hitler is skillful as well as painstaking in working out these tactics of his behavior. He is a master of political method, of "treasons, stratagems and spoils." He knows as well as any modern chief of state has known how to divide his adversaries and destroy each of them in turn. He knows how to bide his time and wait for the best possible moment to act (a quality which less gifted men have often mistaken for an inability to make up his mind). He knows, too, how to advance by such slow stages as never to give his adversary an occasion for taking a stand and effectively opposing him. Yet Hitler understands equally well the uses of effrontery and audacity, of almost never allowing himself to be put on the defensive, but of always and forever attacking—of never giving an enemy in retreat an opportunity to re-form and rally his forces and organize a new resistance.

But most clearly of all is Hitler's evil genius apparent in the skill and unscrupulousness with which, both at home and abroad, he has won over to his side and used for his own purposes those who wield effective power in society as he found and finds it.

THE SOURCES OF POWER

The importance of winning over those who control the real power in society was one of the first political lessons that Adolf Hitler learned. He learned it from Karl Lueger, who was lord mayor of Vienna in the days when Hitler was a starving down-and-outer there before the First World War. After watching and reflecting on Lueger's political methods for only a few months, Hitler perceived what some of the secrets of his success were.

"He attached the greatest importance," Hitler later wrote in "Mein Kampf," "to winning over classes whose will to fight was stimulated rather than paralyzed by a threat to their existence. He also sought to avail himself of all existing instruments of authority and to bring powerful institutions over to his side, in order to gain the greatest possible advantage for his own movement from these well-established sources of power."

Hitler learned both these lessons well, learned them as a youth with no political education and no political training worthy of the name, learned them simply by keeping his eyes and ears open and his wits about him. Politically, this young man obviously was no fool.

Most particularly did Hitler learn the lesson of the advantages to be gained by availing one's self of existing instruments of authority. The most important of these instruments in Republican Germany were two: the first was the government itself, and particularly the army, the police and the other executive and administrative organs of the state, and the courts; the second was the organized right wing of society, which had money and the other implements of power that money was needed to buy, things like the press and the motion-picture industry.

Hitler was greatly helped, in his efforts to avail himself of these instruments of authority, by the fact that influential persons among those who controlled them wanted and were looking for someone like him whom they could use for their purposes, just as he wanted and was looking for them to use for his.

ARMS AND THE MAN

The Reichswehr was the first implement of power of which Hitler availed himself. Hitler stayed in the army until April 1, 1920. During all this time the army fed him, clothed him, housed him and directed his activities.

Officers in charge of Reichswehr political activities in Bavaria discovered that Hitler was an effective speaker with an extreme nationalist point of view, and they used him as an "educational officer" to deliver propaganda speeches to the troops. Considering Hitler's views, this use of him by the military constituted treason against the Republic, but treason was the rule of the day in the German army then and thereafter, and, in this sense, at least, there was nothing remarkable about this relatively un-important instance of it.

Hitler's officers also used him as a spy. On the one hand, the army set out to suppress political activities that it considered undesirable; on the other hand, it undertook to encourage activities that promised, in its view, to rehabilitate the national morale. Hitler was sent out to investigate and report on political activities that seemed to fall into either one of these categories. It was on such an errand, in fact, that Hitler attended his first meeting of the German Workers' Party that he was to take over and build up into the national socialist movement.

Even after Hitler was honorably discharged from the army, he continued to enjoy its support. The Kapp Putsch in the Spring of 1920 failed in Berlin but succeeded in Bavaria. The army ousted the government and installed Gustav von Kahr as prime minister. Bavaria was in effect a military dictatorship, and the military gave Hitler and his party every aid and comfort.

Captain Ernst Roehm was the army's principal agent in extending this aid and comfort. With the consent of his superior, General Ritter von Epp, Roehm enlisted other soldiers in the nazi party, he made grants from the army's secret political funds to help finance Hitler, he provided weapons for arming the S. A. and he let the nazis use armories and barracks to drill in. All this aid was vouchsafed, of course, at the expense of the taxpayers and of the Republic Hitler was sworn to overthrow.

On one occasion the army's support of Hitler even went to the lengths of open defiance of the War Office in Berlin. The *Voelkischer Beobachter* (which army funds had helped Hitler to acquire) called almost openly on the army to revolt against the Republic. The War Office ordered Kahr to silence the paper. Kahr refused to do so. The War Office then ordered General von Lossow, the commander of the 7th division, in Bavaria, to close the *Voelkischer Beobachter*, by force of arms if necessary. Lossow refused to obey this order. The War Office then informed Lossow that he was dismissed and would be replaced by General Freiherr von Kress. Lossow refused to recognize Kress. Such were the faithful servants that the Weimar Republic had—and continued to tolerate—in "its" armed forces. Such were some of the men in the army whose aid and comfort Hitler enjoyed.

The Beer Hall Putsch in 1923 brought this first period of full army support of Hitler to an end. During the "Stresemann period" of treaty fulfillment (of a sort), the army's sympathy was, as Olden puts it, only platonic. But even platonic sympathy was invaluable to Hitler. And when the period of fulfillment ended, important elements in the Reichswehr again displayed an ardor in behalf of Hitler that was far indeed from being merely platonic. Schleicher, who theoretically, at least, controlled the Reichswehr, opposed Hitler, it is true. But Hitler out-maneuvered Schleicher: he went over his head to Hindenburg by making use of another instrument of established power —the organized, conservative right wing, represented by Franz von Papen, which controlled the supreme civil authority in the state.

REVOLUTION BY CONSENT

The civil authorities, in fact, supported Hitler throughout his struggle for power to an extent that was only slightly, if at all, less useful to him than the aid and comfort was that the army vouchsafed. The Weimar Republic was destroyed by traitors among its own officials, sworn to uphold and defend it, using their public offices for public betrayal, as much as it was by its avowed enemies attacking openly from without.

Wilhelm Frick was one of the most important of these traitors. In the early years after the First World War, Frick was head of the political section of the Munich police. Supported by Ernst Poehner, who was chief of police, Frick helped Hitler at every turn. "We held our protecting hand over Herr Hitler," Frick testified at the trial that followed the failure of the 1923 Putsch, "because we saw in him the germ of Germany's regeneration."

Other agents of the state's civil authority also held protecting hands over Hitler. The whole trial at which Frick gave his candid testimony appeared at times, in fact, to be an arraignment of the state by Hitler rather than one of Hitler by the state. This was one of the first conspicuous occasions on which Hitler made effective use of a trick that he was to employ on a much greater stage thereafter: on trial as prisoner at the bar, he turned on those who sought to try him and condemned them as the true criminals instead. At one point in the proceedings Hitler was permitted to deliver a four-hour harangue to the spectators and to "posterity." The court, too, as well as Frick, seemed to see in him the germ of Germany's regeneration.

Hitler was convicted, it is true, and sentenced to five years' detention in fortress. But this, in effect, was an endorsement of what he had done. Everybody knew he would only be detained a few months and that he would be treated like a favored guest at a hotel while he was there. Hitler had led an armed insurrection against the state—and he was "punished" as an officer and a gentleman is "punished" for defending the honor of a lady with his sword.

The authorities continued to hold a protecting hand over Hitler. When his release was proposed after he had served six months of his five-year term, the public prosecutor tried to prevent it. Among other reasons he gave was the fact that Roehm was even then actively engaged in raising a private army in Hitler's name for a new attempt to overthrow the state whose clemency was now invoked. But the Bavarian Minister of Justice overruled the prosecutor. "We must support the national socialists," the minister publicly declared at about this time; "they are flesh of our flesh." Hitler was freed. This obliging minister was Franz Guertner. Like Frick, he was handsomely rewarded later for his betrayal of the state he was sworn to uphold: Hitler made him Reich Minister of Justice.

Beginning with Frick and Poehner and ending with Papen and Hindenburg, a host of public officials placed the established power of the state at Hitler's disposal. Perhaps the most distinguished representatives of authority to do so were the judges of the Reich Supreme Court. At one stage in Hitler's struggle for power they actually laid it down as a principle that in cases involving party clashes it was to be assumed that the nazis and their allies of the right had acted in self-defense and that their Marxist enemies had been the aggressors. Courts all over Germany adopted this principle. Here was a protecting hand

indeed. It is no wonder that Konrad Heiden called the nazi
revolution a revolution by the consent of the Herr Minister
President.

WORD OF HONOR

The support of the established powers and interests that
Hitler enjoyed throughout his career did not simply fall into
his lap. He worked for it, and worked hard.

First he had to convince those with power and authority
at their disposal that he was "their man"—that he shared their
views and deferred to their interests and wanted to further
them. Then he had to convince these people that he was able,
as well as willing, to help them.

Both tasks were often hard. For in the case of a good many
of those whom Hitler sought to win over, he most emphati-
cally was not "their man." Far from it. He was their deadly
enemy. He said so, in fact, publicly, loudly and often. He denounced the right to the left almost as savagely as he denounced the left to the right—in public. Some of those against
whom these menaces were uttered took them seriously. They
were by no means disposed to help the man who made them.

But Hitler was usually able, nevertheless, to win over
enough of those with power and authority for his purposes,
or at least to assure himself of their neutrality, if not of their
active support. He did this, for the most part, by swearing to
these people privately that he did not mean the attacks he
made on them publicly—that, on the contrary, he was their
most devoted friend and ally. Hitler would say anything,
promise anything, forswear anything, to win over those who
controlled the instruments of power. On several occasions he
even privately abjured anti-semitism to people whose support
he thought he could obtain by such a renunciation—or the appearance of it.

Hitler began this practice of duplicity at the outset of his
career. Some time in the latter part of 1922, for example, the
Bavarian Minister of the Interior, a Dr. Schweyer, sent for
Hitler and warned him against doing anything foolish. Hitler
"leaped to his feet," according to Heiden's account, "struck
his breast and shouted, 'Herr Minister, I give you my word

of honor that never in my life will I make a Putsch! Herr
Minister, my word of honor, never in my life a Putsch!'"

Hitler might, perhaps, have argued that when he did make
his bid for power a little over one year later he was not really
engaging in a Putsch because he had the authorities on his side
—or thought he had. Up to a certain point, in fact, they were
on his side. But they betrayed him—a betrayal that was to cost
them dearly, in the end, both as individuals and as a class. No
arguing can explain away the promises that Hitler has made
and broken since, however. Hitler's word of honor is a curious
thing indeed.

He promised to support Papen's cabinet, for example, in
1932, and then attacked and sought to overthrow it. He gave
his word of honor when he himself became Chancellor that
he would retain all the original members of his cabinet even
after the next Reichstag elections, and then got rid of most of
them, on one pretext or another. Hitler's violations of his word
of honor in foreign affairs are notorious. The list of this man's
broken promises is so long it is monotonous.

Some of the victims of Hitler's perfidy learned their lessons
the first time he betrayed them. But even most of these victims
learned their lessons too late. Hitler's duplicity usually served
its purpose by deceiving its victims long enough for Hitler to
achieve his immediate objective. And no matter how often it
has been proven that Hitler has broken his solemn word of
honor, he has always been able to find new victims to accept it,
or to pretend to accept it and to act as though they did. For
these victims have been either, like Neville Chamberlain, incapable in spite of everything of perceiving the realities that
lay behind Hitler's promises, or, like Josef Stalin, they may have
perceived the realities clearly enough but they have thought
they could outwit Hitler. Few in either of these categories
have long survived.

Hitler has been most brilliantly successful in deceiving right-
wing interests, both in the Reich and in the outside world.
The list of his victims of this sort along his path to power is
an impressive one—and it is by no means certain that the list is

yet closed. One of the most typical and most important of these
is Alfred Hugenberg.

As a young man Hugenberg was an official in East Prussia
and took part in the administration of the Second Reich's
attempts to Germanize the Polish parts of the province. It was,
in fact, partly as a result of what Hugenberg told him about
the failure of these attempts that Hitler decided the only way
to do this effectively was to eliminate the Poles completely—
but that is another tragedy.

Later Hugenberg left the government service and went into
big industry in Western Germany and became managing director of Krupp's. As such, he controlled the political funds
of big industry. During the crucial years of Hitler's struggle
for power, Hugenberg was national chairman of the German
Nationalist Party. He also controlled a vast chain of newspapers and news and feature services and the biggest motion-
picture company in Germany.

Hitler succeeded in convincing Hugenberg that he and the
nazis would make valuable allies. Hitler had a big mass following, he was even more nationalist than Hugenberg himself,
if that was possible, and he persuaded this right-wing, conservative leader that his, Hitler's, economic views were as safe
and sound as his political views were. A bargain was struck.
Hitler and Hugenberg—joined by Schacht—agreed to co-operate in a campaign against German ratification of the Young
Plan.

The campaign failed in its immediate purpose. The Young
Plan was ratified. But that was not the most important thing
about the Hitler-Hugenberg partnership. What mattered most
was that it gave Hitler access for the first time to really big
money and to the matchless propaganda machine that Hugenberg controlled, and enabled Hitler to establish himself as a
real political power in North Germany.

Hitler stole the show. From then on he dominated the stage
and Hugenberg receded farther and farther into the background: a funny-looking little fat man who wrote lyric poetry
as a youth and who rose to be the political spokesman of the
vested interests of the whole Reich, but whose role under

Hitler has been limited to abashed appearances at the infrequent "sessions" of the German Reichstag that Hitler summons to applaud his speeches; one of the two or three men present in civilian clothes, looking for all the world like an intimidated sea lion, with his tubby figure in a black frock coat, his close-cropped, graying hair and handle-bar mustache.

The young down-and-outer in Vienna before the First World War learned his lesson from Karl Lueger well.

CRIME AS AN IMPLEMENT OF POLICY

It became unfashionable, after the First World War, to believe in the existence of evil. It smacked too much of theology, and theology had gone out of style.

Both good and evil, people said, depended on the point of view and on time and place and circumstance and heredity and environment. In effect, they said, there really are no such things as good and evil.

Least of all would a good many people believe that conscious, deliberate evil (if there was such a thing) could or would ever dominate the policies of a great European power.

This attitude was due in the first instance to a general collapse of faith and of all moral values. It was strengthened by the excesses of propaganda in the First World War. So many of the allegations of evil conduct made by the allies against the Germans were discredited later that people decided they had been made fools of and swore that they never would believe such tales again.

One of the most important results of this state of mind has been that a good many people have refused to believe that Adolf Hitler and his henchmen in the nazi party are the kind of men they really are. Such evil as is attributed to these men simply does not exist, people have said. Human beings simply do not act the way these men are said to act. Certainly the responsible leaders of a great nation like Germany would not act that way. Besides, the stories of their evil conduct resemble too closely the "atrocity propaganda" of the last war. And—not least among the causes of the incredulity—the stories are so terrifying in their implications that it is much more comfortable to refuse to credit them than it would be to believe them and act accordingly.

Yet evil is an utterly real and utterly terrible thing, and Hitler and the men around him are among the most extraordinarily evil men who ever acquired control of a great European country. And the inability or unwillingness of many of those who have stood in Hitler's way to believe that he was guilty of the enormities he constantly committed has been of the greatest value to him. It has been of value, first, because the people who have refused to believe that he had the evil intentions attributed to him have failed to take the precautions that were necessary to protect themselves against the carrying out of such intentions and have therefore been helpless when Hitler has carried them out. The world's incredulity has been of value, second, because when Hitler has committed one of his enormities and then, as likely as not, boasted of it, people have been paralyzed by shock and horror.

Hitler and his henchmen use crime as an implement of national policy partly because they themselves are evil men and really enjoy committing evil acts. But they use it largely as a matter of deliberate, cold calculation, because of the successes it so often achieves. In every phase of their relations with other human beings, and almost equally among each other, sooner or later the nazis always make use of methods so unscrupulous and outrageous that their opponents are usually flabbergasted and unable to defend themselves.

Douglas Miller relates, for example, how the nazis fleece their foreign creditors. One of their most profitable swindles has been to begin by saying that they have no gold or valuta and therefore could not make payments on German securities expressed in foreign currencies. This has caused the securities to fall to a fraction of their original values. The nazis thereupon have quickly found adequate gold or foreign exchange and bought up the securities at a handsome profit to themselves and a corresponding loss to those who had been so gullible as to believe that the Reich would honor its promises. Barter agreements also have provided an easy way to swindle foreigners.

Miller reports the case, among others, of an agreement by which the nazis promised locomotives, automotive equipment and similar commodities in return for South African wool. The South Africans delivered the wool. They delivered the entire annual clip for three years in succession. But the nazis never sent anything whatever in return.

The nazis' financial swindles, though, are positively benign compared with some of the other uses they make of crime as an implement of policy. Their exploitation of sex, for example, would make a private *souteneur* or blackmailer blush with shame for his inadequacies. To mention only one case, the Wilhelmstrasse makes effective use (or did until these lines appeared) of a house of assignation in Berlin (it is "Kitty's" in the Giesebrechtstrasse) as a source of information that the ladies of the establishment take pains to obtain from such diplomats and foreign correspondents as are so ill-advised as to frequent the house—and the number and rank of those who do are both amazing. So useful is "Kitty's" to the Foreign Office and the Gestapo, in fact, that there are some who believe the nazis actually themselves maintain the establishment. It is, however, probably unnecessary for the nazis to maintain "Kitty's." All they have to do is to exploit it.

The nazis frequently use murder, too, as an implement of policy. They usually call it "assassination," to be sure, or "putting down an incipient revolt," or "mercy killings" of the "mentally unfit," or something else that sounds more respectable, and they often even succeed in persuading the rest of the world to adopt these same less shocking descriptions. But this does not alter the fundamental character of what they do.

One of the most notorious of the many murders the nazis committed during the struggle for power took place in the Upper Silesian village of Potempa. There, late in 1932, five nazis killed an opponent under peculiarly harrowing circumstances. A courageous court sentenced all five to death. Hitler was outraged by the sentence. His honor was involved, he said. He telegraphed the murderers: "United with you in boundless loyalty. Your liberty is from this moment a question of our honor." Hitler became Chancellor in time to set all five men free. Honor, in the end, was satisfied.

The nazis have committed many more murders since they acquired power than they did before. The need, one would have thought, has been less. But the opportunities have been greater. They murdered at least 1,000 men and women the week end of June 30, 1934, alone. Then they cremated the bodies of some of their victims and sent the ashes (or what they said were the ashes) in cigar boxes and paper bags, parcel post, collect, to the victims' families. On at least one other occasion they beheaded a victim (they called it, of course, "execution") and cremated the torso but sent the head to the family—and charged the family for the sack in which the head was sent. They killed several thousand Jews the week end of November 10, 1938. They liquidated approximately 100,000 persons they said were "mental defectives" in 1939 and 1940, and showed no signs of stopping there.

The crimes committed by the nazis in their conduct of the war itself have been so numerous and so monstrous that it is difficult to choose examples to refer to. One suffers from an embarrassment of riches. As good an illustration as any, though, was this:

The nazis deliberately drive civilian populations to the roads to interfere with the movements of enemy armies. Sometimes, however, these masses of civilians hamper the movements of the Germans, too. How do the Germans deal with this problem? On at least some occasions, they simply run columns of tanks right through and over the struggling, densely packed refugees. That solves the problem quickly, if not neatly.

There are Germans, and not only Germans, who persuade themselves that Hitler personally is ignorant of and therefore innocent of the crimes that are committed in his name. But this is nonsense of the worst and most criminal kind, no matter how understandable the unwillingness to face a fact of such ugly implications. The record speaks clearly enough on the worst cases, and in the others, too, Hitler and Hitler alone is responsible for the worst of the enormities of the regime. He has committed some of them himself. He has personally ordered and superintended others. He has publicly endorsed the methods by which they have all been committed. He has chosen and encouraged and upheld the men who have committed them. That is the kind of man Adolf Hitler is. It is one of the essential elements of his character. It is one of the basic factors in his power.

6. Seven Against the World

Like master, like man.

Birds of a feather flock together.

CERVANTES, "DON QUIXOTE"

THE ORGANIZATION of the nazi party is much like that of the medieval Persian League of Assassins, as the (American) Committee for National Morale points out. It is a pyramidal hierarchy, with Hitler at the top, the national leaders of the party just below him, then the armed guard (notably the S. S.), then the party subleaders and, at the base of the party pyramid, the ordinary members. This whole structure rests on the uninitiated masses of the German people and, below them, the enslaved peoples of the subjugated countries.

In theory, and usually in practice as well, the party organization functions in accordance with the so-called "leadership principle." That is, everyone in the party commands those below him in the hierarchy and obeys those above him.

There are, however, exceptions and difficulties in the application of this principle. For one thing, there are a good many parts of the organization where the lines of competence and authority are so confused that it is impossible to know who is to command and who to obey. For another thing, even where the lines of authority are perfectly clear there is also no rule as to who commands and who obeys among members of the hierarchy on the same level of power. Also, there is a ferocious and unremitting struggle for power among the more ambitious of the party, a struggle which Hitler himself encourages, partly because it makes the participants even more dependent upon him than they would be otherwise and partly because he believes that in this struggle the fittest will survive and will be all the more fit because of the struggle. And, finally, advice and suggestions from below are permitted, subject to certain conditions.

Thus while Hitler is the sole true source of authority, and all alike acknowledge, privately as well as publicly, that this is the case, the characters of the principal leaders of the party just below him in the hierarchy, and the parts they play in the organization and in the determination and conduct of policy, are nevertheless important.

The fortunes constantly shift in the struggle for power among these men. Now one and now another of them fights his way to the fore. From time to time one or another is destroyed. Any report on the men who, under Hitler, wield the greatest power in Germany must take account of these changes. Subject to this reservation, however, the leadership of the regime from February, 1938, until Rudolf Hess' flight to Scotland, May 10, 1941, functioned in accordance with this general scheme of authority, and, except for Hess, still does:

Hitler, as undisputed master, stands at the top. Directly responsible to him are three categories of leaders:

First, there are the seven (now six) outstanding, dynamic men who wield the greatest power, except in military matters, and who enjoy Hitler's confidence most, the Seven Against the World, the men who provide the paramount ability and the driving power of the national socialist struggle for world mastery. These men, in approximate order of their importance during this period, are Rudolf Hess, Hermann Goering, Heinrich Himmler, Joachim von Ribbentrop, Paul Josef Goebbels, Robert Ley and Alfred Rosenberg.

Second, there are two groups of military advisers directly responsible to Hitler. One group consists of the regularly constituted heads of the armed forces: Field Marshal Wilhelm Keitel as chief of the High Command of all the armed forces and, under him, Field Marshal Walther von Brauchitsch, commander-in-chief of the army, Grand Admiral Erich Raeder as commander-in-chief of the navy, and Reichsmarshal Goering in his capacity as chief of the air force (although Goering displays great independence vis-a-vis Keitel). The second group of Hitler's immediate military advisers consists of the members of his own personal military bureau, of whom two are outstanding, General Alfred Jodl and General Walter Warlimont.

Third, there are "the technicians," some of them party members of long standing and prominence and some taken into the party relatively late in their careers because of their usefulness, or inactive, no matter how long standing, party members, but all exercising administrative or expert, rather than political, functions. Typical "party" members of this category are Wilhelm Frick, Minister of the Interior; Walther Funk, Minister of Economics and President of the Reichsbank; and R. Walther Darré, Minister of Agriculture. Typical "non-party" members are Fritz Todt, the engineer who built the Reich super-highway system and the West Wall and who later became Minister of Munitions; and Count Schwerin von Krosigk, Reich Minister of Finance.

Of these three groups of leaders, the first group is by far the most important.

HESS: THE RIDDLE FROM THE SKIES

At about 6 o'clock the evening of May 10, 1941, Rudolf Hess strapped himself into a parachute, climbed into a special German long-range reconnaissance plane at an air field in Augsburg, and took off on a journey that was to cause one of the greatest sensations ever occasioned by a human flight since Daedalus and Icarus.

Hess had had an extra gasoline tank installed in the plane. He had also provided himself with a supply of compressed foods. And he had in his pocket a map on which he had drawn, in blue pencil, the shortest route from Augsburg to Dungavel, the estate of the Duke of Hamilton not far from Glasgow, approximately 850 miles distant. Around the point on the map representing Dungavel, Hess had drawn a circle with his blue pencil.

Roughly four hours later, David McLean, a plowman living approximately three miles from Dungavel, heard the motors of a plane flying low overhead and then a crash. He rushed out of his cottage and saw a plane crumpled on the ground 200 yards away and a parachutist coming down to earth. A hay fork was the closest thing to a weapon McLean could find in time, but the parachutist—who injured his ankle when he landed—gave no trouble. He was, on the contrary, very affable, and chatted in good English with his captor. His name, he said, was Horn.

McLean helped the parachutist to his cottage, where his sister and aged mother, wakened by the crash of the plane, were waiting. The parachutist bowed to the women when he entered and chatted amiably with them, too, while they all waited for the authorities to come for him. He even showed them snapshots of his little son. When he was taken away, he thanked the McLeans profusely for their kindness, bowing to the women again as he went out the door.

The man was taken first to Paisley and then to Maryhill Barracks, near Glasgow. There, he identified himself as Rudolf Hess. "I have come," he said, "to save humanity."

He wanted, he said, to see the Duke of Hamilton. As soon as it was established that the parachutist really was Rudolf Hess, the Duke was sent for and Hess was given an opportunity to talk to him. Hess also was interviewed by a Foreign Office official who had served in the British Embassy in Berlin.

But there end the facts of the Hess case, as distinct from rumor and conjecture, that were available up to the time this book went to press. This was the riddle that fell from the Scottish skies the night of May 10, 1941.

Why did Rudolf Hess fly to Scotland?

A final judgment is impossible until all the facts are made known. A provisional hypothesis is, however, perhaps permissible—especially since, in the light of such facts as are available, there is only one possible explanation of the riddle from the skies that makes sense.

This explanation is that Hess, as loyal to Hitler as ever, hoped that by a personal appeal he could induce influential elements among the former "appeaser" group in Great Britain to start a drive for peace that either would actually succeed or at least would confuse and divide the British people and those of the Empire and the United States to such an extent that the British war effort would be appreciably affected.

The argument that Hess intended to put to the former "appeasers," if this hypothesis is correct, must have been, in substance, something like this:

"Germany will win the war, in the end. The cost of victory will, however, be appalling to both of us if you persist in fighting on. For Britain will be crippled for years to come, and even Germany's strength will be seriously impaired. And this will give subversive elements like the communists and inferior peoples like the colored races an opportunity to plunge the world into chaos. Let us, therefore, make peace now, we two great Nordic cousin peoples, let us destroy the bolsheviks and then establish and maintain our joint supremacy, we Germans on the continent of Europe and you British elsewhere in the world."

This hypothesis—and it is only that—is subject to revision and even abandonment if and when further facts should be established that might make it untenable. It has, at least, however, this much merit: it is consistent with what is known of Rudolf Hess and the part that he had played in Germany up to that time.

Hess joined the nazi party in 1920. He soon acquired the name of being Hitler's most loyal and most selfless follower. He was so constantly at Hitler's side, and so solicitous for his leader's welfare, that other party members called him "Fraeulein," the German term for a nurse or governess. (Another and far less creditable reason was sometimes given for the use of this sobriquet; there is no way of determining whether or not this second reason is as valid as the first.)

Hess was sentenced to fortress with Hitler in 1924 and had more than anyone else to do with persuading Hitler to write his autobiography and testament of faith, "Mein Kampf." Hitler dictated the first parts of the book to Emil Maurice, another nazi fellow-prisoner, but Hess soon took over the functions of Hitler's secretary and it was he to whom Hitler dictated the rest of the first volume in the fortress at Landsberg and all the

second volume during the years 1925 and 1926 at Berchtes-
gaden. Hess also edited Hitler's original version of "Mein
Kampf," but the extent of the changes he made is not known.
(Others took a hand at editing "Mein Kampf," too.)

After the nazis were released from fortress, Hess worked
for a time, in order to support himself, as assistant to Professor
Karl Haushofer, of Munich, exponent of the dogma of Lebens-
raum and other geopolitical notions. Hess saw that these fancies
would be useful for propaganda purposes, and he passed them
on to Hitler. Hess was on intimate terms with the Haushofer
family from that time onward. To suggest that either the professor or his son, however, is or was "the brain behind Hitler,"
or anything like it, is ridiculous.

Hitler appointed Hess his private secretary in 1925, but Hess
was so self-effacing (a quality rare among the nazis) that he
was relatively unknown, even in the party, until December,
1932, when Gregor Strasser broke with Hitler and Hitler divided Strasser's authority, which had proven so great as to be
dangerous in the hands of a single man, between Hess and
Robert Ley, naming Hess chairman of the Central Political
Commission of the party.

From then on, Hess' rise was rapid. In April, 1933, Hitler
appointed him deputy Fuehrer of the party and, in December
of that year, Reich Minister without portfolio. In 1934 the
Chancellor decreed that Hess was to take part, either personally
or through appointees, in the drafting of all decrees and legislation, and gave him the power of veto on all and any bills
affecting internal conditions in the Reich. The only right of
appeal against Hess' veto was to Hitler himself, and few cared,
or even dared, to make use of the right.

Hess was given this power partly, if not largely, because it
was he who directed the party's elaborate nation-wide system
for testing the state of public opinion and morale. Every precinct captain in the party reports orally once a week and in
writing once a month on the state of mind among the people
of his bailiwick, and these reports, made up into a mosaic picture of morale all over the country, were laid before Hess. The
consequence was that Hess probably knew more than any other

man in Germany about the national morale and the attitude of the people toward the regime.

In time, Hess acquired a host of other functions. Born in Egypt himself (and therefore sometimes called "The Egyptian"), he was especially interested in Germans living abroad, both in their own welfare and in their uses as implements of nazi imperial and world counterrevolutionary policy. It was he who put Ernst Wilhelm Bohle in charge of all Germans living in foreign countries and encouraged him to organize these Germans, including those who were citizens of other countries, and use them as nazi agents. Hess was also a personal believer in various quaint schools of "faith healing," "nature healing," "magnetic healing" and the like, and this caused him to take a special interest in medicine. He took over the supervision, through deputies, of the entire German medical profession. He further controlled the national leagues of students and teachers.

Hess' most important single function, however, continued to be that of "vice-president and general manager" of the nazi party. It was to his office in the Wilhelmstrasse that the outraged, the disgruntled and the disappointed, both of the party and of the general public, repaired when they wanted solace or redress, and for this reason the office was sometimes called "The Third Reich's Wailing Wall."

And always and forever Hess was the faithful, selfless servant of Hitler. He sometimes seemed to have no will or personality of his own. Hitler trusted Hess, relied on him, confided in him and allowed him an intimacy that he did no other human being. Hess had an apartment in the Chancellory. He was the only one who had a key to Hitler's own apartment, and was allowed to enter it even when the Chancellor was away. "If I ever had a son, he would be like Hess," Hitler once said.

The Chancellor gave two further proofs, after the Second World War began, of his regard for Hess. First he named him a member of the Cabinet Council for National Defense. Second —and this was the final proof of all—he designated him second in the line of succession, after Goering, to the leadership of the party and the nation.

Hess probably has neither the ability nor the force of charac-

ter necessary to rule Germany in his own right long, as Goering
has, but he would serve as a compromise candidate, less en-
tangled than most in inner-party rivalries and relatively un-
smirched by scandal, around whom the others probably would
rally at least for a time.

It is no wonder that when Hess, of all men, flew to Scotland,
the whole world was amazed. Here was a riddle indeed. Hess
was the last man in the whole regime, one would have said,
to do anything he thought was contrary to Hitler's wishes. Did
he flout Hitler when he flew to Scotland? This was the most
significant aspect of the riddle that fell from the skies.

GOERING: THE BLOOD SWILLER

Hermann Goering is the ablest man in the nazi party after
Hitler himself and probably the only other one who is capable
of ruling the Third Reich by virtue (if that is the proper term
here) of his own ability and force of character.

Above all, Goering is an organizer and a man of action—
frequently of violent, bloody action. He first organized the
S. A. He led the nazi deputies in the Reichstag from the start
and ultimately was president of it. His ruthless energy as Commissioner for the Prussian Ministry of the Interior just after
Hitler became Chancellor prepared the way for the seizure of
power that was so soon to follow. Goering created the German
air force. And as Commissioner for the Four-Year Plan he is
czar of the German national economy.

People have misunderstood Goering's true character just as
badly as they did Hitler's, and even longer. Goering is enormously fat, the result partly of disturbances in the functioning
of the ductless glands and partly of his gluttony. He loves
uniforms and display. He flaunts these and other of his all too
human frailties. He can be jovial when he wants to be. He
speaks in a racy vernacular that goes straight to the people's
hearts. On the other hand, it suits both his taste and his purposes to play the part of a "conservative," a role for which he
has a certain background, for he is exceptional among the nazis
in coming from a family with pretensions to gentility. His
father was the first Governor of German South-West Africa.

These several circumstances have conspired to cause most people to misjudge Goering. They have perceived neither his ability nor his reckless, savage brutality.

Actually, Hermann Goering is not only the ablest but also one of the most ruthless and unscrupulous of all the nazis, and the reputation he cultivates for being a "safe," "sound" conservative is a ghastly jest he indulges in at the expense of those (most of whom come from the right wing in both Germany and elsewhere) who are so credulous as to be taken in by it.

It is true that Goering is a sentimentalist about birds and animals, as many Germans are. "He who torments an animal hurts the feelings of the whole German people," he once sententiously declared, and his official biographer writes that in drafting the model game laws that the marshal sponsored, "Goering was determined that it should never occur again that an animal that was wounded should die in slow agony."

Goering's abhorrence of cruelty to animals extends even to frogs. A 66-year-old fisherman of Zweibruecken was once sentenced to six months in jail because he had failed to kill a frog painlessly, as one of Goering's decrees prescribed, before cutting off its legs.

Bengt Berg, the Swedish naturalist, is one of the many who have found this tender solicitude for the birds and beasts commendable and even endearing. "To watch Hermann Goering as he takes up his lion cub and fondles it is to know at once that behind the steely clear gaze of this blond Teuton, warm love of nature and kindness to animals are to be found," Berg once declared in an interview. "Others may judge men by their 'political outlook'; for me their outlook on nature is the most trustworthy guide."

But Goering's solicitude for the birds and beasts does not apply to human beings who happen to get in his way. The 66-year-old fisherman of Zweibruecken is only one of literally thousands who could bear witness to this distinction, or could have done so, if they had survived, and then dared. The fisherman was sent to jail for his cruelty to a frog, in fact, just 10 days after Goering had acted as chief executioner in Prussia in the carnage of June 30, 1934, and Dollfuss was shot and left to die in slow agony only three weeks after that same slaughter—on the very day, as it happened, that Bengt Berg's interview was published.

It all depends, as Berg said, on whether you consider Goering from the point of view of his attitude toward the birds and beasts or his attitude toward his fellow man. If it is the latter that interests you, Goering's record is a violent and bloody one. Party enemies, in fact, sometimes call him "The Blood Swiller."

For years, Goering was a morphine addict. He was once committed for a time to an institution in Sweden. The drug did nothing, of course, to temper his savagery.

"Police officers who in the exercise of these duties [of dealing with anti-nazis] make use of firearms will be protected by me irrespective of the consequences of their use of arms; but if any man through mistaken caution fails to use arms, he may expect to be punished," Goering told the nazi special officers he swore in, as Commissioner for the Prussian Ministry of the Interior, just after Hitler became Chancellor, and this same spirit animates all his other activities.

"My measures are not to be vitiated by legal considerations," he said in a speech, March 4, 1933, in Frankfurt. "I am not in office to dispense justice, but to destroy and exterminate."

Goering has lived up handsomely to these self-appointed duties. He was the principal author of the Reichstag fire. He had so many political opponents and others arrested thereafter that the first concentration camps in the Third Reich had to be established to accommodate the prisoners. He organized the original Gestapo.

"I am in the habit of shooting from time to time," Goering said in a speech at Essen, March 10, 1933, "and if I sometimes make mistakes, at least I have shot. If you call that murder, then I am a murderer."

Shooting is indeed a habit of Goering's—shooting and bombing. He recommended the shelling of the defenseless town of Almeria in the Spanish civil war. And he has outdone even himself since the Second World War came. It is on his personal orders and under his personal supervision that the Luftwaffe has bombed and machine-gunned cities and towns and villages and civilian refugees on the roads and even solitary women and children in the fields. Warsaw and Rotterdam (*after* the city had surrendered) and Belgrade and the plainly marked British Red Cross ambulances filled with wounded on the quais at Dunkirk are only a few of the better-known examples of the handiwork of the Blood Swiller since he got a chance to show what he could really do.

For the rest, Goering is typical in kind, although extreme in degree, of both German sentimentality and German grossness, as well as German cruelty. He has made a cult of the memory of his first wife—whose side he left while she lay dying, to answer a summons from Hitler. Yet he is also capable of a coarseness so startling that it is difficult to describe in print. On one occasion, for example, he entertained members of the diplomatic corps in Berlin and their wives and daughters who were his guests at Karin Hall by exhibiting a pair of bison in the act of mating. And he roared with laughter when a pet lion cub ejected nitrogenous waste all over the evening gown of a lady present at a party for a famous visiting aviator.

This is the man a good many gullible people have thought is much to be preferred to Hitler.

HIMMLER: "GENTLE HEINRICH"

Until the Second World War, it was generally considered impossible to destroy a whole modern European nation. Both the practical and the moral difficulties seemed insuperable.

For to destroy such a nation it would be necessary, first, either to kill off literally millions of human beings or to uproot them from the land on which they lived and send them somewhere else: to lock them up in some great "reservation" or dump them in some wilderness and leave them to shift for themselves. It would probably be necessary, in fact, to do both these things. And, second, it would be necessary to reduce the survivors of this process to a state of brutish serfdom in which they would be useful as slave labor but would be incapable of any spirit of resistance, enterprise or even hope.

These things, most people thought, could not be done. It was hard enough to kill millions of people in the first place.

And how were the bodies to be disposed of afterwards?—the most difficult problem that faces all murderers. And those who would have to be uprooted—where could they be sent? Destroying the trained intelligence of a people seemed almost as difficult as destroying their bodies. And even if it were physically possible to do these things, how would it be morally possible? Where could enough men be found with sufficient resources and authority and with sufficient absolute evil in their hearts to carry out such a project?

But, as has happened so often in other respects as well, people underestimated the nazis. More specifically, they underestimated Adolf Hitler and Heinrich Himmler. For Hitler has now ordered and Himmler set out to do exactly this difficult and utterly evil thing: to destroy whole European nations. The world neither could nor would believe it, even after the process was well under way, and, as usual, the nazis have profited greatly by this incredulity. But the facts speak clearly enough.

Outwardly, Heinrich Himmler, the man who is performing this function, among others, in the nazi regime, seems to be the mildest of men, and to merit well the sobriquet that Gregor Strasser once gave him, only half in jest: "Our Gentle Heinrich." Himmler had succeeded Paul Josef Goebbels as Strasser's secretary and assistant, and Strasser was later to have his gentle Heinrich appointed chief of the S. S., but he had no high opinion of his protégé's force of character. June 30, 1934, the gentle Heinrich would have Strasser murdered, along with at least 1,000 others. That day was still far off, however—and even when it came and even thereafter Himmler continued to seem outwardly to be a mild and gentle creature.

He looks like a young but old-fashioned country schoolteacher. Anemic in appearance, soft-spoken, below average height, he has neutral-colored hair, a Hitler-Chaplin mustache, a weak chin and weak eyes, and wears glasses. Early and late in his office in the Prinz Albrechtstrasse, he is a hard worker. He prefers to remain in the background, and it is said of him that it is harder to get to see him than it is to see Hitler himself.

Himmler cultivates a reputation for simple living and even asceticism. He is a vegetarian and, except for an occasional glass of light Mosel wine, a teetotaler. He drinks no coffee, preferring a mild herb tea. An American acquaintance once introduced him to wild rice and patent breakfast foods, and Himmler liked both. He even made some of the S. S. eat patent breakfast foods for a while. They did *not* like them. Himmler also is a philatelist and has one of the best stamp collections in Germany. Altogether, it is a picture of almost touching purity and diffidence that he presents to the world.

Even in some of his public functions and activities Himmler seems, if not quite harmless, at least not unduly dangerous to the outside world. Thus he is one of the most ardent of believers in the nonsense of Nordicism in its most virulent form, and has encumbered the S. S. with a heavy luggage of runic symbols, pagan ritual and other mumbo-jumbo of the sort. He has also conferred on the S. S. the gentle office of breeding the Nordic supermen of the future, and has established an elaborate system for making sure that the results of these exercises will be satisfactory. He encourages the bearing of children by German girls of "good" blood even out of wedlock.

But these are mere foibles, mere idiosyncrasies, compared with Himmler's other activities. If there is any one man in Germany who is more savage, more ruthless and more unscrupulous than any other, that man is Heinrich Himmler.

As chief of all German police and Reich Leader of the S. S., "Our Gentle Heinrich" commands the Praetorian Guard of national socialism. He disposes of a private army of possibly 250,000 fully trained, fully equipped combat troops (the so-called Verfuegungstruppen of the S. S.). He operates the most extensive and most ruthless secret-police system the world has ever seen, functioning both in Germany and in other countries. He supervises the concentration camps and is responsible for the abominations practiced there. He directs much—and the most effective—fifth-column work that prepares the way for the invasions of the German armed forces. He ordered the killing of persons designated (by means undisclosed) as "mental defectives" to the number of approximately 100,000 in 1939 and 1940 alone. And more than any and all of these things, Heinrich Himmler is the man who has set out to destroy whole nations whose existence Hitler has found incompatible with his plans for the New Order.

Himmler developed his technique by experimenting on the Jews. He is perfecting it in his operations against the Poles. If he gets time, he will apply it to others as well.

His plan for destroying the Poles consists of two main parts. The first part calls for the killing off of several million Poles outright and the uprooting and dumping into a great "reservation" of several million more, many of whom, of course, perish miserably where he dumps them.

Between 250,000 and 500,000 Poles were probably killed in the war itself. Suicides and individual, group and mass executions have probably eliminated as many as 100,000 more. But this is only the beginning. Himmler relies on hunger, thirst and disease to do the major part of his killing for him. The war conditions themselves cause conditions that are bound to decimate the Poles. Himmler sees to it that these conditions become even worse than they were bound to be in any event. Food is taken out of Poland and sent to Germany. Medical supplies are confiscated. Doctors and nurses disappear. Hospitals are seized. There are, of course, other reasons for these measures, too, and other men carry some of them out. But Himmler makes sure that everything that is done also furthers his primary purpose of destroying the Poles, and it is he who orders the measures that do the most toward accomplishing this. Most important of all, Himmler has uprooted approximately 6,000,000 human beings from areas annexed to Germany and elsewhere and shipped them into the so-called "Government General" of Poland, where they necessarily starve and freeze to death and die of disease like flies and at an increasing rate of speed.

Altogether, at least 3,000,000 Poles were liquidated by these several methods within 18 months of the gray dawn when the German armies first struck into Poland. How does Himmler dispose of the bodies? Mass graves and mass bonfires. And if these methods are imperfect and disease lurks at the disposal grounds, why, that helps kill off even more Poles. If Himmler has another year, he will kill off another 3,000,000 of them.

There is another phase of Himmler's attack on the sheer numbers of the Poles: the separation of the men from the women. Even those families that are united have fewer children. Hunger and disease take care of that. And of the children who are born, many die. But at least 1,000,000 of Poland's most vigorous men are kept as prisoners of war and drafted as forced labor to the Reich, and these men can sire no sons at all.

Himmler has undertaken to reduce the survivors of these processes to a state in which they will never be able to cause any serious trouble to the German Master People who intend to rule them. He carefully weeds out all those who seemed capable of any form of leadership. He closes all schools that might train Poles in the uses of the tools and implements that are essential to the maintenance of a modern civilization, to say nothing of a modern army. Such of the tools and implements themselves as are useful are taken out of the hands of the Poles and either reserved for German enterprises in Poland or shipped to the Reich itself. Even works of art that might keep alive a spirit of national culture and achievement also go to Germany.

Himmler is doing his work well. Given enough time, he would utterly destroy the Polish people in Europe. He would also destroy other peoples, too. This is one of the prerequisite conditions for the setting up of the New Order. This is a part of "the wave of the future" that so impresses some gentle ladies elsewhere.

RIBBENTROP: TIN CHANCELLOR

The nazis are fond of saying that democracies are disorderly and riven by internal dissent, whereas in the Third Reich discipline, authority and unanimity under the Fuehrer are the order of the day. This is as utter humbug as any propagated by the nazis—which is saying a good deal.

For in reality the clash of purposes and wills in the New Germany is incomparably more violent and more harmful to the country than any such conflicts could ever become, in the nature of things, in a successful democracy like the United States. The nazi leaders are savage, ruthless men to begin with.

They have fought their way to power by conspiracy, treachery and violence. There are no peaceable, rational means by which any of them can either forge his way further toward the top or be removed and replaced by somebody else. Everything depends on the whim of one single man, and he usually favors whoever has proven his ability to destroy his own rivals, and no questions asked about methods. The consequence of all these considerations is that there is a savage and unremitting struggle for power and for the favor of Hitler throughout the entire nazi party and the country as a whole, a struggle in which the participants literally stop at absolutely nothing to gain their ends.

The story of the rise of Joachim von Ribbentrop to the post of foreign minister and the special favor of the Chancellor is typical of this struggle.

Ribbentrop's first official title was that of Special Commissioner of the Fuehrer for Disarmament Questions. The post itself was of no importance. But even before he had been appointed to it, Ribbentrop had shown that he had a vaulting ambition, and as soon as he acquired a definite responsibility, even so insignificant a one as this, he set about building up an independent organization of his own, a sort of personal Foreign Office, which came to be known as the "Ribbentrop Bureau," and he began to intervene personally and through his agents in a wide variety of matters of concern to Reich foreign policy. This instantly roused the enmity of other nazis who thought that they had, or should have, pre-eminent rights in this domain. It also, of course, roused the enmity of the Foreign Office itself, but this was relatively unimportant.

Alfred Rosenberg was one of the nazis whose hostility Ribbentrop incurred. Hitler had named Rosenberg as Leader of the Foreign Policy Office of the party and (according to Rosenberg, at least) had promised to make him foreign minister in time. While Rosenberg waited for this happy day, he prepared for it and gratified his interests and ambitions by conducting a personal foreign policy of his own through such organizations, agencies and friendships as he had at his disposal.

Ernst Wilhelm Bohle was a second nazi who was roused by

Ribbentrop's activities and apparent ambitions. A young protégé of Rudolf Hess, Bohle was head of the Foreign Organization of the party, which supervised the lives of Germans living abroad. Thus he, too, had an organization. He also had other agencies at his disposal, and he had friends who were willing and even eager to serve him. He was likewise ambitious. And he, too, conducted a sort of personal foreign policy of his own.

Baldur von Schirach, then national Youth Leader of the Reich, hated and opposed Ribbentrop, too, partly because even Schirach wanted to have a voice in foreign policy and engaged in intrigue and subversive activities abroad through his own organization and representatives, and partly because Ribbentrop surrounded himself with enemies of Schirach who had never been members of the Hitler Jugend but had been active in other, rival youth organizations.

These three men disliked and distrusted each other, of course, but they feared and hated Ribbentrop still more. So they entered into a conspiracy to destroy the presumptuous new-comer. They succeeded in enlisting powerful friends in the S. S. on their side, and they mapped out a plan of action.

This plan was, in essence, the standard one employed in most inner party plots against men too close to Hitler or too power-ful for other reasons to be attacked openly and personally. It called for attacks on Ribbentrop's collaborators first. These at-tacks, if successful, would, the conspirators hoped and believed, break the morale in Ribbentrop's organization and perhaps Ribbentrop's own, would discredit him in the eyes of Hitler and would either intimidate him into withdrawing from the struggle or, if he persisted in fighting, would make it possible to attack him openly and personally in the end.

Their plans well laid, the conspirators struck. They made out a case of pederasty against Ribbentrop's second adjutant that was so plausible that he committed suicide while he was home in Kiel for the Christmas holidays in 1934. Ribbentrop inquired if it would be acceptable for him to attend his ad-jutant's funeral, was told it would not, and stayed away.

The conspirators soon struck again. They successfully chal-lenged the political reliability of a second leading member of

Ribbentrop's organization and forced him to resign and go and live in exile in a village in the country.

Time passed, and the conspirators chose another victim in Ribbentrop's Bureau. They resorted again to a charge of pederasty. It was a favorite nazi device, and it succeeded this time, as it so often did. The third victim disappeared into a concentration camp.

The conspirators were delighted. They determined to liquidate one more of Ribbentrop's collaborators. Then, they felt, they would be able to strike at Ribbentrop himself. Accordingly, they denounced a fourth leading figure in the Ribbentrop Bureau, this time on a charge of encouraging the formation of unauthorized clubs and other associations. This charge, too, proved convincing enough to eliminate the victim. The conspirators felt that they were now ready to attack Ribbentrop himself.

But their plans went completely awry. There were several reasons for this. One was that Ribbentrop, far from being unnerved by these assaults, became more determined than ever. Another reason was that while Ribbentrop had been powerless to save these four collaborators, he had succeeded nevertheless in greatly enlarging and strengthening his organization in spite of these casualties. Still another was that Ribbentrop had been able in the meantime to convince Hitler that he knew more about foreign affairs and how to deal with them than any of his rivals. Hitler liked Ribbentrop personally, furthermore. And, finally, the very fact that Ribbentrop was isolated and had so many enemies recommended him to Hitler; the Chancellor liked to have men in such predicaments in certain key posts: it made them utterly dependent on him.

The result: instead of Ribbentrop's being destroyed, he rose steadily in favor and influence with Hitler and became foreign minister, and the conspirators went into at least temporary eclipses.

Rosenberg ceased to exert any real influence in foreign policy. Schirach was "kicked upstairs" and became party district leader in Vienna. And while Bohle continued to be head of the Foreign Organization, he was made an assistant secretary of state in the Foreign Office, under the direct control of the very man he had set out to destroy.

Hitler respects both Ribbentrop's nerve and his judgment on foreign affairs. "Ribbentrop's the man for me!" he once said to party intimates. "He's cold. Nothing influences him." And he sometimes speaks of Ribbentrop as "a second Iron Chancellor," a second Bismarck.

There can be no doubt that Ribbentrop has nerve, of a kind, and that he is cold. He is remarkable, in fact, even among nazis, for his bad manners, his effrontery and his insolence. His habitual bearing in public is one of theatrical dignity, icy reserve and supercilious condescension.

Present on one occasion as guest of honor, with the diplomatic corps, at a dinner given by the Foreign Press Association in Berlin, Ribbentrop took advantage of his position to read both his hosts and his fellow guests a lecture on their failings and to warn them that they both must mend their ways. During the crisis that preceded the Second World War, he acted like a fishwife in a tantrum on more than one occasion toward Sir Nevile Henderson, the British Ambassador. When the Reich invaded Belgium and Holland, and the ministers of those two countries called at the Foreign Office to file formal protests, they were rudely ordered, on Ribbentrop's instructions, to leave the premises and not return until they had learned to conduct themselves properly toward the representatives of the New Germany. When Germany attacked Greece, Ribbentrop achieved a peak of effrontery seldom surpassed even by Hitler himself (whom he assiduously imitates in this as in other respects)—he issued a statement attempting to justify the attack which began, "England is about to commit another crime against Europe." England!

But while Ribbentrop has these qualifications for success in the New Germany, he lacks certain others of equal or greater importance. And while he survived the Rosenberg-Bohle-Schirach conspiracy against him, he soon acquired other and much more formidable enemies who are even more passionately determined to destroy him.

It is hard, for example, to understand why Hitler respects

Ribbentrop's judgment on foreign affairs. Ribbentrop helped to convince the Chancellor that France was ripe for collapse and would prove to be no serious military problem even if the French did enter the Second World War, and in this, of course, Ribbentrop was right. But Ribbentrop also assured the Chancellor that the British could be beaten as speedily as the French. Not only was Ribbentrop proven to be wrong in this, which is bad enough in itself, but he also was proven to have been guessing in both cases, which, one would have thought, was much worse. As a statesman, Ribbentrop is more like a tin chancellor than like an iron one.

Also, Ribbentrop has no popular following or support, he is a very poor speaker, he has no "common touch," and the people find him cold and snobbish.

Nor does Ribbentrop control a political machine of any consequence of his own. He has replaced the older career diplomatists in the Foreign Office and the diplomatic and consular services as rapidly as he could (except to the extent that he has kept some on as a blind for his true character and purposes), but it will be several years before he can eliminate all or even most of these "old school-tie" gentlemen—whose political reliability is doubtful, to put it mildly, to say nothing of their devotion to Ribbentrop personally.

Goering, furthermore, detests Ribbentrop (for a time he had agents at work collecting all the scandal they could find about Ribbentrop's private life, which Goering hoped would some day prove useful), so does Goebbels and so do most of the General Staff and High Command of the armed forces. For Ribbentrop tries to assert himself everywhere and in every phase of policy. "War is the conduct of policy by other means," he quoted when the present conflict began, and he tries to interfere in the conduct of the war as well as in everything else. He has assigned a personal representative to every regimental headquarters in the German army to observe what goes on and report directly to him, and he has even had a special "military" train fitted out as a personal headquarters and has it shifted about as near as possible to Hitler's in the theaters of operations.

If Ribbentrop can retain Hitler's confidence, he will survive as long as Hitler does. If he could acquire a great popular following or build up a powerful political organization of his own or prove that his judgment is so sound that he is indispensable, he might even survive after Hitler is gone. If he lacks these perquisites of power, though, and is ever abandoned by Hitler to face his party enemies without the Chancellor's protection, his chances of survival will depend almost entirely on the friendship of the man who controls the S. S. and the police. It is, therefore, perhaps not altogether personal liking that causes Ribbentrop to cultivate Heinrich Himmler.

GOEBBELS: THE SORCERER'S APPRENTICE

Paul Josef Goebbels is the most disliked and distrusted man in the Third Reich.

His slight stature and his clubfoot inspire distaste among a people who make a fetish of physical size and strength. His Eastern European Jewish appearance, manner and style of speaking inspire ridicule among fellow members of a party dedicated to Nordicism, and dislike among many others. He is an intellectual and something of a socialist—he is probably the only man in the whole party leadership who understands Marxism at all—and these qualities alienate still more Germans. The fact that he and Frick, neither of whom fought in the First World War, joined in ordering that the names of Jewish veterans be removed from war memorials disgusted many. His notorious affairs with women have disgusted more. And the cynicism that is obvious in most of the things he does and says adds still further to the dislike and distrust with which most Germans regard him.

Sneers and jokes at Goebbels' expense abound, and most of the jokes, unlike those told on Goering, are bitter. Ernst Hanfstaengl, who loathes Goebbels, used to refer to him habitually as "that rat down the street." Once when Goebbels appeared at a reception where Hanfstaengl was present, Hanfstaengl quoted in a loud voice the German proverb, "Lies have short legs," and left the room. Other party enemies call Goebbels "The Tainted One." Max Amann, the first business manager of the party, who later became director of the party press, once called

Goebbels "The Mephisto of the party, branded by God with a cloven hoof," and Erich Koch, who was later to become party district leader for East Prussia, once wrote a long and savage attack on Goebbels in the form of an article on "The Consequences of Racial Intermarriage," declaring (without naming Goebbels) that crippled feet were among these consequences, and that persons afflicted with them should be viewed with the gravest suspicion.

This dislike and distrust, however, did not prevent the man who was the object of them from forging his way to the top in the nazi party.

Like Himmler, Goebbels began his political career as secretary and assistant to Gregor Strasser. Like Himmler, also, Goebbels turned against Strasser later when it became apparent that advancement was better to be won under other auspices.

Goebbels excels as an organizer, as a polemic journalist and as a mob orator. He knows both what to say to a mob and how to say it. He has a truly beautiful voice, a magnificent command of German and a pronunciation that is to all practical intents and purposes perfect. It is impossible not to be stirred by Goebbels' speeches even if you hate everything he says. Goebbels also is extraordinarily energetic and he has real physical courage.

He threw himself into the task of winning Berlin and North Germany generally for the party and, first in co-operation with Strasser and later on his own, he was highly successful.

Since the party acquired power, Goebbels has had three principal functions. First, he is national propaganda chief of the party and the government; he operates the German wind machine, or, as unsympathetic persons have said, he is "Chief Hog Caller of the Reich." Second, Goebbels controls the Reich Chamber of Culture, which regulates virtually all cultural activities in Germany. These first two functions often overlap, as Goebbels himself once publicly pointed out. And, third, Goebbels is party district leader for Berlin.

In the first two of these capacities, although not so much in the third, Goebbels is the sorcerer's apprentice rather than a sorcerer in his own right. Hitler supervises propaganda and cultural affairs even more closely than he does most others. For some time, however, Goebbels was nevertheless an able and useful apprentice. The talents that had enabled him to win power and favor in the first place continued to stand him in good stead. He also has always been quick to sense Hitler's moods and wishes, and he has a knack of seeing which way the cat is going to jump and then jumping that way too in plenty of time. When the crisis of June 30, 1934, broke out, for example, Goebbels hastened to Hitler's side and never left that shelter until all danger had passed. Thus from the end of 1932, when Strasser broke with Hitler, Goebbels shared, with Hess and Goering, the distinction of being closer to Hitler and of enjoying Hitler's confidence to a greater degree than any other leaders of the party, and was second only to Goering in authority and power.

Beginning in the Winter of 1937-1938, however, Goebbels went into a political decline that was to last at least until these lines were written. There were two causes of Goebbels' decline. One was a sex scandal. The other was a series of blunders he made in propaganda policy.

Goebbels' affairs with women and his use of his political power to force some of them to yield to his desires had been notorious for years. But while they had caused widespread disgust they had caused nothing worse, and this was of no importance politically. Also, Frau Goebbels either knew nothing about these affairs or pretended to know nothing about them.

Some time during the Winter of 1937-1938, however, an affair that Goebbels was having with an actress exploded in such a serious scandal that it had far-reaching consequences of both a personal and a political nature. For the actress' husband learned of the affair and chastised Goebbels severely. Spread by the minister's enemies, the story swept the country, and shocked or delighted hundreds of thousands, if not millions of people, according to their tastes and morals. Worse still, solicitous friends told Frau Goebbels the story and she fled in tears to Hitler at Berchtesgaden and demanded the right to a divorce.

This was grave indeed. Hitler had always known of Goebbels' sexual excesses, of course. They had left him utterly indifferent, however, and in themselves still did so. But such open scandal, such public ridicule—and the hysterics of Frau Goebbels in his own cherished retreat in the mountains—this was something altogether different. Hitler was distinctly annoyed.

In the end, matters were patched up. Goebbels even allowed it to be understood that he had received Hitler's permission to write the definitive official biography of the Chancellor, presumably as an act of grace and expiation. But Goebbels' position had been shaken. And he still had not rehabilitated himself when the war came and he committed a series of propaganda blunders which made his position still worse. (Nothing more was heard of the biography of Hitler.)

Just after the war began, Goebbels decided to broadcast an appeal to the German people, calling upon them to bear with fortitude the sacrifices that the war would entail. Hitler learned of Goebbels' intention and sent for him. "Do you think, Party Comrade Goebbels, that you are particularly well suited to talk to the German people about sacrifices?" Hitler is reported to have asked. Whether Hitler said exactly this or not, Goebbels at least did not deliver the broadcast.

Nor did he deliver the second great broadcast he prepared. This was to be an attack on certain American and other foreign correspondents in Berlin, whom Goebbels planned to name and revile in his best philippic manner. But this, too, Hitler forbade. The United States and as many other countries as possible were to be lulled into a sense of security at all costs, and it was no part of Hitler's plan to antagonize a single correspondent unnecessarily, especially not a single American. Far from being attacked, the correspondents were to be loved and cherished, Hitler ordered—and most of them were.

Now Goebbels made still a third mistake. The sorcerer's magic got out of the control of the apprentice. For when British warships drove the German pocket battleship *Graf Spee* into the harbor of Montevideo in mid-December, 1939, Goebbels had the German press and radio represent the engagement as a victory for the Reich. The shock to public morale when the *Graf Spee* was scuttled was, accordingly, great. And although the Germans were never told explicitly that Captain

Hans Langsdorf, the commander of the *Graf Spee*, had shot himself, but were given to understand that he had gone down with his ship, the people guessed at the truth anyway, and were even more thoroughly shocked.

Goebbels committed yet another blunder. It was bad enough that a film that featured the actress he had compromised was jeered in Berlin and had to be withdrawn. But now the minister caused a short feature to be made of his family life at one of his luxurious villas near Berlin, and this also roused such displeasure among the Berliners that it, too, had to be withdrawn.

Goebbels was still minister as the war entered its third year. A man as quick-witted as he, furthermore, would always have to be reckoned with, short of unequivocal disaster, especially in a situation where so much depended on the whim of a single human being, and so unpredictable a one as Hitler, in such matters. As of November, 1941, however, it was clear that a major miracle, a major effort or a major reversal of form would be necessary to restore Paul Josef Goebbels to the power and authority that he had enjoyed before.

LEY: THE MESS OF POTTAGE

The nazis rule with less bread and more circuses than any other regime in history. It is Dr. Robert Ley more than any other single person, except Hitler himself, who makes this feat possible.

Ley has several offices. He is national organization leader of the party, he manages the annual party conferences in Nuremberg, he is leader of the Labor Front, and he directs the "Strength Through Joy" organization which provides recreational and cultural facilities for the masses and improves working conditions in offices and factories. It is in these last two capacities that Ley helps perform the prodigy of the bread and the circuses.

Ley seized the German labor unions "brutally and ruthlessly," as he himself described the process, on May 2, 1933, in what was probably the most audacious attack upon organized labor up to that time since the industrial revolution. The attack succeeded; the unions were destroyed. But what was to come next? Could Ley satisfy German labor sufficiently to maintain his position and that of the party? It was a grave problem which faced him.

It was especially grave because Ley not only had destroyed the unions but he also had to induce German labor to accept still further hardships, both material and moral. Prices rose. Deductions from wages and salaries at source for taxes, insurances and party levies also increased. Rates of pay, on the other hand, actually declined below the depression lows. Party members were given preference for jobs. Labor was forbidden to strike, was subjected to work-conscription as inexorable as military service itself, and freedom to choose a trade, to change a trade already chosen, to change jobs within a trade and to move from one part of the country to another—all were severely restricted. White-collar employees had to submit to almost equally disagreeable hardships.

Obstacles like these might have daunted most men, even most men with the Gestapo at their disposal—and Dr. Ley has called in the Gestapo on more than one occasion. But they did not daunt Dr. Ley. He had seized the birthright of German laborers and white-collar employees, and he meant to keep it. But he was a practical man, and he offered a mess of pottage in return. Dr. Ley's pottage consisted of various ingredients:

He promised higher real earnings at some unspecified time in the future, and meanwhile he preached a doctrine he called "The New Socialism," he cracked down on capital almost as convincingly as he had on labor, he went to the workers and employees personally in flying trips all over the country, he took highly effective measures to enhance labor's sense of dignity and self-respect, he improved working conditions in offices and factories and he provided recreational and cultural facilities at very low costs and in many instances altogether free.

What Dr. Ley means by "The New Socialism" is not altogether clear, except that it has nothing whatever to do with public ownership or operation of the means of production or with the right of labor and employees to a voice in the governance of their own affairs. So far as it can be identified at all,

Ley's "socialism" seems, however, to be a form of society something like a highly matriarchal family, with the party in the role of matriarch, and something like a platoon of soldiers, with the party in the role of sergeant major. The emphasis, in any event, is on "soldierliness," with special attention to those two outstanding qualities of the soldier, absolute obedience and low pay.

If this dogma has captivated the workers and employees, there have been no signs of it. This is especially the case, perhaps, because Ley has embellished his dogma with attacks on the 8-hour day as too short, with expressions of the hope that the time will come when everybody in Germany will continue to work until he is 80 years old, and with defenses of wealth.

Ley has afforded satisfaction to labor and employees, though, by the way he has cracked down on capital. It is true that the nazis have always represented themselves as the champions of private property. Owners of property, however, soon found out that this is to be understood in a Pickwickian sense. The citizen keeps title to his property, true enough—provided that he behaves himself and does not run afoul of any too powerful persons in the party. But this is all he keeps. The nazis tell him what to do and what not to do with his property, and they take an increasingly high proportion of its earnings, if any.

It has all been summed up in a wry jest: "What is the difference between communism, socialism and national socialism?" the riddle asks. "If you have six cows," the answer says, "the communists take all six, the socialists take three and leave you three, but the nazis make you keep all six—and they take the milk."

Champions of private property? Of course. The more cows the better.

How much good this system would have done the workers in the long run, nobody will ever learn, because the war has destroyed all the bases for arriving at a conclusion. For the time being, however, the system had at least this advantage, from the nazis' point of view: it did something to persuade labor and employees that national socialism was not, as labor had feared and capital had hoped, the Praetorian Guard of the vested interests.

Ley's national glad-handing tours of factories and offices have had this same merit. German workmen and employees have undoubtedly been impressed, even if only in modest numbers and degree, by the fact that Ley takes the pains he does to seek them out at their desks and counters and workbenches, to talk to them both en masse and individually, and to assure them that the regime has their interests at heart. What politician in any country despises the hearty handshake, the friendly clap on the back and the questions about the wife and kids? Not Dr. Robert Ley, in any event.

Nor does he despise the importance that many human beings attach, or would like to attach, to their personal and professional honor. On the contrary, he has set out to enhance the self-respect of the workmen and employees. Tirelessly he has preached the gospel of the dignity and honor of labor, and he set up "Courts of Social Honor" that interpret the gospel in an exceedingly practical manner by imposing heavy fines on employers found guilty of offending against their workers' and employees' senses of honor, and in some cases even depriving employers of control of their businesses altogether and replacing them by party commissars.

More substantial are the measures Ley has taken to improve working conditions. He has persuaded employers and, when necessary, forced them, to improve and beautify offices, plants and grounds, to install safety devices, to improve lighting and ventilation, to clean up their premises, to provide attractive recreation rooms and restaurants, to install radios and even to put plants and flowers around in shops and offices.

And, best of all, Ley has provided, through "Strength Through Joy," an impressive program of recreational and cultural facilities for workers' and employees' leisure time. He has built two 25,000-ton ships and leased ten others, for example, for workers' and employees' cruises to the Mediterranean, Madeira, the Azores, the Isle of Wight and along the Norwegian coast. He has ordered construction of a gigantic seaside resort for Labor Front members. He has organized excursions and vacations all over the Reich and in Italy. And these and numerous other advantages Ley has made available at only nominal costs and in some cases at none at all.

These are the principal ingredients of the pottage that Robert Ley has offered German workmen and employees in return for the birthright he has stolen. It would be foolish to underestimate the importance of these non-material factors in reconciling the masses of the German people to the regime. Yet it would also be foolish to exaggerate their importance—as Dr. Ley himself does. Ley sometimes talks as if these moral satisfactions were the chief cause for such loyalty—or acquiescence—as there is among the proletariat and lower middle class.

Actually, other factors have been much more important. There has been no alternative to national socialism. Hitler has won victory after victory that have gratified the workers and lower middle class as much as they have everyone else, if not more. And, most important of all, people have earned more money. There has been bread also, as well as circuses. Because while rates of pay have declined, there have been more jobs (between 9,000,000 and 10,000,000 more) at longer hours, and there have been hundreds of thousands, if not millions, of shifts from lower-paid to higher-paid categories of wage rates.

It is no wonder, though, that Ley refrains from emphasizing these material gains. Because the gains are more than outweighed in uncomfortably numerous cases by the hardships that remain. And, besides, it is not Ley who has provided the bread; it is other men altogether. Ley has only provided the circuses.

Apart from his ability, which is great, Ley is also qualified for his responsibilities by enormous energy and conviviality. A stocky, vigorous man with close-clipped, silver-gray hair, Ley shares with Goebbels and Rosenberg the distinction of having it often said that he is partly Jewish—both because of his appearance and because his name is so remarkably close to Levy. The compliment is probably, however, undeserved.

Ley is a notably heavy drinker. He announced in a speech on May 2, 1939, that he had sworn off alcohol, but this was generally regarded as just another of Ley's jokes. Indeed, he was suspected of being under the influence of fiery waters while making this very speech. "Well, he's not drinking quite as much as he was for a while," was all that a high-ranking Gestapo officer who certainly knew the facts would pretend.

In any event, Dr. Ley has continued to go his exuberant, boisterous way, haranguing the workers and employees in a frenzied style of oratory, supercharged with emotion, that splatters his listeners with saliva and adulation of Hitler alike, and Hitler has forgiven him his peccadilloes. After all, he has forgiven other men much worse sins than drunkenness.

The Chancellor once called Ley his "greatest socialist." This is as good a commentary as any on the "socialism" of national socialism.

ROSENBERG: MINOR PROPHET

Alfred Rosenberg is the Dr. Pangloss of the national socialist regime. He is the official philosopher of the party. He teaches a dogma as obscure and as basically ridiculous (although superficially solemn) as that which Voltaire's hero described as "meta-physico-theologo-cosmolonigology." He also teaches that all will be for the best in the best of all possible worlds once the Nordic race (whatever that is) has seized its rightful place as ruler of the earth.

Rosenberg was born a Russian subject, although of Baltic German stock, in Reval. He was studying in Riga when the First World War came, and when the school he was attending was transferred to Moscow, he went with it, ending his studies there early in 1918. The hatred of communism for which Rosenberg has since become celebrated may have had its origins in Russia during the First War, but the record does not show that he gave any proof of it then. All that the record does show is that Rosenberg never served in the German army and that he not only stayed on in Moscow for several months after the red revolution without displaying any undue anguish of spirit but that he actually took part in demonstrations, of loyalty to the Russian government, although it is not altogether clear whether this was the Czarist, the Kerensky or the communist regime.

Rosenberg has said since that he tried to enlist in the German army during the war but was rejected. He has also claimed that he took part in the demonstrations of loyalty, with fellow members of a student club, in order to deceive the Russian authorities as to his true sentiments and thus to try to save the club from dissolution, its property from confiscation and its members from arrest if not worse.

It was evitable, however, that many would find these assurances unconvincing. Once, before the nazis came to power, for example, Rosenberg was guilty of the really startling effrontery of challenging the patriotism of Chancellor Bruening. That ordinarily reserved man turned on Rosenberg in a cold fury of contempt. "I should like to remind the gentleman," he said, "that I was lying behind a machine gun on the Western Front for four years at a time when he did not even know what his Fatherland was."

Rosenberg took some time, in all conscience, to decide what his Fatherland was. The war was still going on when he ended his studies in Moscow, but he went, not to Germany, but to Paris. This phase of Rosenberg's life also is obscure, and enemies make the most of the opportunities this fact gives them. Goering, who dislikes and despises Rosenberg, once exclaimed, "I'd like to know what that fellow was doing in Paris during the war!" Others think they do know: they say flatly that Rosenberg was acting as a spy for the French.

Whatever Rosenberg was doing, he left Paris and went to Germany in 1919, settling in Munich. There he began to write pamphlets attacking the Jews, the communists, the Roman Catholic church, the Freemasons and assorted others, all of whom, Rosenberg proclaimed, were engaged in a gigantic conspiracy against the Nordic Master People in general and the German Reich in particular. He soon enlisted under Hitler's banners.

Hitler was much impressed by his new recruit's intellectual pretensions. He thought Rosenberg was a great thinker, and adopted most of his ideas. After all, they were similar to his own. Rosenberg's "metaphysico-theologo-cosmolonigology" became the national socialist philosophy of life, and Rosenberg himself became, successively, editor of the *Voelkischer Beobachter*, Commissioner of the Fuehrer for the Supervision of the Philosophical Education of the National Socialist Movement, and chief of the National Office for the Advancement of German Literature, a gigantic censorship bureau whose authorization must be obtained before any book can be published in the Reich.

Rosenberg also aspired to be German foreign minister, and for a time he was Hitler's leading adviser on foreign policy. It was announced on April 1, 1933, that the Chancellor had authorized Rosenberg to set up a Foreign Policy Office for the party, and Rosenberg said privately that Hitler had promised to appoint him Reich foreign minister in time.

Hitler may well have meant to keep this April Fool's Day promise. But time and circumstances and Rosenberg's enemies in the party and Rosenberg's own inadequacies made it politically impractical, if not impossible, to do so.

It would be inaccurate to say that Rosenberg is his own worst enemy. He has too many other more effective ones. But his own deficiencies are nevertheless impressive.

He is personally unattractive. He has heavy, doughy features, fishy, lack-luster eyes and a habit of rarely looking directly at people when he is speaking to them. He is cold and arrogant and he has a positively Olympian regard for his own intellect. His most pretentious book, "The Myth of the Twentieth Century," a confused and tortuously written hodge-podge of racial abracadabra, inaccurate "history," plagiarized religious scandals and polemics and false logic, Rosenberg considers one of the most important philosophical works of modern times, if not the most important, and of "Mein Kampf" he once remarked condescendingly that it was "a freshly written work."

Rosenberg might have gone much further in spite of his repellent personality if he had had any real judgment on foreign affairs and had been an able fighter in the catch-as-catch-can struggle for power within the party. He was scarcely unique among nazis in having an unlovely personality. But he knew nothing about foreign affairs and he was no fighter, and he soon demonstrated beyond much doubt that this was the case.

His political feebleness became apparent early in the history of the party. When Hitler was sentenced to detention in fortress in 1924, he named Rosenberg his deputy. But the other party leaders ignored Rosenberg's patent of authority and rode rough-shod over him. Roehm called him a "noisy moral hero," and Max Amann, who was business manager of the *Voelkischer Beobachter*, thought so little of his editor that the two communicated only by means of written notes.

Rosenberg's defeat at the hands of Ribbentrop has already been reported. He has also been defeated by most of the other important party leaders, too, at one time or another, or at least by such of them as have thought it worth their while to trouble themselves about him. Goering, for example, once put Rosenberg in his place by arresting several of his collaborators and even his mistress. Rosenberg did not persist, as Ribbentrop had done when attacked. He came to terms and made his peace.

Nor did Rosenberg have much judgment in foreign affairs. His commission as Leader of the Foreign Policy Office of the party freshly signed by Hitler, Rosenberg set off in May, 1933, to pay a visit to London that was intended to pave the way for his later appointment as foreign minister. But the trip was a disastrous failure.

The British were hostile in the first place, the Foreign Office in Berlin and the German Embassy in London both did what they could to sabotage the visit, and Rosenberg's own ineptitude did the rest. There was a demand in Parliament that he be deported. A wreath he laid at the Cenotaph was first slashed and then thrown into the Thames by a British officer who gladly paid a fine in police court for the satisfaction. The newspapers attacked Rosenberg enthusiastically. Even some of the German press, probaby egged on by Goebbels, took advantage of the occasion to discredit Rosenberg by publishing mock-indignant denunciations of the British whose real purpose was to acquaint the German public with the resounding failure of the mission.

This trip to London put an end to whatever chances Rosenberg had ever had to become the first national socialist foreign minister of the Reich. He retained his literary and philosophical functions, and he continued to act as Leader of the Foreign Policy Office of the party. But his power in foreign affairs was restricted to minor functions of propaganda, espionage and subversion through various ostensibly literary societies of no consequence which he maintained abroad. The Foreign Policy Office soon came to be referred to as "the ghost of something that died long ago."

In November, 1941, Hitler found a new imposing position for Rosenberg: he appointed his greatest Russia-hater governor of the areas seized from the Soviets. The post must have gratified Rosenberg enormously. But his inadequacies were bound to make him more of a figure-head than a true governor. Rosenberg might reign in Russia, but he is incapable of effective rule. The real governors will be the much abler—and even more ruthless—men whom Hitler named Rosenberg's deputies and assistants.

Alfred Rosenberg is the prophet of national socialism. But he is an exceedingly minor prophet.

II

Brave New World

7. No Private Lives

For prying into human affairs, none are equal to those whom it does not concern. VICTOR HUGO

This philosophy is acclaimed as the essence of modernity; actually, it marks a reversion to the oldest state of affairs of which our anthropologists have any knowledge, for it is exactly the philosophy of the priests in savage societies. The nazis have reconstructed the taboo system in its entirety—the system in which every part of the social structure depends on an unquestioning acceptance of the edicts of the priests.

STEPHEN H. ROBERTS, "THE HOUSE THAT HITLER BUILT"

IN A DICTATORSHIP, as has been remarked, everything which is not forbidden is compulsory. For a dictatorship is an authoritarian, totalitarian state, and authoritarian means that the dictator tells everybody else what to do and what not to do, and totalitarian means that this extends to everything—almost literally everything—that everybody else does or wants to do and everything he does not want to do.

It extends in nazi Germany, for example, to the question whether the citizen may marry or not and, if he may, the person whom he may marry, and the kind of wedding rings he and his bride may exchange. It extends to the question whether the citizen may have any children, and what names he may give them and how he may bring them up. It also extends to the question what the citizen may keep in his attic, how many evenings he ought to spend away from home every week, how long his shirt tails may be, how many pockets he may have in his trousers, who may be president and treasurer of his chess club and what kind of a funny paper he may read.

The individual does not decide these things for himself in Germany under the nazis, even in times of so-called "peace." The party decides them for him.

It also decides whether or not his son may fly kites, whether his daughters should have their hair bobbed or wear it in pigtails, what kind of jokes he may tell and what he may say in general, even in the bosom of his own family. The party asserts the right to challenge the legitimacy of the citizen's children, that of his parents and his own at any time during life and at any time after death.

If the citizen's son was killed in any of the "little wars" that preceded the Second World War, or if he is killed in the greater conflict itself, the party forbids the family to make undue display of grief. And when civilians, as well as soldiers, die, the party asserts the right to determine the kind of clothes in which they may be laid out and the kind of tombstones they may have over their graves.

These are only a few examples of the respects in which the nazis interfere in the lives of the German people. The examples could be multiplied almost indefinitely, because there is almost no limit to the extent to which the nazis regulate the citizens' affairs.

THE VOICE OF COMMAND

This degree of interference in people's lives, this issuing of so many orders on so many subjects to so many human beings on so many occasions, creates innumerable problems. The first and most obvious of these is the problem of how the orders themselves are most effectively to be given. For manifestly in a country where the whole population is either commanding or being commanded most of the time, the giving of commands becomes an art of the greatest importance.

Others might have left the development of this art, the solution of this problem, to the individual giver of orders. But the nazis, partly because they are nazis and partly because they are Germans, do not believe in leaving anything to the individual. Also, they have profound respect for scholarship and science in all things. So they turned to the doctors and professors for a solution of the problem. What, they asked science, is the most effective way to give commands, to order people around?

The doctors and professors, assembled in solemn conclave at the International Congress for Singing and Speech at Frankfurt in October, 1938, gave answer. Professor Dr. Loebell of Muenster gave answer most to the point.

Professor Dr. Loebell had investigated the specific problem of what the Germans call "the voice of command"—the sounds emitted by the human being engaged in shouting orders—and what sort of men are most likely to have good voices of command and how these voices can be used with greatest effect. He had studied the organs of speech and other physical features and characteristics of 22 officers of a German infantry regiment, and his research had yielded valuable data on this all-important problem.

Generally speaking, big, broadly built men have better voices of command than small, narrow-chested men, Professor Dr. Loebell reported on the basis of his studies, and the bigger the chest expansion, the bigger the parade ground on which the officer can make himself heard. Thirteen of the officers studied had chest expansions of 8 centimeters or more, Professor Dr. Loebell said.

Heart and lungs also must be sound if the voice of command is to be suitably authoritative, the scientist found. The lung capacities of the 22 officers varied from 3.8 liters to 5 liters, he said. Some of the officers could sound an uninterrupted "O" for as long as 40 seconds.

Twelve of the officers had inflamed vocal cords, Professor Dr. Loebell told the congress. This condition is often found among actors and singers, he pointed out. Most of it, he said, is due to uneconomical use of the breath. Even after shouting a command in a loud voice, some of the officers could still breathe out more than 2 liters of air, he reported. He deplored this as wasteful use of the lungs.

The voice of command is often two full octaves above the ordinary speaking voice, according to Professor Dr. Loebell. This, he said, puts a heavy strain on the organs of speech. He urged greater clarity of pronunciation, which, he said, would make it unnecessary to shout so loudly and at such a high pitch.

Thus was the aid of science invoked in the nazis' exercise of totalitarian, authoritarian power. Thus were the physical attributes of the voice of command established, the voice with which the nazis could most effectively tell everybody what to do and what not to do on every possible occasion.

The nazis were gratified by these contributions to their knowledge of a highly practical subject. They hastened to make the most of them. It was announced that the Strength Through Joy organization of the Labor Front would make a special study of the training of voices for giving commands.

THE TOTALITARIAN SPRING

It is peculiarly appropriate that the Labor Front should be especially interested in the voice of command. For while each and all of the multifarious officials and agencies of the party and government have their part in issuing orders to the German people, in telling them what to do and what not to do, Dr. Robert Ley, the head of the Labor Front, has more commands to shout and more orders to give by other means than any other single man in Germany. As head of the Labor Front, Dr. Ley regulates the working lives of the German people. As head of the Reich Organization of the party, the great octopus of power whose tentacles reach into every city and town, into every shire and village in Germany, Ley regulates the people's (previously) private lives. He regulates them so thoroughly, in fact, that he long ago destroyed them. There are no private lives in the Third Reich, as Ley himself has frequently affirmed.

Like all good nazis, Ley has a low opinion of the masses of the people. "The peoples," he has said, "and the individual human beings within each people, are like children." It follows from this that the people must be treated like children. Dr. Ley does not shrink from this logic. On the contrary, he embraces it, lovingly. "The politician," he once announced, "must supervise everything."

Dr. Ley's supervision extends to every human being in Germany. "We have developed a leadership of the people," he declared several years ago, "which makes it possible to investigate and examine every last citizen and tell him how . . . on grounds of reason, he must act." And the nazis do tell the citizen how to act—how to act in every phase of life. "This revolution," Dr. Ley has said, "is totalitarian and must be totalitarian. It can recognize no exceptions, even if its authors wished to do so."

In this respect, the national socialist revolution is like Spring, according to Dr. Ley. "We are experiencing the Springtime of our people," he once said, "and just as every Spring is totalitarian, so is this renewal of our people totalitarian. Spring takes in every tree and every bush, and no tree can say, 'I'll wait and see if this is a real Spring.' Neither can anybody hold back and say, 'I'll wait and see if this revolution is a real one.' "

The implications of these authoritarian, totalitarian qualities of the national socialist Spring are clear: "There is no such thing as a private individual in national socialist Germany," Dr. Ley proclaims. "The only person who is still a private individual in Germany is somebody who is asleep." On occasion, Dr. Ley does not even allow this exception. "In Germany," he has said, "nothing is a private matter any more."

But suppose there are unreconstructed citizens who do not agree with Dr. Ley as to how they, "on grounds of reason," should act? Suppose there are people who do not perceive the beauties of being taken in by the national socialist totalitarian Spring, who do not always want to be told by Dr. Ley's precinct captains what to do?

Dr. Ley is ready for these Germans, too: "Everyone *must* go with us, must accept our spirit, or he won't get air to breathe any more," he once said. "We shall deny him every possibility of making a living. He will waste away. . . . If somebody says he wants to be left in peace: No, my friend, I shan't leave you in peace. I wouldn't think of doing such a thing."

Dr. Ley has more than 1,000,000 precinct captains, ward leaders and other political bosses who make good his promise.

A MOTHER DOES NOT UNDERSTAND

The first few years the nazis were in power, they concentrated their interference in the private lives of the citizens primarily on members of the party. Beginning May 1, 1936, however, the authority of the "political leaders" was extended to cover the lives of all citizens equally, whether they were party members or not. All households in Berlin, for example, were grouped into "blocks" of 40 to 60 families each, and a "block leader" was put in charge of each group, with power to interfere in every phase of the lives of the families in his block.

The leaders' exercise of this power encountered a certain "lack of understanding" on the part of some citizens, according to a statement issued in mid-November of 1936 by Party Comrade Dr. Schach, of the Berlin leadership of the party, and Dr. Schach undertook to enlighten the citizens.

The authority of the precinct captains, ward leaders and other party bosses covered the whole life of the family, Party Comrade Dr. Schach explained in an interview. In his own words, the authority covered "the situation in the household" in general, the "social [in the larger sense] interests" of the individual and his "care" and "instruction and direction" in matters of "philosophy of life" and "questions of everyday life."

Party Comrade Schach gave an example of the "lack of understanding" of the "necessity" of the party's interference in the citizens' lives which had been encountered. A "political leader" had called on a housewife subject to his jurisdiction and had requested detailed information about the affairs of the members of the family, including particulars as to how the housewife was bringing up her 8-year-old child. The woman had refused to answer the "political leader's" questions. The matters he asked about were the purely private affairs of the family, and none of the "political leader's" business, she had said.

But there are no more private matters in Germany, Party

Comrade Schach declared, and the mother who did not understand was speedily set aright by superior party authorities.

"The block leader in future must care for all his national comrades," the mother was told, in the words of Dr. Schach, "and therefore naturally must know all about the situation in the family. It is self-evident that the questions about the child were justified, since the block leader must concern himself with the whole social status of the household."

The justification for the party's interference in the citizens' lives apparently was not so "self-evident" to some Germans as it was to Party Comrade Schach, however, for the *Voelkischer Beobachter* reported 12 months later that "most of the people" still did not "understand" it. The *Voelkischer Beobachter*, accordingly, asked Dr. Ley himself for an interview which might further inform the citizens. Dr. Ley obliged.

The party, he said, intended to "care for" every human being in Germany. This "care," he explained, consisted of two elements, "supervision" and "training." To conduct this supervision and training, Dr. Ley said, the party must be in direct personal contact with every individual in the country. It must have complete information regarding everyone's affairs and be in a position to intervene at any time to guide him in their management.

The system of surveillance of the people's lives that the party had employed up to that time had proven fairly satisfactory. Dr. Ley said: "The party can form a picture of the lives of all citizens of all classes and occupations, including every house and family."

But Dr. Ley was a perfectionist. "The fact that we are again a herd is not enough," he said on another occasion at about this same time, "not nearly enough." The party's supervision of the citizens' affairs would have to be increased still further, he told the *Voelkischer Beobachter*. And therefore, naturally, the party's surveillance of the people's lives would also have to be intensified. A new "intelligence service" was, accordingly, being organized to report to the party in the greatest possible detail on the life of every German, Dr. Ley announced.

NAMES WRIT IN WATER

Dr. Ley has been as good as his word. He has been aided and abetted, furthermore, by the whole regime. For he spoke for the whole regime. The nazis' interference in the people's lives begins, in fact, before birth and continues after death, and omits almost nothing in between. Dr. Ley spoke truly when he said there is no such thing as a private matter in Germany any more.

The nazis begin by deciding whether you may be born or not. For they decide who may marry and who may not and who may marry whom and who may have children and who may not. They sterilize most of those they decide should not have children, kill a good many, and castrate the rest.

After the citizen has obtained the nazis' permission to marry and their approval of the person he wants to marry and their authorization to have children, he also has to secure their consent to the names he wishes to give his children.

The basic principle by which the choice of names is regulated is that names must reveal as clearly as possible the racial, national, sexual and family identity of the individual.

Thus Jews must have "Jewish-sounding" names and gentiles "Aryan-sounding" ones. Gentile parents are forbidden to give their children such names, for example, as Esther, Judith, Samuel, Abraham and Joshua, because the nazis say they sound too Jewish.

Not all "Nordic" names are, however, acceptable for German children either. "In this connection, insofar as such first names as Joerns, Knut, Bjoerns and Sven are concerned, they are no more desirable than other foreign names," says Wilhelm Frick, Minister of the Interior, who issued these regulations.

"On the other hand, first names of foreign origin which have been used in Germany for centuries, and which . . . are not looked on as foreign, but are fully 'Germanized,' may continue to be used without objection, for example, Hans, Johann, Peter, Julius, Elizabeth and Maria." German children may not, however, be named Charles except when the name is a family tradition, as in some Huguenot families.

Boys must be given names the nazis consider suitably masculine, furthermore, and girls such as are officially ruled feminine. Thus no German boy may be named "Maria," as is a common custom in some Catholic regions—witness Carl Maria von Weber, the composer—unless he is also given another and masculine name, and this must be the one commonly used.

The authorities also limit the number of names that may be given a child and, if more than one name is allowed, the father must state which one will be commonly used.

The nazis regulate the changing of names as closely as they do the original giving of them. On the one hand, the individual who wants to take a new name must satisfy the authorities that his reasons for doing so are adequate and obtain their approval of the new name he proposes to take. On the other hand, the nazis may change people's names for them, whether the people want them changed or not, and may cancel a change previously allowed and compel the citizen to revert to the use of his original name.

If there is doubt as to the names individuals should use, the Reich Ministry of the Interior decides the matter. These regulations apply to both given and family names. The authorities, furthermore, may order changes even after the person concerned is dead, which also automatically changes the names of such persons' children. Changes can be made effective merely by notification in a daily newspaper. The Germans' names are indeed writ in water.

The fact that a person dislikes his name is not an adequate reason for allowing him to change it, Frick has ruled, and neither is the claim that a new name would help the individual get along better in life. Changes are, however, permissible in cases where original names are ridiculous or offensive.

In deciding on a new name, the first choice should be the name of an ancestor, Frick has provided. Names of celebrated historical, literary or political figures may not be taken. Use of hyphenated names is also discouraged, except when an extra name is wanted to add to one so common that it affords only inadequate identification, such as Meyer, Mueller, Schmidt or Wagner. Gentiles with Jewish-sounding names are allowed and, in fact, encouraged, to change them. Persons of "hereditarily inferior" stock, on the other hand, are not allowed to take the names of "hereditarily superior" families.

BAR SINISTER

But the nazis' insistence upon clearly establishing the identity of every German by no means ends with their determining how he may be named. For the individual's racial, national and family identity obviously depend in the first instance on who his father was. And this point, too, the nazis assert the right to investigate and establish whenever they decide there is any room for doubt on it; they assert the right to challenge the legitimacy of every German, in the case of both the living and the dead.

"It is well known that a large proportion of first-born children are conceived before marriage," Dr. Schmidt-Klevenow, an official of the Central Bureau for Race and Settlements of the S. S., wrote in a Berlin newspaper December 17, 1936. "The party, the state and the other members of the family must have the right to challenge the legitimacy of a child."

A law giving the authorities this right was promulgated in April, 1938. It empowered the government to institute proceedings to establish paternity whenever this should be "considered desirable in the public interest or in that of the child," even in cases where neither parent had ever questioned the child's legitimacy and where both parents protested against the question's being raised.

The law also provided that certificates of legitimate birth could be canceled after they had been issued if it should be "established" later that the issuing of the certificates had been a mistake.

When the authorities challenge the paternity of a child they are empowered by the law of April, 1938, to require the mother of the child and all men the authorities think might possibly be the father to submit to blood tests and other examinations calculated to help to establish paternity.

If the courts rule on the basis of the evidence adduced by the authorities that the man previously assumed to be the father actually was not, but that some other man was, the courts have the power to remove the child from its home and place it in the custody, either of the nazi youth office, or of the father as determined in the proceedings.

The nazis lost no time in exercising these powers, according to Dr. Rexroth, an official in the Reich Ministry of Justice. Writing in an official legal journal in May of 1938, Dr. Rexroth announced that the authorities would investigate the paternity of adults as well as that of children—and of dead persons as well as living ones.

Dr. Rexroth made no estimate of the number of either living or dead persons whose paternity would be called into question under the new law. He said, however, that the number would be "large." And his interpretation of the powers conferred by the law made this seem extremely likely.

"Whenever a large number of persons share the belief that a child is not the offspring of the man whose legitimate child it is supposed to be," for example, the authorities would feel justified in instituting proceedings, Dr. Rexroth said. The state would also intervene, he said, "in cases in which official inquiries yield clear indications of the illegitimacy of a child born in wedlock and in those in which only a slight probability of legitimate descent exists."

Under earlier German legislation, the husband of a child's mother was the only person who had the right to institute proceedings challenging the child's paternity under any circumstances, and he could exercise the right only within the 12 months following the child's birth. If he failed to act within this time, his right to do so lapsed.

Under the new law, however, the legal father may challenge at any time within 12 months after becoming aware of circumstances which cause him to doubt that he is the child's real father. A child may develop characteristics at any time during its life which rouse suspicion in the legal father's mind, Dr. Rexroth said, and even if the legal father learns of suspicious circumstances after the child has died, he may still institute proceedings.

Cases would probably occur in which a husband suspected or even knew that he was not the father of his wife's child but would wish to overlook his wife's "misstep" and accept the child as his own, Dr. Rexroth wrote, but the state could not allow this concealment of a child's true origin. Not even this is a private matter in the New Germany.

Most of the instances in which the state intervened would be those where it would be considered necessary to establish whether a person was really of Jewish or gentile origin or whether he was hereditarily sound in the meaning of nazi legislation, according to Dr. Rexroth.

HITLER TAKES THE CHILDREN

The nazis have never revealed the number of persons whose legitimacy they have challenged. But while Dr. Rexroth said the number would be large, it nevertheless must constitute a very small proportion of the total population. In other respects, however, the nazis interfere in everybody's life, and in the most intimate phases of it. The party's regulation of the individual's affairs has only just begun when the regime has decided whether the citizen may marry and whom he may marry and whether he may have any children and how he may name them. For the party now tells the citizen how he must bring up his children, too.

"We have begun, above all, with the youth," Hitler said in a speech in Berlin, May 1, 1937. "There are old idiots out of whom nothing can be made any more [laughter]. . . . But that causes us no concern. We take their children away from them. We bring them up to be new German human beings and we bring them up thoroughly.

"When a child is 10 years old it does not yet have any feeling about its birth and origin," said the bachelor Chancellor. "One child is like another. At that age we take them and form them into a community until they are 18 years old. But we don't let them go then. They enter the party, the S. A. and S. S. and other formations, or they march directly into the factories, the Labor Front, into the Labor Service, and they go into the army for two years."

Children live at home in Germany, even after they are 10 years old, much as children do elsewhere. Parents have the privilege of feeding and housing them. But they have few other privileges. The nazis keep a watchful eye on what goes on in the home, and if they think that children are not being brought up in accordance with the party's ideas on the subject, they take the children away from the parents altogether.

A court deprived one German mother of custody of her 15-year-old son in February of 1937, for example, on the grounds that the boy was not being brought up in a properly "manly" way, and the Ministry of the Interior commended the court's action in a circular sent to all local officials throughout Germany.

In November of 1937 two more cases were decided by nazi courts in much this same spirit. In the first case, a divorced mother was deprived of the custody of her children because she wished to educate them in Catholic convent schools. This, the court held, was "in no way in the children's interest." In the second case, a court in Waldenburg, in Silesia, took children away from their father and mother because the parents were members of the International Bible Students' organization and did not accept the national socialist philosophy of life; they also taught their children not to give the Hitler salute and were themselves pacifists.

"The law as a racial and national instrument entrusts German parents with the bringing up of their children only on the condition that they bring them up in the manner that the nation and state expect," the court said. "It is above all necessary that a realization be wakened in children that they are members of a mighty nation, bound to their fellow citizens by uniformity of opinion on fundamental matters. Whoever wakens in children opinions which bring them into conflict with this racial and national unity has not fulfilled the condition on which he was entrusted with their bringing up. For reasons of general policy this right must be taken from him."

THE SIX SECOND CHILDHOODS

It is not only children, however, on whose conduct the nazis keep a close watch. The party is at least equally zealous in the surveillance it exercises over adults' lives, too. The seven ages of man are all childhoods in Germany, in nazi theory and practice, a first childhood and six second childhoods, and the party supervises and regulates them all.

Criticism of the regime is, of course, strictly forbidden. "Who are the people who criticize?" Dr. Goebbels demanded in a speech in Berlin, November 23, 1934. "Party members? No. The rest of the German people? They should consider themselves lucky still to be alive. It would be too much of a good thing altogether if those who live at our mercy should be allowed to criticize."

But surely the citizen may grumble just a little in the bosom of his own family? Surely there is some last vestige of privacy at least there? By no means. The Reich Supreme Court itself has made this point clear. Both ordinary slander and criticism of the regime are punishable even if the offending remarks are uttered in the most intimate family circle—by a husband to a wife, for example, or by a parent to a child—and even if the person to whom the remarks are made is pledged to secrecy, the court ruled in September, 1937, if the remarks are repeated in spite of the pledge of secrecy.

The court recognized only two forms of utterance that could be considered really private and therefore (regrettably, from the nazi point of view, it is to be presumed) not actionable. One is soliloquy. A citizen may not be punished, the court held, for things he says while talking to himself without intending to be overheard and in the belief that he cannot be and is not being overheard. The other form of privileged utterance recognized by the court consists of entries in a diary which nobody else is expected to see. Even if such a diary should fall into the hands of others by chance or due to negligence on the part of the author, in spite of his intentions, remarks in the diary would not be actionable, the court held.

This, then, is what freedom of utterance—and privacy— amounts to in the Third Reich: a citizen may talk to himself, in either written or spoken words, and not be punished for what he says. Not, at least, by the Supreme Court. What the Gestapo thinks on this point may, of course, be altogether different.

Apart from what the citizen says while talking to himself in adequate solitude, however, there is little that he may either say or do that is not subject to the party's advice and consent. "Privacy"? The nazis have no more inhibitions in invading and destroying privacy than they do in invading and destroying anything else.

How many evenings should a husband spend away from home every week? It is a question, one would think, best left to the husband and wife concerned. Not so in the New Germany. Here, as everywhere else, the party knows best.

The question is a live one in the Third Reich. For so busy are the nazis regulating everything and everybody on every possible occasion that they have to work long hours to get it all accomplished. Party husbands are liable to be on duty more evenings than they are at home—or at least to say that they are on duty—and party wives often complain that the regime has made "political widows" of them.

A Dr. W. Weimar, of Cologne (or someone signing himself so), once reproached "political widows" for complaining. Writing in a Berlin newspaper, June 1, 1937, Dr. Weimar laid down general rules for the number of evenings a husband had the right—and the duty—to be absent from home on party business. It is true, he conceded, that wife and children should not be altogether neglected. But it is a husband's duty to take part in party activities, and a wife who makes trouble on this score gives grounds for divorce, Dr. Weimar warned.

The number of evenings a party husband may and should be away from home varies with circumstances, Dr. Weimar said. The wife must not complain, however, if her husband devotes two evenings a week to party activities. "Nor do Sunday mornings always and exclusively belong to the family," he said. Special circumstances and occasions may require still more of the husband's time, Dr. Weimar wrote: for example, an election campaign, an S. A. parade, an official visit by a foreign statesman, or the annual party congress at Nuremberg.

The most important thing is, Dr. Weimar declared, that the wife must view her husband's party activities with "love and understanding," for his party work is in the service of the community and therefore, by this same token, in the service of his family.

THE POLITICAL STOMACH

"Service to the community" is a favorite nazi phrase. It is invoked to cover a multitude of—activities and deprivations and interferences in the lives of the citizens. It is invoked, for example, to cover, not only the number of evenings a husband spends away from home, but also the kind of clothes both husband and wife alike should wear and the kind of food they should eat and even how they should eat it. These matters, too, are regulated in accordance with the principles of "service to the community." They, also, are not private in the Third Reich.

The official party news, editorial and feature service, *The Nationalsozialistische Korrespondenz,* devoted itself as early as November, 1936, to the question of diet control. The German people require, it said, "a political stomach," that is, a stomach that willingly, not to say gladly, accepts and makes the most of such foodstuffs as the nazis decide it should have, and does not yearn for others.

"Not only is the way to a man's heart through his stomach, but so is the way to his politics, if he wants it to be so," the *NSK* said. "It sounds comical, but it is bitterly serious—the German people need a political stomach."

If any German has failed to acquire a political stomach since then, it has not been for lack of the opportunity. The nazis, at least, certainly have seen to it that the Germans have had a "political diet"—a diet, that is, determined more by government regulation and less by personal preference and habit than the diet of any great European people had been for generations for such a long period before a war.

The nazis have exercised as much as possible of their diet control by persuasion, by propaganda. They have urged the citizens to eat less fats and meat and more fish and vegetables, for example, and to prefer black bread to white—and to chew each mouthful longer, for that, they have said, would provide more nourishment from less food. Overeating, party spokesmen have declared, is a form of treason to people and state.

These reforms in diet have not only been advisable in the interests of the government's foreign trade policy—and possibilities—but they also are good for the national and individual health, the nazis have said.

What the regime has not been able to accomplish by persuasion, it has undertaken to do by compulsion. Foodstuffs were rationed long before the war began, mostly by controls of imports and of distribution to dealers, although to a certain extent also by the direct food-card system—and rationed down to the smallest detail. Everything possible has also been done from the first to increase domestic production of foodstuffs. Attempts were even made, for example, to develop a new type of bee with an especially long proboscis so that it could get more honey from the flowers. But most citizens have felt the impact of nazi policy in this sphere primarily in the rationing of foodstuffs rather than in their production. And in this, too, no form and no detail of regulation has been too insignificant to be overlooked.

The maximum number of dishes of each category that may be offered on restaurant menus was fixed long before the war. Bread could be sold only after it was at least 24 hours old, on the theory that it would be less appetizing then than when it was fresh and that people therefore would eat less of it. The amount of chocolate that could be used in making Easter eggs was prescribed in detail with all the authority and majesty of the law. And magicians were forbidden to use eggs, milk or other foodstuffs in their tricks. (They were also forbidden at the same time to explain their tricks to their audiences; if people began to expect explanations of sleight-of-hand, where would their expectations end?)

With the passage of time, the Germans came increasingly to need a political skin as well as a political stomach. For not only the food they ate but also the clothes they wore were regulated in greater and greater detail by the nazis. The wearing of fine clothes was denounced as no less treasonable than overeating. Schoolboys were forbidden to make symbolic bonfires of their caps. Pleats and trains were damned with particular vehemence because they required so much material. The length of men's shirt tails was fixed. So was the number of pockets men might have in their trousers.

Even the clothing of the dead was regulated, in at least one instance. The mayor of Pirmasens gave out a statement on May 18, 1937, which read as follows:

"It has been noted repeatedly that the dead have been laid out in expensive clothing and decorations. I call your attention to the fact that it is the duty of every citizen to see that the dead shall not be buried in expensive materials."

WILL TO RULE

The cycle of life in the totalitarian, authoritarian state is thus complete. The nazis intervene at every point in every segment of it; from birth and before to death and after. There is no private life in Germany.

There are several reasons why the nazis assert the right to exercise these powers and do exercise them. One reason is that the nazis were preparing for war from the time they seized power in Germany, and preparations for modern war require a great degree of interference in the lives of the people.

This is the primary reason why the nazis tell the people what they may keep in their attics, for example, whether or not they may fly kites, and the extent to which they may show grief if their sons are killed. For inflammable materials in attics multiply the damage caused by incendiary bombs, flying kites on long strings causes hazards for low-flying planes (or at least so said Hermann Goering, who issued the order requiring permits for flying kites) and the display of excessive grief can harm morale.

(Nobody knows this last fact better or exploits it more fully than the nazis themselves. One of the myriad ways they attacked French morale before the big offensive in the Spring of 1940 was to send agents out on the streets of French towns and cities in deepest mourning and giving every sign of soul-shattering grief. This, the nazis calculated, would prey upon the fears of French families with men at the front.)

A second reason for the nazis' interference in the citizens' lives is the economic predicament in which the country has found itself ever since the nazis seized power—and before. Even pre-nazi governments had instituted far-reaching controls of the national life in an attempt to fend off disaster, and the economic policies which the nazis adopted, even the non-military measures, to the extent that it is possible to make a distinction, would have led to more and more government interference in "private" life in themselves, even if the regime had not been preparing for war at the same time.

Among the gravest economic problems which have weighed upon the country have been a lack of gold and foreign exchange and a raw-material shortage. Aggravated by the preparations for war, these deficiencies have dictated the necessity of choosing, not only between guns and butter, but also between guns and most other things as well. That is why the nazis regulate the amount of gold that may be used in making wedding rings, the amount of textiles that may be used in making clothes—and even the kind of clothing that may be used for laying out the dead, because that clothing is "wasted."

The interferences in the people's lives resulting from the attempts to solve Germany's economic problems and those resulting from the nazis' preparations for war soon led in themselves to the necessity of still more regulation and therefore still greater interference, furthermore. For no matter how necessary it may be, or appear to be, government interference creates a vicious cycle: whether or not it solves the problems it is intended to solve, it is extremely likely to create new problems which also must be dealt with in their turn.

These principal reasons for the nazis' interference in the lives of the citizens apply similarly, in greater or lesser degree, in any country, with any kind of a regime, that finds itself in the kind of economic predicament that the Reich found itself in or that sets out to prepare as speedily as possible for war. They do not necessarily have anything whatever to do with national socialism.

The nazis have reasons of their own for destroying private life in Germany, though, reasons independent of their prepara-

tions for war and of their economic difficulties. For the nazis
are revolutionists, and are trying to convert the German people
to a whole new philosophy and way of life. They are even trying to breed a whole new race of human beings. The nazis,
furthermore, have a lust for power, both for its own sake and
for the privileges, prerogatives and property with which it en-
dows them, or enables them to endow themselves, and they are
determined to keep power. And, finally, the nazis are Germans,
and therefore addicted by nationality, as well as by party motives,
to the most thorough possible regulation of everything and
everybody anyway.

These are the considerations that explain the most intimate
and most bizarre interferences in the lives of the German people
in which the nazis indulge themselves. For if they are going to
breed a new race of people, then the nazis obviously have to
determine who is to marry whom and who is to have children
and who is not. If they are going to train the people in a whole
new "Nordic"-Germanic outlook and way of life, then they
have to see to it—or, being Germans, as well as nazis, think
they do—that children have suitably Germanic names and that
mothers refrain from having their girls' hair bobbed in what
the nazis declare is a "French-Jewish-American" manner and
that they keep it, instead, in truly Germanic pigtails. They also
have to take every conceivable pains to establish everyone's
paternity, lest racial outsiders be smuggled into the national
blood community. If the nazis are to reap the greatest possible
profit from their power, furthermore, they must lay their hands
on all kinds and quantities of loot available, even the treasury
of the neighborhood chess club. And if they are to keep the
power they cherish so, they must seize every vantage point
where opposition of any kind might conceivably gain a foothold,
and prevent the expression of any form of opposition whatever,
whether it is in a funny paper, a joke, or even a protest uttered
in the bosom of the family.

But the lengths to which the nazis go in interfering in people's
private lives cannot be altogether explained by logic, not even
by nazi logic. The most grotesque of these interferences are due
simply to the fact that the nazis lust after power for its own

sake, that they love to wield it just for the sake of wielding it, whether there is any other and more valid reason for doing so or not.

Only this can explain, for example, why the nazis insist on regulating tombstones.

THE CO-ORDINATION OF THE TOMBSTONES

In the Third Reich, the nazis have proclaimed, cemeteries are to be considered "cultural treasures of the community of the people." It is, accordingly, necessary that they be "dealt with in a worthy manner." This mission was entrusted, in January, 1938, to the nazi Chamber of Art, a section in the national Chamber of Kultur, presided over by Dr. Goebbels, and the chamber immediately set about co-ordinating the dead as effectively as the living also are co-ordinated in Germany.

Every cemetery must have a basic landscaping and artistic plan, the chamber prescribed. The sizes and kinds of gravestones that may be set up in each part of the cemetery must be regulated in accordance with this plan. Stones must be of approximately the same heights and colors. Conspicuously dark materials may not be used. Graves must not be "artificially adorned" with metal wreaths, paper figures or potted plants.

"The bereaved chooses a gravestone in accordance with these considerations," a semi-official statement explained. "It will be well, even before ordering a stone, to discuss one's plans with the duly authorized art adviser of the cemetery [duly authorized by the nazis, that is], in order to make possible a pleasing co-ordination of all the stones in any one part of the cemetery.

"May love and care be devoted once again to our cemeteries," the statement concluded, "so that our cemeteries will testify, as cultural treasures, to a single, common will."

There is no privacy, even in the grave, in the New Germany. Name, legitimacy, clothing and even tombstone are subject to review by the national socialist party.

"We have the will to rule," Dr. Ley once proclaimed. "We delight in ruling."

Clearly, it could not have been better said.

8. Man's State

The National Socialist movement is in its nature a masculine movement.   GOEBBELS

Philosophers never concern themselves by whom women have children, provided they have them at all.   VOLTAIRE

THE NATIONAL SOCIALIST STATE is a man's state.

"The German woman from now on will live in a state formed and led by the masculine spirit," a nazi wrote soon after the party came to power, "in a non-parliamentarian and conservative state in which, for a long time, she will not have any direct influence as formerly."

The implications of this fact—for it is a fact—have been far-reaching. Not only was the status of women themselves changed radically almost over night, but the whole tone and atmosphere of all life in Germany altered—and altered for the worse, as even the nazis themselves admitted in the end.

Women were virtually banished from public life, and strongly discouraged, when they were not altogether deterred, from entering the professions and from engaging in advanced studies for any purpose at all. Women's clubs and other organizations, which had reached a state of development at least as advanced as those of any other country, and more advanced than most, were either suppressed or taken over by the nazis. Under the new dispensation even the women's "own" organizations are directed by men.

156

Dr. Erich Hilgenfeldt is head of the central office of the great, all-inclusive women's organization, the Frauenschaft, and, as such, superior to Frau Gertrud Scholtz-Klink, the so-called Reich Leader of Women. The nazi organizations for German girls are ruled by the Reich Youth Fuehrer, who is a man. And all women's organizations of all descriptions are subject to the "patronage" of Wilhelm Frick, Minister of the Interior.

But the changes that the nazi revolution wrought in women's existences went far beyond these.

THE DOUBLE STANDARD

German women soon found, for example, that in the new male Reich a distinctly barrack-room, parade-ground air and manner dominated life. Actual open brutality toward women is, in fact, far from being altogether unknown among these men who profess such adoration of the "truly feminine" woman— that is, the wife and mother.

No brutality is too outrageous to be inflicted on Jewish women or on "Aryan" women who associate with Jews. In Nuremberg, one Sunday in August, 1933, S. A. men seized a gentile girl of 19 who was out walking with a Jew, cut off her hair, shaved her head and hung a sign around her neck reading, "I have given myself to a Jew." Then they paraded her through the streets, forced her into one cafe after another and made her stand on the stage in each one while the S. A. men shouted the text of the sign and vile abuse at her. Shortly after this experience, the girl went hopelessly insane and had to be committed to an institution. When the nazis seized Austria, Jewish women were forced to clean out men's public toilets with their bare hands in Vienna. Outrages on Jewish women have been even worse and even more numerous since the war began than they were before.

But even simon-pure "Aryan" women having no associations with Jews cannot be sure of immunity from nazi brutality. On one occasion before the nazis seized power, a social democratic woman deputy was jeered at by a nazi deputy because she spoke with grief of the loss of her son in the war of 1914-1918. "That's what you nanny-goats were made for!" he shouted at her on the floor of the Reichstag itself.

Outbursts like these are exceptional, however revealing they may be of the character of the men who rule Germany. Few women—even relatively few Jewesses and social democrats—have had such experiences. But many and perhaps even most German women feel another consequence of the exclusively, not to say excessively, masculine spirit that dominates life in the Third Reich under nazi rule: For the nazis have re-established the double standard of morality in all its primitive simplicity.

The sexual morals of the men who rule the New Germany are no better than their morals in other respects. Woman's place, they say, is in the home, and her function is to have and care for children. But it does not by any means follow from this that man's place is in the home, too. Many nazis, in fact, find home a dull place at best.

They have power, furthermore, and they have money, and what is the use of having these things if you stay home all the time? You can't use power and money to greatest advantage at home. Nor are home-body wives always the most amusing of companions outside the home, either. So the nazis go out, and they go out with—and to—other women.

Hitler's own interests in this sphere are obscure at best. It seems to be the case, however, that they are, in any event, sub-dued. Yet even he likes the company of pretty young dancers and actresses. And among other nazis, whose vigor is anything but subdued, lubricity achieves positively startling proportions. Blondes, orchids, champagne, lobster and silver-fox capes are not rationed in Germany. There is never a lack of any of them in nazi party circles.

Besides the nazis with heterosexual interests there are also others with homosexual ones. *Das Schwarze Korps*, official organ of the S. S. and the police, reported in March of 1937 that when the nazis came to power they found that approximately 2,000,-000 men belonged to homosexual clubs and associations of one kind or another in the Reich. Even pederasty was organized in Germany. At the same time, there must also have been many other homosexuals who were not members of such associations. The nazis themselves numbered at least their share of these members of the third sex in their ranks, some of them high in the party's councils, especially in the S. A.

Until June 30, 1934, these men flaunted their tastes in the most public possible manner. After the slaughter of that week end, pederasty fell into political disfavor. It had been used as one of the principal pretexts for the slaughter. And besides, as *Das Schwarze Korps* pointed out, pederasty withdrew at least 2,000,000 men from the campaign to raise the birth rate, and this was intolerable. Instead of being something to boast about openly, as it had been before in the party, pederasty became instead a favorite pretext for destroying political enemies. Anyone who is sufficiently useful to the regime, however, and is moderately discreet, can continue to belong to the third sex with impunity, and a good many nazis do.

THE BARRACK-ROOM MANNER

It took the nazis five years to decide that they wanted German women to be pretty, after all, and then the idea of doing something about it had to be postponed indefinitely because of the war.

Considerations of race and class morality alike seemed to conspire to convince the nazis in the early years of their rule that German women should be as unattractive as possible—which was saying a good deal. Even population policy entered into the conspiracy, for it was officially established in Germany, as it had been long before in Italy, that a slender figure is often incompatible with the bearing of many children, and since the men who rule Germany demand many children above all things, they called upon German women to cease from troubling about their figures.

A few voices were raised in dissent even then, to be sure:

A new German Fashion Institute was founded, and Frau Goebbels became its president. "I am trying," she said, "to make German women more beautiful."

Rudolf Dillenz, who was associated with Frau Goebbels in the Institute, also took a position in favor of beauty.

"I take this opportunity [one he had made for himself]," he said, "to deny certain 'atrocity stories' which have been spread abroad regarding national socialist ideas on women's dress. It is not true that we have forbidden or shall forbid the use of make-up, jewelry and other adornment. We must unite against the saboteurs who spread the report that the national socialist movement does not want German women to be well-dressed and beautiful."

Even Captain Ernst Roehm, then chief of the S. A., denounced the busybodies who were trying to make women give up cosmetics.

But these were voices crying in an esthetic wilderness populated in truly amazing proportions by shiny noses, straggly hair, flat-heeled shoes and sack-of-potato figures in severe and forbidding dresses. And even these few voices were soon stilled. Frau Goebbels resigned from the Fashion Institute, nothing further was heard from Dillenz—and Captain Roehm was a notorious pederast, and therefore easily discredited as an authority on the charms of women.

The lower middle-class morality that dominates the rank and file of the party was the principal cause of the perverted Puritanism that now held almost undisputed sway as far as outward appearances were concerned. Also, there was a feeling that fine feathers and even good manners were somehow not altogether in keeping with the best revolutionary tradition.

Mussolini had not known how to use more than one fork when he had become prime minister, and had not excelled even with that one, and this seemed a fitting and even an admirable quality in a son of the people, and one to be emulated.

Most of the party leaders have lived like pashas, ever since they first laid their hands on enough power and plunder to do so, but they have always protested that they still remain the same rough, simple-hearted fellows they have always been. And if the pasha is a plain fellow, and no nonsense, then the pasha's wife manifestly must be even plainer—his *wife*, that is, not his concubines. If the pasha's wife did allow herself a touch of lipstick now and then, in the early years of party rule, she was careful about it, for the Janissaries and their wives were sensitive on this subject, and quick to suspect that where there was scarlet there must also be sin.

(The nazis' whole attitude toward women was, and is, in fact, oriental and smacks strongly of the Old Testament.)

But apart from considerations of class morality and the birth rate, there were reasons of race policy, too, it appeared, why German women must be unattractive. Allure, it was semi-officially proclaimed, was definitely non-Nordic.

"Close contact with the southern world," a nazi woman official wrote, "has enticed the German people far from their own values and subjected them to the dangerously decadent influences of foreign civilizations. This is the case also in respect of women's dress; the following of foreign examples has had injurious physical and spiritual effects, leading to national corruption and racial disintegration. . . .

"Not only have foreign races different ideals of physical beauty, but the position of women in foreign countries is different, too," this authority asserted. "Race decides whether a woman is a free being or a plaything. Such fundamental conceptions determine women's dress to a considerable degree.

"The southern 'exhibitionist type' adapts her dress to the desire for display, the Nordic 'achievement type' adapts hers to her sphere of activity.

"The southern feminine ideal is the youthful beloved. The Nordic, the motherly woman.

"The 'showing-off' motive leads to distortion of the body. The motive of action demands the cult of the body."

Fashions which distort or exaggerate the lines of the body are a sign of alien influences, the writer went on, in which the "showing-off" motive plays an important part.

"When signs of sex confusion show themselves in women's clothing—the emphasis on narrow hips, for example, which represents an approach to the male physical structure—these are the decadent influences of an alien race, hostile to procreation and therefore disruptive."

"Face-painting is blatantly un-German," too, according to a (male) nazi official of Breslau. "This type of make-up may be suitable to the sensual faces and thick lips of oriental races—Jewish and Russian girls," he wrote in the *Voelkischer Beobachter*, "but the worst and most unnatural thing we can encounter in the streets is the German woman who, disregarding all laws of beauty, has painted her face with oriental war colors which are in utter contradiction to her character and her way of thinking, and which deform her clearly-limned Nordic lips and light eyes by harsh and formless daubs of color."

This, then, was the official party line on feminine beauty when the nazis first took over the country. And, generally speaking, German women adhered to it. Some of them did because they had to. The way of life in the girls' Labor Service was regulated in accordance with these principles, for example. The girls were trained in Spartan severity and "taught to do without cosmetics and to dress in the most simple manner and not permitted to display any individual vanity," *Der Arbeitsmann,* official journal of the men's Labor Service, reported, and were "trained to sleep on hard cots and forego all culinary delicacies for the sake of general hardening."

Even girls and women who were not actually compelled to do so hewed to the party line to a considerable extent also, in outward appearance, if in nothing else. Were not the Germans accustomed to and reverent toward authority? Were they not also a remarkably sturdy people, able to endure the most excruciating hardships and anguish?

THE ORGANIZATION OF BEAUTY

The esthetic results of all this were depressing to an outsider from the beginning, and the longer the era of the barrack-room manner and shiny noses lasted, the more depressing did it become. In the end, even the nazis themselves began to be affected —or disaffected.

Perhaps they finally perceived that their logic was faulty even from the point of view of their own population policy. For if women are to have as many as possible babies, then presumably they must attract men, and if they are to attract men, then they should not be deprived of the most effective implements of attraction. Sex appeal is a national necessity and therefore a patriotic duty under such circumstances. But whatever the reason, a reaction set in.

Dr. Goebbels, the most sophisticated of all leading nazis, led the van:

"Now that the national socialist spirit permeates the entire nation," he told propaganda officials congregated in Munich in February, 1936, "you must be especially careful not to elevate to the level of ideological problems matters that need not be appraised from this point of view.

"We must find a healthy style for our social life," he said. "The revolutionary is not distinguished from the non-revolutionary according to whether he wears a workman's overalls, a uniform or a swallow-tail coat, but by the heart that beats beneath his shirt."

This was cautious, in all conscience, but at least it was a beginning.

Emboldened, possibly, by the drawing in such an exalted quarter of this distinction between the revolutionary shirt-front and the revolutionary heart, others, too, raised voices in a similar sense. Some of them even went so far as to advocate openly that women should be attractive in spite of everything.

The month after Goebbels' address, for example, *Das Schwarze Korps* denounced the mannish woman and said flatly that women should be "truly feminine."

The *HJ*, official organ of the Hitler Youth, went even further. It approved evening dress for nazi girls.

The (nazi) League of German Girls was still suspicious of the evening gown, the *HJ* said, because of the "stale spirit of yesterday that still clings to it." But, the *HJ* went on fearlessly, "we must not act like the men whose socialism is so great that they must go to the opera in knickerbockers although they have a dark suit hanging in the closet at home, who march across the room in heavy boots and ridicule the conductor's evening clothes.

"No," said the *HJ*, "that is not the way. The League uniform in its place, namely, on duty; the folk costume where it belongs, namely, in the meadows. But on festive occasions which carry us outside the circle of our comrades we should adorn ourselves in a festive spirit and enjoy pretty clothes . . . without hesitation."

The protest against the barrack-room manner grew. By January, 1938, *Der Arbeitsmann* had advanced so far that it even denounced its prevalence among men.

"It is a mistake," *Der Arbeitsmann* said, "to believe that heel-clicking is the only proper deportment or that the man begins with the manual of arms. The well-known 'rough but hearty tone' customary in soldierly comradeship is not everywhere in place, especially not in the company of women. There is no reason to feel that one is at all times wearing high boots, even when one is really wearing laced shoes."

The wheel was now to come full circle. After five years of shiny noses and the barrack-room manner, the nazis repented and recanted. German women, it was officially announced, were to be beautiful. It remained only to make the new ideal effective. This was speedily undertaken, and in the best authoritarian manner. In the New Germany such things are not left to chance, or even to persuasion. Beauty, too, was organized—officially organized:

On January 19, 1938, Baldur von Schirach, then Reich Youth Leader, proclaimed the launching of a program to make German girls beautiful whether they liked it or not. A new organization was created as of that date within the Hitler Youth for carrying out the program, Schirach announced, and membership would be compulsory for all German girls between 18 and 21. The organization was named "Work, Beauty and Faith." Among other things, rhythmic and other exercises would be taught, to improve bearing and general appearance.

"Elegance and the care of the body are necessary parts of the education of feminine youth in this period," said Schirach. "The more beautiful German girls become, the prouder and more self-confident will they be. With the absorption of cultural values and care of the body, feminine youth will express its faith in an ideal of behavior and self-respect."

THE RETURN OF EVE

But tragedy was to halt this program before it could get well under way, the tragedy of the war. For even before the war itself began, the more thorough the preparations for it became and the longer they lasted, the more serious became the shortages of both raw materials and labor, and the more serious these shortages became the less justification could the nazis see, even those so recently converted to beauty, for devoting either men or materials to the manufacture of the properties and appurtenances of allure.

Das Schwarze Korps, in June of 1939, urged that workers be shifted from the cosmetics industry to jobs where they would be more useful. All cosmetics are "humbug" anyway, said *Das Schwarze Korps*. "There is no need for 200 different kinds of facial creams," it declared. "Ten are enough." It further proposed that the number of beauty parlors be reduced.

Das Schwarze Korps also assailed the whole idea of styles in women's clothes. "German women," it said, "should learn that one puts a dress aside when it is worn out or no longer suited to one's age, not when it becomes 'out of fashion.' What is really becoming to a woman one Spring is just as becoming to her the next Spring and the one after that as well, if it is made of good material and well cared for."

Precisely at this time, however, it was becoming increasingly difficult to get good material, or, in fact, any material at all. Early the same month of *Das Schwarze Korps'* pronouncement, the Ministry of Economics informed a meeting of textile manufacturers that German women would be unable after July 1 to buy cotton lingerie or printed goods because materials would be needed for "more important national-military purposes." Manufacture of sheer silk stockings probably also would be stopped in the near future, the ministry said. Sheer silk stockings are "trashy," the ministry declared. They look well, it conceded, but they are expensive and they last only a short time. Their manufacture, therefore, represents "an unnecessary waste of raw materials."

In time, even colors were rationed. In July of 1940, at the request of the high command of the armed forces, an official "register" of 100 "especially useful" colors was compiled, and it was indicated that these approved hues should be preferred to any others.

The campaign for making German women beautiful continued despite these difficulties. The steadily worsening shortages of textiles made it seem more and more likely, however, that beauty was destined to end in a state of nature in the Reich.

There was, in fact, a distinct increase at this same time in the public display of the female integument, of the tendency to view with tolerance, if not with downright pleasure, the exhibition of feminine beauty with a minimum of encumbrances, and often with none at all—in special portfolios of photographs, in magazines and books, in paintings and drawings and even on the stage.

A mammoth official party spectacle in Munich in 1938 culminated in what was called a "Night of the Amazons," in the course of which the Amazons performed in an open arena the most varied feats of daring and agility (or at least of violent motion), both on foot and on horseback, with virtually no clothing whatever to interfere with their activities or clog the functioning of their pores, and a revue playing in Berlin the season of 1939-1940 actually offered a diffident variation of a strip-tease act—which was accomplished so speedily, however, that, as one ribald witness reported, "She stripped, all right, but she certainly didn't tease."

Most of these displays of nakedness are justified on grounds of "esthetics" or of the love of nature or of sport. They are offered in the interests of "art" or "outdoor life" or "health" or "athletics." Some authorities have even discovered that nudism is, in fact, markedly characteristic of the Nordic race, and one book and magazine and portfolio of pictures full of naked Nordics has followed another in the bookstores and on the newsstands. This, it is explained, is a "healthy" eroticism that has nothing to do with the evil pornography that flourished in the bad old days of the Republic.

It is amazing, all the same, how closely the nazi Eve resembles the Republican Eve, when stripped of her nonessentials.

THE NATURAL IMPULSE

But, apart from "healthy" eroticism and public manners, what is the position of women in the New Germany?

Nazi policy in this sphere consisted originally of two main parts. First, women were to be relieved of the necessity of doing "unwomanly" work. Second, they were to marry and have homes of their own and each woman was to have at least four babies. The nazis often suggested, in fact, when they did not say openly, even before the war, that women should have babies whether they married or not.

"The program of our national socialist women's movement has only one point," Hitler himself has said. "That point is called the child." Nor is the Chancellor above more direct encouragement. At the annual party congresses at Nuremberg, he had some of the stalwart youths of the Labor Service parade in only boots and trousers and, referring to this in a speech to women and girls at the congress of 1935, he said, "When the women see the fine Labor Service boys, dressed only in trousers and with breasts all bare, surely they must say, 'What fine fellows they are, and how nice for the women!'"

Lesser nazis—but only slightly lesser—are considerably more outspoken. The German people, Alfred Rosenberg has said, never could have survived some of the darkest periods of their history if they had not resorted to polygamy, and, "The German Reich of the future will regard the woman without children—whether she is married or not—as a member of the community having only inferior rights. In this connection, sexual relations out of wedlock which result in the birth of a child should not be punishable by law." Rosenberg is Commissioner of the Fuehrer for the Philosophical Education of the National Socialist Movement. When he discusses population policy he therefore presumably speaks ex cathedra.

There are enthusiasts to whom this is as nothing. An official journal of the Labor Front argued on one occasion that illegitimate children are more likely to be good racial specimens than children born in wedlock, because the illegitimate children must necessarily be the tokens of a greater love. "We oppose old, outworn prejudices," said Dr. Ley's editor. "Marriage must not be allowed to become an obstacle to the natural impulse."

Utterances like these sound natural enough to some German ears, and more like simple descriptions of the status quo than anything else. For in some parts of the Reich the proportion of children conceived before the marriage of the mothers has long

been high. According to an official of the Swiss Federal Bureau
of Statistics, writing in the *Frankfurter Zeitung* of August 21,
1936, out of 100 first-born children, the following numbers
come into the world less than nine months after the marriage
of the mothers: France 17, Italy 27, Switzerland 29, Australia
and New Zealand 37, and Saxony 51.

As an official nazi legal journal said in March of 1937: "It
cannot be denied that among wide circles of our people cohabi-
tation of engaged couples is not considered impermissible, to say
nothing of immoral. It is only necessary to recall that in some
parts—and by no means in the worst parts—of the peasant population it is customary to marry a girl only after she has shown
her fiancé, by conceiving, that she can present him with children,
and above all with heirs for the farm." This, said the legal
journal, was "certainly [an] unobjectionable ethical-moral custom." It is, perhaps, not surprising that the nazis attach such
importance to establishing paternity.

But the nazis are no more prepared to let nature take its
course than they are to let anything else do so. Particularly
since the war began, and many of the nation's most vigorous
men have been otherwise engaged—and it must be expected that
some of them will never return—the highest official encouragement has been given the view that, in the words of the Labor
Front journal, "marriage must not be allowed to become an
obstacle to the natural impulse." Both Hess and Himmler gave
their blessing to this thesis early in the war.

"In war, which demands the lives of so many of the best
men," said Hess, "every new life is of special importance to the
nation. When, therefore, racially unobjectionable young men
who go to war leave behind them children who bear their blood
on for future generations, the children of equally hereditarily
healthy girls of suitable age, whose marriage was impossible for
some reason, pains will be taken to care for these precious national treasures.

"Misgivings that are justified in normal times must be set
aside," said Hess. "Higher than principles laid down by men,
higher than all morals that may be expressions of recognized
customs but not the expressions of true morality as such, higher

than all prejudice, stands the life of the nation. The highest service that women can render the community is to contribute to the maintenance of the nation through racially healthy children."

Said Himmler: "Beyond the borders of possibly necessary bourgeois laws, customs and views, it will now be the great task of German women and girls of good blood to become, even outside the marriage bond, and not in frivolity but in deep moral earnestness, the mothers of the children of soldiers going off to war."

The available statistics afford no indication of the influence, if any, that the expression of these views may have exerted. The number of children born out of wedlock remained approximately the same the first few years of nazi rule (about 100,000 per year). But figures on the number born less than nine months after the marriage of the mother do not seem to have been published—and the whole problem, in the nature of things, does not lend itself to close scrutiny and study.

In any event, in spite of their untrammeled utterances, the nazis really prefer legitimacy to illegitimacy, and, generally speaking, their policies and legislation reflect this preference. And regardless of what the nazis prefer, most German men and women, like most men and women elsewhere, want their children to be legitimate, too.

The nazis have moved heaven and earth in the pursuit of this part of their program—to increase both the marriage and birth rates—and they have succeeded notably. The marriage rate rose from 7.9 per 1,000 inhabitants in 1932 to 9.4 in 1938 (the last full calendar year before the war) and living births from 15.1 to 19.7 per 1,000 inhabitants during that same period.

Obstacles or no obstacles, the natural impulse has triumphed.

WOMEN MUST WORK

But while German women have gotten the husbands and babies the nazis promised them, they have not gotten some of the other things that they were also promised.

For one thing, being relieved of the necessity of doing "un-

womanly" work has turned out in practice to mean being relieved of the best jobs but continuing to keep the worst.

Women have been banished from the Reichstag, and their
access to other public office has been made so difficult as to be
virtually impossible. "It is clear," said Rosenberg, "that the
continuing influence of women in the affairs of state, admitted
in principle, must be the beginning of open decadence," and this
threat to public institutions the nazis speedily checked.

In the Reichstag that was dissolved on July 31, 1932, there
were 38 women deputies. Thirty-five women were elected deputies in the balloting in November of that year, and 30 were
elected in March of 1933. But since the nazis established their
monopoly of power not a single woman has been a deputy.

Nor was what Rosenberg called "the beginning of open decadence" allowed to proceed in other public offices. The Prussian
government, in an order of April 27, 1934, cited by Kirkpatrick,
ordered the dismissal of all married women officials who could
be adequately supported at home, and this and other pretexts
continued to be invoked to reduce the number of women officials
to a minimum.

The nazis even seem to consider teaching in girls' schools
"unwomanly" work. They have dismissed many women from
such posts, at any rate, and have replaced them by men. There
were 11,370 women teachers in higher schools for girls just
before the nazis seized power, according to Kirkpatrick; by
1935 this had been reduced to 9,941. Out of 5,888 teachers in
institutions of higher learning the semester of 1935-1936, only
46 were women, Kirkpatrick reports, and none of these was on
a full-time, permanent basis.

The number of women engaged in social-welfare work has
remained approximately the same, Kirkpatrick believes, and the
number of women doctors actually has increased under nazi
rule. In both professions, however, men soon took over the
most influential positions, and in many cases they have shown
a hostility toward women's engaging in the professions that
bodes ill for the future. "We will strangle higher education for
women," said the late Dr. Gerhard Wagner, then nazi boss of

the entire German medical profession, at a meeting in Berlin in December, 1934. Men in the audience cheered.

Higher education for women, in fact, if not strangled, has, at least, been severely restricted. A law of April 24, 1933, provided that, by limiting new enrollments, the total number of students in all German universities was to be reduced to 120,000. Of this total, only 12,000, or 10 per cent, could be women.

The last semester before the nazis seized power, 21,829 women were enrolled in German universities. This constituted 19.2 per cent of the total. Thus the nazis purposed to reduce by almost 10,000 the number of women to be allowed to engage in advanced studies in Germany at any given time.

This particular limitation was abolished February 9, 1935. Women are still discouraged by a variety of means, however, from going to German universities.

What is "womanly" work, then, if it is not public service, social welfare, medicine, or even teaching in girls' schools? What are German women to do if they may not study in universities?

The nazis have always been vague on this point. They have said, though, that domestic service is "womanly" work, and they have adopted several measures calculated to induce more women to become nurses, governesses, housekeepers and maid servants.

Employment in factories and offices, on the other hand, the nazis say, is definitely not "womanly." Partly on these grounds but chiefly to provide jobs for men, the nazis set out, when they seized power, to reduce the number of women working in these "unsuitable" jobs.

While there was much sound and fury on the subject, however, the campaign to relieve women from the necessity of doing "unwomanly" work was a failure.

The number of women registered at government employment offices as engaged in gainful occupations rose from 4,272,-487 in January, 1933, to 5,337,573 in 1936, an increase of 1,065,086, according to figures cited by Kirkpatrick, and it kept on rising. The number of women industrial workers rose by approximately 350,000 during this same period. The number of married women employed in industry apparently did not decline. And women continued to be paid less than men engaged in the same occupations.

There were two main reasons why the campaign failed. The first reason was that after the nazis seized power, as before, married men did not earn enough to support their families. The second reason was that the nazis' preparations for war caused a labor shortage, and women workers were required in the national economy whether they needed extra money for themselves or not. A certain number of women were, in fact, drafted out of their homes and even from relatively "womanly" positions in stores and offices and forced to work in factories and on farms instead, long before the war.

Woman's place may be in the home in theory, but in fact she was needed at the workbench and in the fields as well, even before the war began. Women have had to go on doing "unwomanly" work in even greater numbers than before.

NO PLACE LIKE HOME

The results of the nazi program for providing German women with homes of their own also have left much to be desired. For one thing, while people have married and have had babies in gratifying numbers, they have had the greatest difficulty in finding a place to live, for there is a severe housing shortage in Germany.

The shortage is due in the first instance to the virtual cessation of dwelling construction during the First World War, but it also is partly due to failure on the part of the nazis to undertake anything like an adequate housing program. The Weimar Republic performed prodigies in providing low-cost housing. The nazis, however, beginning with Hitler himself, have proclaimed that public structures are more important than dwellings, and they have concentrated most of their building activity on palatial government edifices—including a vast, luxurious new Chancellory for Hitler himself, who decided almost before he had finished moving in that it was not adequate and began immediately planning an even vaster and even more luxurious one.

In the New Germany, not even enough dwellings have been

built to keep up with the growth in the number of families which the nazis have done so much to encourage, and with the disappearance of buildings that have been torn down and become uninhabitable for other reasons, to say nothing of enough to do anything toward relieving the original shortage. Except for the shortage, housing conditions for those in the lowest earnings category are incomparably better in the Reich than in most parts of the United States. There is almost no such thing as a real slum in Germany. But it was Bismarck's Reich and the Weimar Republic that accomplished this, not the nazis. In the Third Reich, the housing shortage has steadily grown worse—while Chancellories, stadiums, ministries and other public structures have sprouted like so many mushrooms on every side. "What is man, that thou art mindful of him?" the nazis have said—and built another palace.

Morally, too, as well as physically, the promise of homes for German women has fallen short of fulfillment. For what kind of a "home" is it where there can be no privacy? Where the local political boss can intrude whenever he chooses, ask any questions he wishes and indulge in whatever "supervision" and "training" (to use Dr. Ley's words for the process) strike his fancy? What kind of a home is it in which the authorities may challenge the legitimacy of the children and dictate how they must be brought up? This is indeed "no place like home" in a new and bitter sense.

But of course the final judgment on the nazi "home" must wait for the war to end, and for some time thereafter. German women have married and have had their babies and have done the best they could to keep house in whatever dwellings they have been able to find (and most of them have kept house miraculously well, too, in spite of everything) and have fended off the impertinences of the ward heelers as well as has proven possible. But this has all been part of a prelude to disaster. For just when the babies were beginning to grow up, the fathers had to go off to another war. If Germany should win the war and not too many German men should be killed and maimed in the process, and not too many children should get tuberculosis and rickets for lack of proper nourishment, perhaps this part, too, of the nazi program for women—the providing of real homes—could be accomplished later, after all. Like so many other things in Germany—like almost everything—it depends on the generals.

9. The Decline of the West

> *Why is it that we rejoice at a birth and grieve at a funeral? It is because we are not the person involved.* "PUDD'NHEAD WILSON"

IN THE TWENTIETH CENTURY, most of the white peoples of the earth have lost the fecundity that characterized them for some time following the industrial revolution.

With only a few exceptions, birth rates in the United States, the white portions of the British Empire and Central and Western Europe began to decline about 1900 and were still falling when the Second World War began. On the eve of the war so few babies were being born that the populations of these countries either actually had begun to shrink or would do so, if the trends of that time continued, within 10 or 20 years. And unless the fall in the birth rates is stopped in other white countries, their populations, too, will begin to shrink within a generation.

This threat of a decline of the white races of the West was concealed for a time, because death rates fell faster than birth rates, and total populations, therefore, continued in most cases to increase. But these increases were only due to the fact that people were living longer. The white races are aging. And too few babies are being born to take the places of the older people when they die.

This was already the case, when the Second World War came, in the United States, England and Wales, Australia, France, Belgium, Sweden, Norway, Denmark, Switzerland, Bohemia and Moravia, Hungary and Germany, including Austria.

In Holland, Ireland, Italy, Poland, Portugal, the Balkans and Russia more than enough babies were being born to maintain populations. But the birth rates in these countries, too, were steadily falling, except for Italy, where a slight increase had occurred. Within a generation these countries, too, will begin to show deficits in their ledgers of national life and death unless the declines in their birth rates are checked.

Among countries for which statistics are available, only the yellow peoples seem to be flourishing biologically. Japan has only one-half the population of the Reich exclusive of Austria, but twice as many babies were being born in Japan every year as were in the Reich before the nazi revolution, and the excess of births over deaths was four times as great. Even Korea, with a population less than one third that of Germany before the Anschluss, had a greater excess of births over deaths than the Reich did in 1933.

As a result of the decline of the Western peoples' biological vitality, as expressed in birth rates, shifts have begun to take place in the balance of population power all over the world and among the white peoples themselves. If pre-war tendencies continue, these shifts will become more and more important with the passage of time and will cause more and more profound changes in the balance of population power and therefore in the character of civilization itself.

Both Germany and Austria suffered the worst declines in birth rates of all the countries of Europe, up to the nazi revolution, and the decline in Austria continued up to the Anschluss with the Reich in 1938. This threat to the numbers of the German people was aggravated by the biological consequences of the First World War.

THE MORTGAGE OF DEATH

A mortgage of death hangs over the German people. It is a mortgage contracted during the First World War. It remains to be seen whether the War of 1939 will put a second mortgage of death on Germany.

Approximately 1,775,000 Germans were killed during the

First World War. The blockade starved to death another 1,000,000, according to an estimate by Dr. Friedrich Burgdoerfer, director of the Reich Statistical Office. Dr. Burgdoerfer's figure may be high. He has, after all, no interest in minimizing the effects of the blockade. But even if his estimate is cut in half, the biological results of starvation from 1914 to 1919 are still noteworthy. And 3,500,000 fewer babies were born during the war years than would have come into the world under normal circumstances, Dr. Burgdoerfer believes.

It is the loss of these 3,500,000 unborn babies that created what Dr. Burgdoerfer calls the German mortgage of death. For the fact that they were never born meant that 21 years later there were 3,500,000 fewer men and women in Germany (minus a certain proportion who would have died in the meantime) to have babies of their own. The "war classes" that came of age from 1936 to 1941 were only 50 to 60 per cent as strong numerically as normal "classes" are.

The Germans are a "people without youth"—to use another phrase of Dr. Burgdoerfer's—in a further and even more serious sense, too. Because, for more than a generation, and apart from the special circumstances of the First World War, while more and more people lived longer in Germany every year, fewer and fewer babies came into the world. The result was that a larger and larger proportion of the population was made up of people past the ages when they had children, and past the ages of their best energies and achievements, and a smaller and smaller proportion was made up of youths and of people at the ages when they did have children, people at the height of their powers.

The average length of life in Germany increased by more than 20 years from 1871 to 1938, and by more than 11 years over the average for the period 1901-1910. The total population of Germany increased by 8 per cent between 1910 and 1925. The number of persons over 65 increased by 26 per cent. But the number of children under 15 actually declined by 8 per cent. Before the First World War, one third of the population of Germany consisted of children under 16. In 1938 only one fourth of the population did.

The collective aging of the German people struck at the national vitality in two ways. Not only did the number of persons of marriageable age begin to decline, but the number of deaths began to increase.

As early as 1933 the aging of the German people began to add 15,000 each year to the number of deaths in the Reich, and this number tended to increase steadily. For the larger the number of people became who lived to older ages, the more prevalent did diseases of old age become: cancer and other malignant growths, tuberculosis, apoplexy, paralysis, heart diseases and especially senile decay. Eighteen per cent more persons died of senile decay the first quarter of 1935 than had during the corresponding period of the year before.

The long-term decline of the birth rate in the Reich and the biological consequences of the First World War combined to constitute this threat to the numerical strength of the Germans: that if the trend continued that was well under way when the nazis seized power, the population of the Reich would begin to shrink in 1945.

Germany needed 1,400,000 live births per year to maintain its population as of 1932. In 1900 there had been approximately 2,000,000 live births in the Reich. But in 1932 there were only 993,126 and in 1933 only 971,174. Put another way, Germany needed 21 live births per 1,000 inhabitants per year to maintain its population. In 1900 there had been 35.6 live births per 1,000 inhabitants. In 1901 this had risen slightly to 35.7. But in 1932 there were only 15.1 live births per 1,000 of population and in 1933 only 14.7. Put still another way, Germany needed an average of 3.4 children per family to maintain its population. But in 1932 only 16.7 per cent of German families averaged more than 3.4 children each, only 20 per cent averaged just that number, and 62.9 per cent averaged fewer. The national average was only 2.3.

Such were the omens of decline that threatened the German people when the nazis seized power.

MYSTERY OF LIFE

The nazis set out to check this decline with characteristic energy and thoroughness—and with characteristic disregard for those who disagreed with them. They set out to stop the fall in the German birth rate and to raise the rate enough to guarantee an indefinite increase in the population of the Reich.

The real, basic causes of changes in birth rates are part of the mystery of life itself, and scientists are slow to be sure that they can explain them. But since the nazi revolution something certainly has happened to the German people that has caused an enormous (as such things are measured) increase in the birth rate in the Reich, and it seems probable that this "something" has been the national socialist population policy.

Up to the time that the Second World War began, the nazi campaign to raise the birth rate had only succeeded in postponing for 20 years the day of reckoning when the population of Germany would begin to decline. Too few babies were still being born in the Reich, in spite of all the nazis' efforts, to maintain a population growth after 1965. But the nazis have at least been more successful than any other regime in raising the birth rate. So what the nazis have done is important for the rest of the world. For what the nazis have done, others probably can do, too, if they want to and are willing to pay the price.

What the nazis have done is important for another reason, too. For it has given Germany an advantage in world power politics over other countries with continuing lower birth rates. It has affected the balance of population power, that is, and thereby the balance of cultures and of military and political power.

But there is a qualitative as well as a quantitative phase of nazi population policy. The nazis do not want all Germans to have more children. They only want certain kinds of Germans to do so. There are three chief categories of persons whom the nazis discourage and, in some cases, prevent altogether, from having children: first, persons of certain races and race mixtures; second, persons afflicted with certain diseases and other physical and mental disabilities; and third, persons whose moral and social characteristics the nazis find undesirable. The nazis are engaged in the greatest program of selective human breeding in all modern history. They have set out to change, by controlled procreation, the whole character of the German people. Obviously this aspect of national socialist policy, too, will bear study.

10. Delirium of Race

*. . . Of course there are no pure races left; not
even the Jews have kept their blood unmingled . . .
Race! It is a feeling, not a reality . . . No such
doctrine will ever find wide acceptance here in Italy
. . . National pride has no need of the delirium of
race.*   BENITO MUSSOLINI

"I can't believe that!" said Alice.
"Can't you?" the Queen said, in a pitying tone.
*"Try again; draw a long breath and shut your
eyes."*
*Alice laughed. "There's no use trying," she said:
"One can't believe impossible things."*
*"I dare say you haven't had much practice," said
the Queen.*   LEWIS CARROLL, "THROUGH
THE LOOKING GLASS"

THE RACE to which a person belongs affects "the deepest and
most unconscious impulses of his soul" and its influence "pene-
trates deep into the most minute fibers of his brain," two leading nazis write in an official commentary on the party's race
program. "Race sets its imprint on man's spiritual features no
less than on his outward form. It determines his thoughts and
perceptions, his powers and his instincts. It decides his character
and his nature."

Here, summed up in its most official form, is the first proposition, the central idea, of national socialist race dogma. Here is
the basic concept of a theory on which the nazis claim they base

much of their whole program and, more specifically, on which they say they base the application of a principle of racial selection to marriage and child-bearing in the Third Reich.

The race to which a human being belongs conditions his whole physical, mental and moral character, the nazis say, and they go on from this to argue that therefore the races with the kinds of characters the nazis like should be encouraged to have as many children as possible, and the races with the kinds of characters the nazis do not like should be discouraged and, in some cases, prevented altogether, from having any children at all.

THE NON-ARYAN NUT-BROWN MAID

"I am convinced that the different races have their different rhythms—in character and conduct, in music and in the dance," Alfred Rosenberg once said.

"A certain type of music or of the dance cannot be carried over from one race to another because it would not suit the other," Rosenberg said. "It is exactly the same in language. The rhythm of one language cannot be applied to an entirely different language.

"One country has its folk songs in major keys, another in minors. This is no mere accident, but corresponds to an inner rhythm of the soul."

Support for this racial theory of rhythm was forthcoming from a nazi scientist within a few weeks of Rosenberg's utterance. Dr. Gerd Cehak, of the Biological Institute of the Reich Academy for Sports and Gymnastics, announced that each race does indeed have its own characteristic speed of speaking, walking and moving in general. Dr. Cehak called this speed the "normal psycho-motor tempo." Nordics have the slowest psycho-motor tempo of all the races Dr. Cehak studied, he reported, and brunette Ostics have the fastest. Dinarics have a tempo somewhere between those of the other two races, according to Dr. Cehak.

Thus relentlessly do the nazis pursue the logical implications of their race theory, the theory which holds that in all things, both great and small, race makes the man.

Even the colors men prefer are racially conditioned, according to Professor Dr. Hans F. K. Guenther, leading nazi academic authority on race questions. Each race has its own "soul colors," Guenther says.

"The colors to which the Nordic inclines," Guenther writes in one of his books, "and which are appropriate and agreeable to his soul, and which (more clearly in the case of women, less clearly in that of men) the Nordic favors for clothing and decoration and for house furnishing and in the choice of objects of art, and which are most becoming to the person concerned— as such 'soul colors' the Nordic prefers blue and pale green." The "soul colors" of the Westic race are red and yellow, according to Professor Dr. Guenther, those of the Dinarics are dark green and red-brown and those of the Ostics are brown and violet.

Ideals of beauty, too, are determined by race, according to Rosenberg, and it is the Nordic ideal, described by Rosenberg as a tall, slender, blue-eyed figure, which has dominated Western civilization, he says—which is only natural, in nazi logic, to be sure, since the nazis assert that all Western civilization has been created by the Nordic race.

Professor Dr. Guenther gives a useful hint, in this connection, for a rule-of-thumb test for determining the purity of a people's racial ideals and therefore of their race itself. Any people that sings songs in praise of "Nut-Brown Maids" has at least begun to fall prey to race mixture and disintegration, Professor Dr. Guenther says, because Nut-Brown Maids are not Nordics, but daughters of a darker race, he explains, and any people that admires dark beauty has ceased to be inspired by the superior Nordic racial ideal.

Not only is woman's complexion conditioned by her race, furthermore, Professor Dr. Guenther writes, but her posture, as well. Nordic women keep their legs together when sitting in railway carriages and street cars, for example, according to Professor Dr. Guenther, who apparently has devoted considerable attention to this problem, whereas Ostic women spread their legs apart.

The freckle, too, may be a Nordic racial characteristic, Professor Dr. Guenther believes. He refrains from laying down a positive rule on the point. He says with true scientific caution that adequate data are not yet at hand. But he reports that among other races the Ostics, at least, seem to be unable to raise freckles, and he suggests that freckles may indeed be a sign of Nordic blood.

Men's beards, also, as well as their ability to raise freckles, are influenced by their race, Professor Dr. Guenther says. The question of the forms of beards characteristic of the various races is still an almost virgin field for scientific research, he writes, but he is satisfied on at least one point: Nordics prefer full, red, spread-eagle whiskers. Witness Barbarossa.

SUPERMAN

Once upon a time, long ago, in a region centering in Luebeck and extending as far north as Stockholm and as far south as Brunswick, a heroic race of men were born who, setting out from this region, have since created everything the world calls civilization. These supermen were tall, long-legged and slender, with broad shoulders and narrow hips, their hair was blonde, their skins fair and their eyes pale, usually blue or blue-gray.

This race was—and is—the Nordic, or Aryan, race, according to nazi teachings. This is its origin, these are its outstanding physical characteristics, and these, succinctly summarized, its achievements, as the nazis report them. This is the race the nazis say they want to preserve and increase as part of their program of selective human breeding.

This is the second proposition of nazi race dogma: the proposition that the Nordics are the greatest of all the races.

"What we see about us today of human Kultur, of achievements in art, science and technique, is almost exclusively the creative product of the Aryan," Hitler writes in "Mein Kampf." "Precisely this fact, however, justifies the conclusion that he [the Aryan] absolutely and alone was the founder of higher humanity, and therefore constitutes the original type of what we understand by the term 'human being.' If he is eliminated, deep darkness will again descend upon the earth, perhaps in only a few thousand years, human civilization will disappear and the world will revert to desert."

The Aryan created Japanese culture, for example, among others, Hitler writes. It was American and European Aryans, according to Hitler, who conferred civilization on Japan. If the stimulating Aryan influence should be withdrawn, the Chancellor says, Japan would relapse into the cultural "sleep" from which the Aryans wakened it.

Perhaps the only useful part that inferior, non-Aryan peoples have played in the cultural achievements of the Nordics has been to provide the necessary labor supply, Hitler declares. Thus the non-Aryan subhumans have served much the same purpose as horses. In fact, the Aryans have sometimes used their inferior subject peoples literally as draft animals, the Chancellor reports:

"Only pacifistic fools can regard this as a sign of depravity, however," Hitler writes, "failing to understand that this development was necessary in order finally to achieve the position [of advancement] from which these apostles inflict their drivel on the world today."

Outstanding virtues have enabled the Aryan-Nordic to perform the prodigies for which civilization is indebted to him, the nazis report. Among other things, for example, the Nordic excels physically, and is a great natural sportsman, according to Professor Dr. Guenther. So convincing was the theory of Nordic supremacy in sport, in fact, that Julius Streicher, the formerly eminent Aryan of Nuremberg, published a cartoon on the first page of his pornographic, anti-Semitic journal, *Der Stuermer,* just before the Olympic Games in 1936, showing a brutal, degenerate figure labeled "Jew" glaring with envy and hatred at a Nordic-looking Olympic victor crowned with laurel. When Jesse Owens and other presumptive non-Aryans conspicuously excelled at the games shortly thereafter, the nazis were intensely annoyed, and Hitler refused to shake hands with the colored winners.

Another of the Nordic's outstanding qualities is physical cleanliness, according to Professor Dr. Guenther. He asserts in this connection that both soap and the hairbrush are Nordic inventions.

THE DISAPPEARING NORDIC

Only 6 to 8 per cent of the German people are Nordics, according to Professor Dr. Guenther, and this is probably the highest proportion of Aryans to be found among any people on earth.

But if even the nazis themselves say this is all the Nordics there are in Germany, and in the world, then what has become of "The Great Race," as one American specialist in these matters calls it? What lessons do the nazis say must be learned from the decline of the Nordics? And how do the nazis apply these lessons in their program for selective human breeding?

A whole series of disasters have befallen the Nordics, the nazis say, with dreadful consequences for the German people and, indeed, all civilization:

Throughout the world the Nordics (being braver) have been killed off in wars more than members of other races, the nazis say.

The Reich has lost many of its Nordic sons by emigration, the nazis say.

And even the Nordics who have stayed at home in Germany have died at younger ages than men of other races and have had fewer children than the others, the nazis say.

But even more important than these factors in the decline of "The Great Race," is the fact, as the nazis see it, that the Nordics have mixed their blood with that of other and therefore, in nazi eyes, necessarily inferior races. Thus although the nazis say that only 6 to 8 per cent of the German people are pure Nordics, they also say that at least one half the blood that flows in the veins of the Germans as a whole is Nordic blood, mixed with that of other races.

The Nordic's very virtues have played important parts in causing his decline, in the opinion of leading nazi racial anthropologists. Thus the greater modesty which nazis attribute to Nordic women, their later ripening and the reserve of both sexes in their relations with each other which the nazis report, have contributed to the virtual disappearance of pure Nordics, Professer Dr. Guenther believes. Even when Nordic men do marry Nordic women, they marry relatively late in life and have relatively few children, according to Professor Dr. Guenther. And, what is even more serious, Nordic men are very likely to marry the dark and "diabolically alluring" women of other races, Professor Dr. Guenther writes. The innocence and magnanimity of the Nordic, he explains, help betray him into committing this sin against racial purity.

Still another characteristic of the Nordic has played a part in his undoing, the nazis announce: It appears illogical, in view of the formidable list of virtues which the nazis attribute to the Nordic, but party students of these matters report that the Nordic is especially prone to commit suicide. This, too, presumably, has helped to reduce his numbers in the world.

PEACE

"The result of every mixture of different races, very briefly stated, are the following," Hitler writes in "Mein Kampf":

"(A) The decline of the level of the superior race and

"(B) Physical and spiritual retrogression and therewith the setting in of a slow but sure sickliness."

Therefore, the Chancellor adds at another point, "there is only one supremely holy law: the most sacred obligation, namely, to see to it that the blood is kept pure."

This is the third proposition of nazi race dogma: the proposition that all race mixtures are bad.

3

But if this is the case, then in all logic the consequences for human history of all the mixtures that have taken place must have been far-reaching. And this is indeed so, the nazis say:

"The mixing of blood and the sinking of the racial level which it causes are the sole reason for the dying out of ancient cultures," in fact, Hitler writes. This is most especially true of the Aryans, or Nordics, according to Hitler: The conquering Aryan remained master and created great cultures as long as he ruthlessly maintained his position as ruler and kept his blood pure. But "history shows with terrifying clearness that in every mixture of the blood of the Aryan with that of inferior peoples the outcome was the end of the bearer of Kultur [that is, the Aryan]," he says.

For it is a law of nature, Hitler reports, that peoples of racially mixed blood lack the virtues of their best blood and have no will power. This in turn gives the pure races an advantage over mixed peoples and leads to the decline and fall of the latter. This fate, says Hitler, the mixed peoples can escape only by bringing about the "bastardization" of the superior Aryan or Nordic race. And this, the Chancellor solemnly asserts, is precisely what the racially inferior peoples have set out to do, and with considerable success.

Before the nazis seized power, Hitler writes, "corruption" of the blood of the German people threatened to destroy the last Nordic values. So far had the process gone, in fact, the Chancellor declares, that the danger was imminent that Germany, at least in its big cities, would be reduced to what Hitler describes as the low racial level of Southern Italy.

The Germans' carelessness about mixing their blood with that of inferior peoples has, indeed, had the most sweeping consequences, not only for the Germans themselves, but for the whole world, according to Hitler, for it has cost Germany world mastery:

"The blood poisonings which have affected our people, especially since the Thirty Years' War, have led to a decomposition not only of our blood, but also of our souls," the Chancellor declares, "with the result that in critical moments the German people disintegrate. The German people lack that sure herd instinct which is based on unity of blood and which, especially in moments when danger threatens, protects a nation against destruction, in that among such a people then all minor inner differences disappear and the closed ranks of a united herd confront the common foe.

"On the separate existence side by side of our basic racial elements which have remained unmixed is based that which is described among us as hyperindividualism. In times of peace this may sometimes be valuable, but taken all in all it has cost us world mastery.

"If the German people had possessed in their historical development that herd-like unity by which other peoples profited, then the German Reich would be mistress of the globe today.

World history would have taken another course, and no one can know whether that would have been achieved which so many deluded pacifists today hope to obtain by whimpering, blubbering and begging: a peace, not supported by the waving of palm leaves by tearful, weeping women, but founded by the victorious sword of a master people seizing the world in the service of a higher Kultur."

COMPLIMENT

The total number of persons in Germany (exclusive of Austria) with one-fourth or more Jewish blood in their veins was between 800,000 and 1,000,000 a year before the outbreak of the Second World War, according to an official nazi estimate made at that time. Of this total, between 500,000 and 625,000 were believed to be full Jews, 200,000 to 250,000 half Jews and 100,000 to 125,000 quarter Jews.

Thus the nazis themselves report that full Jews amounted at that time to only between seven-tenths and nine-tenths of 1 per cent of the country's population, half Jews to between two-tenths and three-tenths of 1 per cent and quarter Jews to only a fraction over one-tenth of 1 per cent, a total of between 1 and 1.4 per cent.

The German Jews were dying out even before the nazi revolution, furthermore, according to German figures:

There were 41.05 births per 1,000 of population (including the Jews) in the Reich in 1880 but only 32.26 per 1,000 among German Jews that year, according to Heinrich Silbergleit. By 1910 there were only 33.05 births per 1,000 inhabitants of all races and only 16.55 per 1,000 among German Jews. This birth rate was already too low to maintain the Jewish population of that time.

Between 1911 and 1925 the excess of deaths over births among Prussian Jews totaled 37,093, according to E. H. Schulz and Rudolf Frercks, and there was probably a proportional excess of deaths over births among Jews in other parts of the Reich.

On the nazis' own showing, therefore, the Jews amounted to only a minute fraction of the German people, and were steadily shrinking to an infinitesimal one, even before the nazis seized

power. Yet the nazis claim that the Jews are Germany's most
dangerous enemies. This pretense is the fourth proposition of
nazi race dogma, and one of the fundamental points in their
whole campaign for selective human breeding.

How does this minute and diminishing fraction of between
1 and 1.4 per cent of the total population threaten the very
existence of the remaining more than 98 per cent?

It is seldom that the nazis can be induced even to pretend
to give a rational answer to this question. When they can be
prevailed upon to try to answer it, though, they usually give
a reply consisting of three main points:

First, the nazis say, the Jews unless checked seize control
of key positions in the country and exercise influence out of all
proportion to their numbers.

Second, the nazis say, the Jews are such a virile race that
even one of them is too much for 99 gentile Germans.

Third, the nazis say, this is especially the case because it is
not merely the Jews in Germany itself who are so dangerous,
but the Jews of all the world, united in a great plot against the
Reich.

Whatever else may be said of this theory about the Jews, it
surely is one of the greatest compliments ever paid a people.

PAINFUL POSITION

There is only one people on the face of the earth today who
may possibly be racially pure, according to Professor Dr.
Guenther—the Eskimos. As for the others, "racial anthropology
is in the painful position of being obliged to declare that by
far the greatest part of the peoples of Europe are mixed
breeds," Guenther adds, and he says that this is also the case
among other white peoples as well.

This painful truth applies to Germany, too, according to
Guenther and other nazi authorities. "The German people constitute a unified race just as little as other peoples do," says
Wilhelm Frick, for example. The Germans, in fact, according
to nazi dogma, are a mixture of no fewer than nine different
races, as the nazis define the term "race," and have strains of

two other special stocks that the nazis say do not constitute separate races but special racial mixtures.

The nine different races represented in the German people are the Nordic, Ostic, Dinaric, East Baltic, Falic, Westic, Sudetic, Inner Asiatic and Negro races, according to Guenther and others. The two special stocks whose blood has also entered into German veins are the Jews and the gypsies, the nazis say. This racial description of the German people constitutes the fifth and final proposition of nazi race dogma.

The Negro strain in Germany results for the most part from intermarriage with Southern European and Mediterranean peoples who had previously intermarried with African Negroes, according to Guenther. The Inner Asiatic strain is evident above all in the eastern marches inhabited by the German-speaking peoples of Europe, Guenther writes.

The Negro, Inner Asiatic and Sudetic strains in the German people are insignificant, Guenther believes. The "Gypsy Problem," on the other hand, some nazis consider a grave one.

"Gypsies constitute a biological and sociological danger whose proportions must not be underestimated," according to Dr. Rodenburg, chief of the section for questions of race and heredity in the Reich Committee for the Public Health Service. "From the viewpoint of race biology the danger should not be held inferior to that which threatened us through mixture with the Jews."

Gypsies multiply faster than Aryans, according to Dr. Guenther, mayor of the town of Berleburg, and tend to be "anti-social," and he demanded on one occasion that a large proportion of all gypsies, men, women and children alike, should be sterilized.

The official party news, editorial and feature service, *The Nationalsozialistische Korrespondenz,* for its part, says that gypsies constitute a serious social and criminal problem, and it denounces "irresponsible" persons who represent the gypsies as romantic.

Romantic or not, however, and "anti-social" or not, "pure-blooded" gypsies in Germany number only approximately 6,000, and persons with one-fourth or more "gypsy blood" only approximately 18,000, according to the best official estimates, and orthodox party opinion holds that the "Gypsy Problem" is not tragically serious.

The overwhelming proportion of the German people are altogether free of infiltrations of Jewish, Gypsy, Negro and Inner Asiatic blood, the nazis say. The vast majority of Germans, they say, consist of various mixtures of the six "European" races. Guenther gives the following figures for the proportion of each of these several kinds of blood in the veins of the German-speaking peoples of Europe as a whole:

	Per Cent
Nordic blood	50
Ostic blood	20
Dinaric blood	15
East Baltic blood	8

In addition, Guenther estimates that approximately 5 per cent of the blood of Northwestern and Southern German-speaking peoples is Falic and 2 per cent Westic, and that 2 per cent of the blood of German-speaking peoples in Eastern regions is Sudetic and Inner Asiatic.

11. Blood and Spoils

A state which in an era of race poisoning devotes itself to the preservation of its best racial elements must some day become master of the world.

ADOLF HITLER, "MEIN KAMPF"

ONE OF THE FIRST RESULTS of the nazi revolution was an enormous increase in the sale of peroxide.

For in a state ruled with an iron hand by a party that believes in the supremacy of blonde Nordics, it obviously pays to be blonde. Even if you can't be a Nordic, at least you can look like one.

The state would speedily set about breeding Nordics, in accordance with its race theory, it was widely believed. Had not Wilhelm Frick, Reich Minister of the Interior, announced that "it is sought to maintain and increase the Nordic blood" among the people? But this breeding program would profit only future generations, not those already born. And, obviously, those already born wanted to profit, too. So they rushed off by the thousand to the beauty parlors, the barber shops and the drug stores in search of bleaching substances.

The peroxide Nordic craze assumed such proportions that official statements were issued deploring it:

"We must not tolerate this epidemic of blondeness which already has caused rivers of peroxide to flow," said Minister Dr. Staehle of Wuerttemberg. "Not even the purest of blondes is necessarily a pure German, and in many a person with dark hair there is concealed a heroic soul."

Even so powerful a regime as the nazis', however, could not stop recourse to the peroxide bottle. Heroic souls were all very well, but there was no use overlooking the obvious advantages of purest blondeness. And other short cuts to Nordicism were discovered, too.

THE LASCIVIOUS LEMON

Friedrich Bernhard Marby of Stuttgart was one of the pioneers in this field. For a consideration, Marby undertook to reveal to the citizens certain mystic formulas which, if repeated according to a system of his devising, were guaranteed to change the patient's physical characteristics into those of simon-pure Nordics. The incantation of these formulas Marby called "rune gymnastics." Marby did not promise heroic souls, but in a book entitled "Rune Gymnastics as a Way to Racial Uplift" he quoted testimonials from grateful customers who reported that they had changed the shapes of their heads, the colors of their eyes and hair and the quality of their blood in a few days by the chanting of his incantations.

Other citizens looked to their diet as a means of racial uplift—encouraged, perhaps, by the *Fraenkische Tageszeitung*, a newspaper in Franconia, which attacked the lemon as a corrupter of German blood:

"The species, its character and its achievements, are bound to the quality of the blood," said the *Tageszeitung*, "and blood is bound to the soil. Only the products of German earth create German blood," the *Tageszeitung* said. "Only through it [the German earth] are those finest vibrations transmitted to the blood, and thereby to the body and soul, which are decisive for our German species, which is unique in the whole world because there is only one German soil."

But the lemon does not grow in German soil. So: "Farewell, lemon!" said the *Tageszeitung*. "We need thee not. German rhubarb will replace thee altogether. . . . Begone, unwanted Southerner, from our German homes and countryside! Lascivious creature, we wish to see thee no more!"

Still other citizens sought more direct means of dealing with their racial difficulties, and the forging of birth and marriage certificates purporting to prove Aryan descent flourished like the green bay tree. Aryan grandmothers could be obtained at relatively fixed prices, depending only on the evidence of other ancestry to be overcome and on the ability of the citizen to pay.

These short cuts to Nordicism may have gratified those who took them, but they threatened to cause all kinds of complications and perplexities, too. For how could a peroxide Nordic, full of lascivious lemons, armed with a forged Aryan grandmother—and perhaps an honor student of Professor Marby's courses in rune gymnastics—be distinguished from a real, or rhubarb, Nordic?

It is not surprising that some citizens were confused. A flood of anxious requests for enlightenment and documentation poured into churches and government offices.

"I looked up 'Aryan' in the dictionary, and it says they live in Asia," one citizen wrote to a sexton's office in Zehlendorf, a borough of Greater Berlin. "There isn't any branch of my family there. We all come from Prenzlau."

"I am of agrarian origin, which I ask you to certify," wrote a second.

"God be praised, my grandmother was illegitimate, so I don't have to have her marriage certificate," wrote a third who considered himself blessed beyond most.

THE CASE OF THE ARYAN SIOUX

American Sioux Indians are Aryans, the official nazi Chamber of the Press ruled in a decision it handed down in 1938.

Rulings on other Indian tribes are lacking. Nobody apparently knows whether the Navahoes, the Iroquois or the Chippewas are Aryans or not. The question of their status seems never to have arisen. But the question of the status of the Sioux did arise, and it was officially settled. The case came up in this way:

Two generations ago Hans Mueller (which was not his real name) emigrated from Germany to the United States and, in the course of time, married a full-blooded Sioux squaw. The couple's children, when they grew up, all married persons of white, gentile, European stock, so that the grandchildren of

Hans Mueller and the squaw were one quarter Sioux and three quarters white, gentile and "European."

As long as the family stayed in America it didn't matter particularly whether the squaw was considered Aryan or not. But one of the grandsons went to Germany some time after the nazi revolution and decided to stay there, take out German citizenship and become a journalist, and then it immediately mattered a great deal whether or not the Sioux grandmother was considered Aryan. For anyone who wants to become a citizen of the Third Reich must prove that all his grandparents were Aryan, and anyone who wants to become a journalist must prove that all his ancestors were Aryan back to 1800.

The question came before the Chamber of the Press, which passes on applications for licenses to practice journalism. Weaker spirits might have quailed before the responsibility of making this decision. But the chamber did not quail. Its proceedings are secret, and the legal and anthropological considerations on which it based its decision are therefore unknown. But give a decision it did: The Sioux Indians are Aryans, said the chamber, and no nonsense about it, and therefore the descendant of a Sioux squaw and of other ancestors who were of white, gentile, European stock is an Aryan, too, and may become a citizen and a journalist in the Third Reich, other considerations permitting.

The Case of the Aryan Sioux seems to be unique in nazi race theory and practice. The number of Sioux and of other American Indians intimately affected by German racial legislation is presumably small. But the problem of the Sioux grandmother is typical of many perplexities which arose when the nazis set out to implement their race theory as a part of a program of selective human breeding. For the question of the Aryan or non-Aryan status of other peoples also speedily arose.

THE CHINESE FARE BADLY

One of the first of these questions to arise concerned the Japanese. When the welkin began to ring with official uncomplimentary remarks about non-Aryans, the Japanese ambassador in Berlin went to the Foreign Office and asked if by any chance these remarks were intended to apply to the Japanese people—and to their Emperor.

That was before the founding of the German-Japanese-Italian alliance, but the Foreign Office chose discretion as the better part, nevertheless. The uncomplimentary remarks about non-Aryans were by no means supposed to apply to the Japanese, the Foreign Office said. In fact, it said, the nazis considered the Japanese Aryans, too.

The Japanese professed themselves satisfied by these assurances. But this was only the beginning of the trouble. For others wanted to know where they stood, too.

Close on the heels of the Japanese ambassador, the Chinese minister appeared at the Foreign Office. He also wanted to know if the official insults of non-Aryans applied to *his* people. The Chinese fared badly, however, according to their own account of what happened. For the Foreign Office declined to give them the same sort of assurances that it had given to the Japanese. The Chinese have never succeeded in obtaining a certificate of Aryan status.

The Japanese were understood to be doubly gratified by the drawing of this distinction between themselves and the Chinese. Their gratification was, however, short-lived. For not long afterwards Hitler himself proclaimed in a speech at Munich that the white races are destined to rule the colored peoples. The Japanese neither asked for nor obtained assurances this time. Nobody hastened to say that the Japanese were not only Aryans but white as well. The government in Tokyo was annoyed and said so publicly.

Other rulings on Aryan status caused less travail. The Finns, the Armenians, the Poles and the Wends were officially declared to be Aryan and nobody apparently objected.

A reservation was made, however, in the case of the French. For there were some colored and colonial troops in the army of occupation the French sent into the Rhineland after the First World War, and these troops sired a certain number of children. To make sure that none of these makes his way into the German racial community, the nazis require that anyone whose father was a member of the French army of occupation must submit extra proofs that his father was Aryan.

The Egyptians were banned from Aryanhood as uncompromisingly as the Chinese. Early in the history of the Third Reich a government office in Berlin sent out confidential instructions that Turks were to be treated as Aryans but Egyptians as non-Aryans. The Turks were thus honored because they had fought on Germany's side in the First World War, it was explained. The Egyptians, on the other hand, had fought on the side of the allies and therefore were to be denied Aryan status. The Egyptian minister, like his Chinese colleague, made representations, but, also like his Chinese colleague, was rebuffed.

THE REVOLUTIONARY MYTH

Revolutionary myths "must be judged as instruments for acting upon present conditions," Georges Sorel wrote in "Reflections on Violence." They "enable us to understand the activities, the feelings and the ideas of a people preparing to enter into a decisive struggle," he added in a letter to Daniel Halevy. "They are not descriptions of facts, but expressions of will."

Sorel was talking about his own myth of the general strike as the decisive instrument in the class struggle and the whole socialist movement. What he said about the myth of the general strike, however, also applies in many ways to the nazi myth of race.

For there are at least two essential questions to be asked about the nazi race theory. The first question is: "Is the theory sound? That is, does it describe and explain the relevant facts?" The second question is: "Whether the theory is sound or not, what are the results of its adoption and implementation by the nazis? As an instrument, that is, how does it act upon conditions?"

The answer to the first question is, of course, "No." The theory is not sound. The "facts" it purports to describe and explain are not facts at all, but fantasies, and their description and "explanation" are therefore doubly false.

"There is no such thing as an Aryan race and . . . the Germans are neither Aryan nor Nordic nor a race," says S. K.

Padover, writing in *Foreign Affairs* in as good a brief summary as any of the case against the nazi "delirium of race." "The German scientist Virchow called the theory of an Aryan race 'pure fiction.' Reinach dubbed it 'prehistoric romance.' And Max Mueller, the German scholar who was responsible for the word 'Aryan,' bluntly rejected the distortion of his concept. 'To me,' he wrote, 'an ethnologist who speaks of an Aryan race, Aryan blood, Aryan eyes and hair, is as great a sinner as a linguist who speaks of a dolichocephalic dictionary or a brachycephalic grammar. It is worse than Babylonian confusion of tongues— it is downright theft. . . . If I say Aryan, I mean neither blood nor bones nor head nor skull. I mean those who speak an Aryan language.' "

Not only is the nazi race theory nonsense, furthermore, but it is criminal nonsense, for it is motivated by and it incites the basest of human passions.

"Next to the outright imprisonment, torture or execution of opponents," persecution of minorities is "the most ancient, most direct and most immediately efficacious of political devices," Schuman writes in this connection. "Fear of government is transmuted into detestation of those branded by the government as public enemies," he says, and thus persecution "affords to those disgruntled strata near the bottom of the social hierarchy the emotional satisfaction of being able to 'look down upon' a group which is still lower in the social scale."

In the modern world, anti-semitism has most often served this purpose of a social lightning rod for deflecting dissatisfaction onto a helpless minority, Schuman observes, and he quotes Bismarck as telling the merchant Bleichroeder in 1880 that he tolerated anti-semitism in the Second Reich because it provided a safe discharge for the anti-capitalistic feelings of the lower middle class.

There still remains, however, the second question: No matter how false and no matter how criminal the theory is, what are the effects, not only in Germany itself, but in the rest of the world as well, of the nazis' adoption and implementation of the theory?

In answering this second question, Sorel's remarks about revolutionary myths are illuminating:

For the nazi race dogma is most certainly a revolutionary myth.

It is one of the most powerful instruments ever devised for acting upon present conditions.

As few other single features of national socialism could, the race theory enables the world to understand the activities, the feelings and the ideas of the German people, or at least of the nazis among them, at a time when they were entering upon a struggle which would be decisive for a whole civilization.

Even if it is not a description or an explanation of facts, the nazi race theory is certainly a violent expression of a violent will. And this violent expression of a violent will is having profound effects on tens of millions of people outside Germany, as well as on the 80,000,000 within the Reich itself.

LOOT

To seize and keep and wield effective power in the modern world, a political movement must be inspired by fanatical faith in some revolutionary idea, Hitler writes in "Mein Kampf."

"The lack of a great creative idea always means an impairment of fighting strength," he says. "The belief in the right to use even the most brutal weapons always depends upon a fanatical faith in the necessity of the victory of a revolutionary new order on earth. A movement which does not fight for such highest goals and ideals will therefore never resort to the last weapon."

The nazi race theory is the revolutionary idea which serves these purposes, among others, in the Third Reich, just as the Marxist theory serves similar purposes in the Soviet Union. And this aspect of nazi race theory is at least as important to the world as the more immediate effects of the application of the theory in the sphere of race and population policy in Germany itself. Because the nazi race theory not only helps explain how the nazis came to power in the Reich; it also helps to explain how they extend their power over other countries as well.

Consider the merits, from the nazi point of view, of the race theory as a revolutionary idea:

It informs the German masses that they are more nearly Nordic than any other nation, and therefore God's chosen people. This gratifies those among the masses who believe it.

It delivers up, helpless, to the masses an "enemy" to be held responsible for all their miseries and to be punished accordingly —the Jew; his job, his property, his self-respect, his liberty and sometimes his wife or mistress to be taken away from him, and he himself to be driven into the outer darkness. This consoles the masses. It also affords them the opportunity to compensate themselves at the "enemy's" expense for the harm the "enemy" is officially proclaimed to have done them.

The nazis talk a great deal about "blood and soil," and some ingenuous Germans may actually think primarily in terms like these. The nazis, however, are disingenuous above all things. They are much more interested in loot than they are in earth— the loot that they have plundered and still hope to plunder from the world's helpless Jews (as well as others). The device of nazi anti-semitism should be, not "Blood and Soil," but "Blood and Spoils."

DAZZLING VISION

The nazi race theory also arms German foreign policy with a powerful weapon. For it holds out the dazzling vision of nothing less than world mastery, and is calculated to enlist the support of 25,000,000 human beings in more than a score of other countries who are promised a share in it.

World rule by the Germans is to be achieved by two principal means, nazi race theory holds:

First, by the union of all the Germans in the world. This union is to take two forms: Germans living on the Reich's frontiers are to be annexed outright, as the Austrians and Sudetens were. Others, living remote from the Reich, are to be "morally annexed." They are to be—and are being—organized in German blocs, ruled from Berlin in reality, no matter what the outward forms of citizenship and sovereignty, and playing a part, and often a decisive part, in determining the policies of the countries where they live.

Second, world rule is to be achieved by the victories which the thus united Germans are bound to win, owing to their "superior" blood (and numbers) over other peoples. The Germans will inevitably conquer the others because the others are racially inferior and corrupt, the nazis say. The United States, for example, is only a "mush" of different racial elements, in the words of one nazi writer, and as for France, it is composed largely of despised Westics, it is impregnated with Negro and other non-European blood, it works hand in hand with world Jewry, and therefore on racial grounds alone France must be destroyed, the nazis announce.

Nazi race dogma is a potent theory in a continent where every sixth human being speaks German as his mother tongue and in which 14 different states (as of before the Second World War) have important German elements in their populations— and in a whole world in which anti-semitism is latent even when it is not active.

12. No Nordics Could Be Bred

It is a condition which confronts us, not a theory.
GROVER CLEVELAND

It is silly for fanatics to have the idea of breeding Nordics," says Dr. Friedrich Bartels, of the health department of the Reich Ministry of the Interior. "It is also entirely immaterial whether or not another ['Germanic'] racial strain predominates. The truth is that there are several different racial strains in the German people, and we must accept this fact. The ideas of the national socialist party are far above any notion of making a rabbit-breeding farm out of Germany."

Just how far, if at all, the national socialist party's ideas are above making a rabbit-breeding farm out of Germany will be considered later. It may be noted at the outset, however, how significantly the voice of experience, the voice of the practical administrator, differs from the accents of some of the more cloistered apostles of pure race theory.

For when the nazis set out to put their theory into practical operation as part of a program of selective human breeding they found that the theory had to be modified in order to fit certain facts. Even the "facts" related by some parts of the nazis' own theory seemed to make it difficult, if not impossible, to implement other parts of the same theory.

THEORY INTO FACT

In its original form the nazi race theory may be summed up in five articles of faith:

1. Everything about a human being is conditioned by the race or races from which he comes.

2. The Nordics are the best of all the races.

3. All race mixtures are harmful.

4. The Jews are the deadly enemies of the German people.

5. The great majority of the Germans consist of a mixture of six "white, European" races, in the following order of importance: Nordic, Ostic, Dinaric, East Baltic, Falic and Westic. There are also slight strains of Jewish, Negro, Inner Asiatic, Gypsy and Sudetic blood in the German people.

Definite principles of racial selection for a program of controlled human breeding were clearly implicit in the first four of these articles of faith:

For if everything about a human being is conditioned by his race, then clearly everybody's racial identity should be established with the greatest possible accuracy.

If the Nordics are the best of all races, then Nordic elements in the Reich should be encouraged to keep their blood pure and to hand it down to as many children as possible.

If all race mixtures are harmful, then marriage, childbearing and all other sexual relations between persons of different races should be prevented.

And if the Jews are the deadly enemies of the Germans, then clearly every trace of Jewish blood should be eliminated from Germany; the Jews should be prevented from having sexual relations with Aryans, discouraged from having children even among themselves, and in the end be driven out of Germany altogether.

But the fifth article of the creed put difficulties in the way of the practical application of the first four principles. Because the fact, as reported by the nazis themselves, that the German people are a mixture of nine different races and two other special racial stocks, made it difficult, if not impossible, even to determine the exact racial identity of the individual, to say nothing of breeding pure Nordics, preventing all racial mixtures and eliminating all traces of Jewish blood.

The Germans are so thoroughly mixed racially that it would be impossible to distinguish and separate the various stocks.

And even if this could be done, the various stocks could not be bred separately. It would be impossible from a practical administrative point of view, even among a people with as highly trained a civil service as the German. It would provoke at least passive resistance, even among a people as respectful toward authority as the Germans. And it might force the German birth rate down still lower than it already was when the nazis seized power.

So in working out a program for effective action the nazis had to adapt their pure theory to the practical necessities of the situation. They had to devise standards and definitions and methods which would work.

From the qualitative point of view the nazis had to decide which racial elements could and should be distinguished from each other in actual practice, which could and should be encouraged to have children, and which could and should be discouraged from doing so, and which should be allowed to have sexual relations with which others. They had to define terms and work out methods which the German civil service could understand and use in administering a practical program.

From the quantitative point of view the nazis had to decide how to classify the individual racially. How much Jewish blood must an individual have in order to be classified and treated as a Jew? How little must he have to be classified and treated as an Aryan?

And, finally, the nazis had to work out some way of identifying the various races and measuring the proportions of their blood present in each individual. Failing laboratory tests, how was it to be decided whether or not the blood in any given individual's veins was Jewish blood?

The initial recourse to the peroxide bottle, to rune gymnastics, to the forging of Aryan grandmothers' birth certificates and to other short cuts to Nordicism, and the complications which developed in Germany's foreign relations owing to the proclamation of the pure race theory, showed how necessary it was to make certain adjustments in the theory as a matter of practical politics.

THE END OF THE ARYAN

The first modification which nazi race theory underwent when it was adapted to practical administration was that the terms "Aryan" and "non-Aryan" and "Nordic" and "non-Nordic" were abandoned as legal designations. The nazis adopted, in their places, the terms "persons of German blood," "persons of similar blood" and "persons of alien blood."

"The concept 'German or similar blood' replaces the previously general concept 'Aryan descent,'" says a commentary on nazi race legislation written by two high officials of the Reich Ministry of the Interior. "Persons of German blood and persons of similar blood are included together under the designation, 'German-blooded.'

"The German people consist of the members of different races (the Nordic, Westic, Dinaric, Ostic and East Baltic races) and their mixtures among each other," the commentary says. "The blood thus present in the German people is German blood.

"Blood similar to German blood is the blood of those peoples whose racial composition is related to that of the German people. This is the case among all peoples settled in closed regions in Europe and among their descendants in other continents who have retained their purity of kind [that is. of race]. . . .

"Alien blood is all blood which is neither German blood nor similar blood. In Europe, as a rule, only Jews and gypsies are of alien blood."

This change-over from "Aryans" and "Nordics" to "German-blooded" and from "non-Aryan" and "non-Nordic" to "persons of alien blood" is the most important "reform" the nazis adopted in reshaping their race theory in order to put it into practical operation. It represented an adjustment to "realities," as understood by the nazis, of two of the principles of the party's theory in its original form: the principle that pure Nordics should be bred in Germany, and the principle that all race mixtures should be prevented. It constituted a confession that pure Nordics could not be bred and that all racial mixtures could not be prevented.

For the time being, at least, the nazis have given up the idea of breeding Nordics and preventing all race mixtures. They have even discovered that all race mixtures are not harmful, after all, but only certain kinds of mixtures:

"The German people are composed of members of various races," Frick has said. "It is characteristic of all these races, however, that their blood mixes well—in contrast to alien blood —and causes no disharmonies or other difficulties."

Thus as a matter of practical selective breeding the nazis distinguish between two kinds of race mixtures, one kind which they say is deleterious and which they prohibit, and another kind which they say is harmless and which they allow.

Subject to certain other principles of selection, white persons with no Jewish and no gypsy blood may marry each other and have children in the Third Reich. They are, in fact, strongly encouraged to do so.

Jews, gypsies and colored persons, on the other hand, may not marry or have other sexual relations with non-gypsy, white gentiles and are strongly discouraged from even having children among themselves.

This is the principle of racial selection which the nazis have put into practical operation in Germany.

There still remained, however, the quantitative problem and the problem of identification. Was a half Jew to be treated the same as a full Jew? And what of a quarter Jew and an eighth Jew? And how was it to be determined whether or not the blood in an individual's veins was "alien" blood or "German" blood?

This is how the regime solved these problems:

CASTE

The nazis divide all Germans into three main castes, according to the proportions of "alien" and "German" blood the nazis say the citizens have in their veins. Each of these castes, in turn, is divided into subcastes.

Persons with four white gentile grandparents and with no

gypsy blood are classified as "German-blooded." These are the blessed of the new caste system.

Persons with three or four Jewish, gypsy and/or colored parents are classified as "persons of alien blood." These are the damned of the new caste system.

Between these two castes of the blessed and the damned, the nazis have provided for a third category of persons who are neither altogether blessed nor altogether damned but partly both and partly neither. Persons in this category consist of those with either one or two grandparents of "alien" blood; they are officially and legally designated "mixed breeds." Persons with two "alien" grandparents are "first-degree mixed breeds" and persons with one "alien" grandparent are "second-degree mixed breeds."

Under certain circumstances, a person with two "alien" grandparents and even a person with only one, may be classified as "alien" himself, but cases of this sort are few.

Only fully "alien" grandparents count in this new caste system. A person who is three-eighths Jewish is classified with those who are only one-quarter Jewish, for example, and a person who is five-eighths Jewish is classified with half Jews.

This is the nazis' solution of the quantitative problem of practical racial selection, the problem of deciding what proportion of "alien" blood is enough to warrant classifying the individual himself as an "alien." These are the three basic categories of the new caste system, a system as elaborate and rigid as India ever dreamed of.

But how was "alien" blood to be identified?

The nazis insist that the blood itself is what matters in race—not religion, for example, or any other factor. A baptized Jew is still a Jew, the nazis say. Yet nobody has yet found a way to identify the racial qualities, if any, of blood. So in the end, as a matter of practical administration, the nazis fell back on the religious test after all.

Some kind of test had to be found if the program of selective breeding was to be launched at all. And besides, three generations ago most persons who were Jewish by race were also members of the Jewish religious community. So the nazis ruled that anyone who now professes or ever professed the Jewish faith is to be presumed to be of Jewish blood as well, and, accordingly, classified as a Jew in the new caste system.

Using these rules and these definitions, the nazis have promulgated an elaborate series of regulations intended to prevent all but business relations—and to reduce even these to a minimum—between "German-blooded" persons on the one hand and "persons of alien blood" on the other. These regulations apply to gypsies and colored persons as well as Jews, but it is the Jews who are the most numerous and most important in this connection, and it is their experience which will be considered here.

13. The Untouchables

> *As Benjamin Constant points out, caste rests on the religious idea of an indelible stain resting on certain men and the social idea of certain functions being committed to certain classes. . . . As the daily intercourse of men in trade and industry presents numberless occasions on which the stain of real or fancied impurity may be caught, the power of the religious class who define the rules of purity and the penalties of their violation becomes very great.*
>
> ENCYCLOPÆDIA BRITANNICA (NINTH EDITION), ARTICLE ON CASTE

THE JEWS are the Untouchables of the nazi caste system of race.

The nazis seldom even try to justify their anti-semitic policy. When they do try to do so, however, they pretend that the policy is based on their race theory: The Jews, the nazis say, are the deadly enemies of the German people. They seek to destroy the Germans by every possible means. And one of the Jews' methods, the nazis say, is to "corrupt" the German blood by mingling their own blood with it, by intermarriage and other sexual relations. Therefore, the nazis say, all sexual relations between Jews and gentiles must be prevented.

But this is only the beginning of the nazi program for degrading and destroying the Jews. For the "superior" "German-blooded" person is tainted by any contact at all with a Jew, the nazis proclaim, and they try, accordingly, to see to it that no such contacts occur.

EROTIC APPROACH

There are four principal points in the nazi policy of preventing all sexual relations between Jews and gentiles:

1. Intermarriage of Jews and gentiles is forbidden.

2. Divorce is made easy for gentile partners in marriages between Jews and gentiles concluded before the nazis forbade such marriages, and in some cases the nazis force gentile partners to divorce their spouses whether either partner wants a divorce or not.

3. Sexual relations between Jews and gentiles out of wedlock are prohibited.

4. All other approaches and familiarities between persons of the two racial categories are forbidden.

The "moral" and legal concept the nazis have invented for making effective their policy of reducing the Jews to the status of Untouchables is the concept of "Rassenschande." This word is as ugly in the meaning the nazis have given it as it sounds; it means "race defilement," and the nazis use it to describe all relations, even innocent acquaintanceships, between Jews and gentiles, with the sole exception of business dealings.

Thus a gentile who dances with a Jew, no matter how decorously, is "racially defiled," for example, a court in Breslau has ruled, citing a pronouncement to this effect by Hans Kerrl, Reich Minister for Church Affairs, and playing cards with a Jew also "racially defiles" the gentile who does such a thing in Germany today.

In this kind of "delirium of race," it obviously is all the more "true" that a gentile girl who is kissed by a Jew is "racially defiled," and decisions of at least two nazi courts to this effect are indeed on public record:

Judges in both Darmstadt and Hildesheim sentenced Jews to terms of imprisonment some time ago for kissing "German-blooded" girls—although in both cases the girls themselves testified that they had known the men were Jews and had not in the least objected to the kisses.

"By kissing an Aryan girl, the Jew has insulted, not only

the girl herself, but also the entire German nation," the court roundly declared in the Hildesheim case.

In Magdeburg the concept of "race defilement" was invoked to penalize an even far more remote salute: A 22-year-old Jew was waiting for a friend one day outside the apartment building where the friend lived, when a "German-blooded" girl appeared and began to wash the windows of the apartment on the first floor of the building. Attracted by the girl, the Jew asked her what she was doing that evening and if she would go to a movie with him. The girl not only rejected the invitation but also had the Jew arrested, and a court sentenced him to four weeks' imprisonment.

"Any erotic approach" by a Jew to a "person of German blood" is forbidden, the court declared, and an invitation to go to a movie constitutes an "erotic approach."

THE CRIME OF DR. SERELMAN

But if the "erotic approach" is dangerous to the purity of blood and therefore prohibited, what of the scientific approach: what of blood transfusions? For if blood determines race, then surely the most effective way to change a person's race is to inject a different kind of blood directly into his veins? Racial identities to suit would thus be available by the pint or quart through a rubber tube, subject only to the supplies of the various kinds of blood that could be obtained.

"Madness?" Yes, of course. "Such things don't happen—couldn't happen?" But in the New Germany, they do happen. Consider the case of Dr. Hans Serelman, a Jewish physician of the town of Niederlungwitz:

One day in the relatively happy epoch when Jewish doctors were still allowed to treat "German-blooded" persons, one of Dr. Serelman's gentile patients was stricken by a condition so imminently dangerous that the patient's life could only be saved by an immediate blood transfusion. Dr. Serelman knew that his own blood was of the same group as that of his patient, and was otherwise suitable for transfusion, so he gave enough from his own veins and saved the patient's life.

There is no record of the patient's reaction to the transfusion, except that he lived. There is a record, though, of the reaction of some of Dr. Serelman's "German-blooded" colleagues of the medical profession in Niederlungwitz: they said that transfusing "Jewish blood" into the system of a gentile constituted "race defilement" of the patient, and they denounced Dr. Serelman to the Gestapo on this charge. The Gestapo found the charge convincing, or at least adequate, and they arrested Dr. Serelman and sent him to a concentration camp.

This and other cases which seem to have occurred at about the same time moved at least one responsible official to correction: Professor Dr. Loeffler, of the Race Policy Office of the party, gave out a statement tartly denying that an infusion of "Jewish blood" could impair the racial qualities of the recipient. Dr. Serelman was released after having spent seven months in the concentration camp.

Professor Dr. Loeffler to the contrary notwithstanding, however, the crime of Dr. Serelman still outraged his "German-blooded" colleagues in Niederlungwitz. They still burned with a passion for race purity and for Dr. Serelman's practice, and they decided to denounce him anew to the Gestapo. It was only a warning conveyed to him by a grateful gentile patient that enabled Serelman to flee in time. (The identity of the patient must be kept a secret to preserve *him* from a concentration camp; whether or not it was the man whose life Dr. Serelman had saved by the blood transfusion cannot be revealed.)

Professor Dr. Loeffler's statement had no more effect in other quarters than it did in Niederlungwitz, furthermore. Following the Anschluss, for example, Vienna hospitals adopted the practice of using only blood certified as having come from gentiles for transfusions performed on "German-blooded" patients, and only certified "Jewish blood" for those performed on "persons of alien blood."

And no matter how the question might finally be settled as to whether or not a mixture of bloods caused by transfusion could constitute "race defilement," the ruling of the Breslau court in the case of "defilement by dancing" represented the broad official rule: "Any friendly relations with one of alien blood, especially with a Jew, going beyond exclusively business dealings," said the court, "constitute 'race defilement,'" and, as such, are punishable by law.

THE PROTECTION OF THE PROSTITUTES

But the crime a gentile commits in Germany by playing cards or dancing with a Jew, or the crime a Jew commits by kissing a gentile girl or inviting her to go to a movie with him, is only a secondary crime, in spite of everything. It is a crime only because the nazis call it an "erotic approach," because, they say, it may lead to sexual relations in the more (or most) intimate sense of the term. The primary, paramount crime of "race defilement" consists of the offense the Jewish partner commits in consummating a sexual union with a gentile. The Jewish partner, that is, "racially defiles" the gentile partner. The offense committed by the gentile partner in such a union is not "race defilement," because, in nazi logic, a gentile cannot defile a Jew. The gentile's offense the nazis call "race treason." Such are some of the obscene refinements of the greater, all-inclusive obscenity.

This distinction between "race treason" and "race defilement" is held by nazi jurists to be especially important when the offending relationship is one between a Jew and a "German-blooded" woman. Such a relationship, says Roland Freisler, Undersecretary in the Reich Ministry of Justice, for example, is more criminal than those between "German-blooded" men and Jewesses, because they "defile" the "German-blooded" woman, who is "the protectress of the purity of German blood." Apparently it is harder to defile a male German than it is a German female; or maybe it just doesn't matter so much if he gets defiled.

The penalties which the nazis inflict upon those who consummate "mixed unions" vary in accordance with these fine distinctions. Thus a Jew who consummates a union with a "German-blooded" woman is punished much more severely than a "German-blooded" man who consummates one with a Jewess. The law provides no penalty at all for the woman in either case —a fact which naturally leads to a good deal of blackmail, even though the authorities do sometimes send the offending women to concentration camps in spite of the lack of any legal basis for doing so.

This is especially the case because the nazis have even extended their new caste system to commercialized vice. Even "German-blooded" prostitutes are "protected" by the law, and Jews who have had relations with them have been found guilty of having "racially defiled" the women and have been sentenced to terms of imprisonment for their sins against "German blood."

The Jew is responsible for making sure that the woman with whom he has such a relationship is also Jewish. The Reich Supreme Court once rejected an appeal from a Jew who had been convicted by a lower court of "race defilement" and who pleaded that the woman in the case had said she was a Jewess and that he had taken her word for it. The Jew must obtain definite proof that a woman is Jewish before he may enter into intimacies with her, the court declared.

The most complete report on convictions for "race defilement" that ever seems to have been published in the Reich was one printed by *Der Stuermer* covering 358 cases of Jews found guilty and sentenced by German courts during 1936 on charges of having consummated sexual unions with "German-blooded" women. In the cases cited in this report, 127 of the defendants were sentenced to a total of 226 years and six months' penal servitude, an average sentence of 21.4 months, and 231 were sentenced to a total of 215 years and five months' imprisonment, an average of 11.1 months. The longest sentence was one of five years' penal servitude.

THIRTY-ONE RULES FOR LOVE

But while the nazis strictly forbid sex relations out of wedlock between Jews and gentiles—love that the rest of the world, too, calls profane or illicit, although for very different reasons—the regime is particularly concerned to prevent marriage between Jews and gentiles: love that the rest of the world calls sacred. There is no such thing as sacred love between Jews and gentiles, in the nazi view: It is all illicit and it is all profane, because it all "defiles" the race.

There are 31 different rules of law regulating marriage between Jews and "persons of German or similar blood" in the Third Reich, 31 rules for love between the races. Depending on the proportion of Jewish blood in each of the partners, 18 of these rules expressly permit marriages between persons of certain castes, nine forbid marriages between persons of other castes, and four require special permits for marriages of persons of still other castes.

The laws themselves are complicated, but the purpose they are intended to serve is simplicity itself. This purpose is the breeding of persons who are predominantly or altogether of "German or similar blood" on the one hand and of persons who are predominantly or altogether of "Jewish blood" on the other hand, and the prevention of the breeding of persons of relatively equal proportions of both Jewish and "German or similar blood."

Thus persons all four of whose grandparents were white gentiles without any gypsy blood may marry freely among each other, subject to other principles of selection. And persons with three or four Jewish or gypsy or colored grandparents may marry freely within their own caste, too. But marriages between members of the two castes are forbidden.

Marriages of "mixed breeds" are regulated in much more detail: A person with one "alien" grandparent may marry a partner who is entirely "German-blooded" but he must have a special permit to marry a person with two "alien" grandparents, and he is forbidden to marry another person with one "alien" grandparent. A person with two "alien" grandparents, on the other hand, may marry a person with either three or four "alien" grandparents or another person with two, but must have a special permit to marry a person with only one "alien" grandparent or a person all four of whose grandparents were "German-blooded."

These, then, are the rules of law by which the nazis regulate human breeding in the Reich according to race, the rules by which they have set out to breed out of the whole German people persons with relatively equal proportions of gentile and Jewish (and other "alien") blood, and, by this and other means, to eliminate "alien" blood from Germany altogether.

If the nazis remain in power long enough, they will succeed. Because from now on the vast majority of children born in Germany will be either purely Jewish or purely non-Jewish; a very small additional number will be either one-eighth or less Jewish or three-fourths or more Jewish; and only an infinitesimal number will have relatively equal proportions of Jewish and gentile blood between these extremes. As a result of other nazi anti-semitic measures, furthermore, most persons of half or more Jewish blood will disappear from Germany within a few years. Some will die from natural causes, some will emigrate, some will be deported and some will be killed.

In fifty years, therefore, if nazi rule endures, almost everybody in Germany will be overwhelmingly or altogether of "German or similar blood," there will be almost nobody of "alien" blood, the Jews will have virtually disappeared from Germany, and "race mixture" as defined by the nazis will be at an end in the Reich.

MARRIAGES OVER THE BORDER

For a time after the laws regulating "mixed marriages" were promulgated, a certain number of couples tried to evade them by getting married abroad. A few even arranged "frontier weddings," in which the couple stood just inside the frontier on German soil and the clergyman stood just over the frontier on foreign soil and the ceremony was performed across the line.

But these attempts to evade the law were few in number. Because nazi legislation was held to apply to foreign and "frontier" weddings as well as to those performed within the country itself, and violations of the law are punishable by penal servitude up to 15 years.

The nazis also threatened not only to invoke this penalty but also to charge offenders with engaging in inter-racial sexual relations out of wedlock as well, a separate crime under nazi law and one carrying further heavy penalties.

In the country itself elaborate proofs of racial identity must be submitted before a marriage license can be obtained: the birth certificates of both partners and their four parents and their eight grandparents, and the marriage certificates of parents and grandparents as well, a total of 20 official documents.

Violations of the laws have therefore seldom occurred. There are few "frontier marriages" in either the literal or the figurative sense—across the borders of either states or "races." Racial selection, by means of the most ambitious attempt the world has ever seen to regulate human sex life, is a reality in Germany.

14. Sterilization: the Nazis Pick the Unfit

> *As though there were a tie*
> *And obligation to posterity.*
> *We get them, bear them, breed, and nurse:*
> *What has posterity done for us?*
>
> JOHN TRUMBULL, "MC FINGAL"

> *How convenient it would be to many of our great*
> *men and great families of doubtful origin, could*
> *they have the privilege of the heroes of yore, who,*
> *whenever their origin was involved in obscurity,*
> *modestly announced themselves descended from a*
> *god.* WASHINGTON IRVING, "KNICKERBOCKER
> HISTORY OF NEW YORK"

THE NAZIS apply physical, mental and moral principles in their program of selective human breeding, as well as racial principles. Not only do they encourage certain racial elements to have as many children as possible and discourage or prevent certain others from having any children at all, they also encourage persons of certain physical, mental and moral characteristics to have as many as possible and discourage or prevent certain others from having children, too.

The nazis employ four principal means in their program for eliminating those they say are unfit: Some they kill; others they allow to live but castrate or sterilize or forbid to marry.

The regime has never openly admitted killing off the unfit, but responsible officials acknowledge it freely in private, and the facts are too well known to admit of any real doubt. Ap-

proximately 100,000 persons seem to have been disposed of in
this way during the years 1939 and 1940 alone.

The Gestapo is in charge of these killings. Most of them
seem to have taken place, as both Shirer and Harsch have reported, at Grafeneck, not far from Stuttgart; at Hartheim,
near Linz; and at Pirna, near Dresden. Of the first 100,000
to be killed, most or all seem to have been taken from institutions. Neither the patients themselves nor their families are
consulted or informed in advance as to what is to be done.
Families are only told afterward that the patient has died suddenly and unexpectedly. No reliable information is available
as to the grounds on which these supposedly unfit are chosen
for execution, or of the methods employed in the killings.

DEGENERACY

Almost 2,000,000 persons in Germany suffer from physical
and mental diseases and defects which seriously interfere with
their ability to earn a living and which the nazis say are hereditary. Of this total, approximately 1,155,000 are supported
wholly or in part by the taxpayers at a total cost of 1,151,-
000,000 marks yearly, the late Dr. Gerhard Wagner, nazi
"Leader of Reich Physicians," once estimated. Mental cases
receiving state care number approximately 880,000, or 76 per
cent of the total, and cost the taxpayers 631,000,000 marks
yearly, or 54 per cent of the financial burden.

In Germany, furthermore, as elsewhere, the diseased and
otherwise unfit—and the criminals—tend to breed faster than
the healthy and the law-abiding. Feeble-minded couples averaged four times the number of children that normal couples
did in the Reich before the nazi revolution. In families in which
one or both parents were convicted criminals, the number of
children averaged 4.9. In families of habitual criminals with
several convictions the average was 4.4. The average in normal
families was 2.2.

Facts like these, which are typical of most if not all other
countries, too, show that the German people were beginning to
degenerate, the nazis say. And they accordingly adopted far-
reaching measures to counteract the trend toward degeneration

and, as they themselves describe the process, to "regenerate" the nation.

The most drastic of these measures, apart from the killings which came later, was compulsory castration of certain kinds of persons the nazis said should not be allowed to have any sex lives at all. Officials say they castrate only certain types of sex criminals. No check is possible on this claim, however—nor on any of the nazis' other claims, either, if it comes to that. In choosing this category of the "unfit" to be castrated, as in choosing the other categories to be killed, to be sterilized and to be forbidden to marry, the nazis allow no investigation of their methods. The world—and the "unfit" themselves—must take the nazis' word for it that the picking is wisely and fairly done.

The only exact official figures to be given out on the number of persons castrated in Germany are for the years 1934 and 1935, when 996 are reported to have been emasculated. The Race Policy Office of the party has estimated, however, that between 1,500 and 2,000 persons altogether were castrated between January 1, 1934, when the law providing for compulsory emasculation went into effect, and the outbreak of the war.

NO GREAT LOSS

Sterilization plays a much more important part in the nazi program for selective human breeding than castration does:

Up to the time the Second World War began, the regime had sterilized approximately 375,000 persons. The diseases or defects for which sterilization had been ordered, and the approximate number of operations for each, were as follows:

Congenital feeble-mindedness	203,250
Schizophrenia	73,125
Epilepsy	57,750
Acute alcoholism	28,500
Manic-depressive insanity	6,000
Hereditary deafness	2,625
Severe hereditary physical deformity	1,875
Hereditary blindness	1,125
St. Vitus' dance	750
Total	375,000

Only round figures can be given, because the nazis refuse to make precise ones available. These estimates are based on a series of special studies and statistics published in official and scientific journals, however, and on information obtained from competent party sources, and are believed to be close to the exact figures.

Sterilization as a means of eliminating the unfit is provided for in the "Law for the Prevention of Hereditarily Diseased Offspring," which the nazis promulgated only five months after seizing power. "Any person suffering from a hereditary disease," this law provides, "may be rendered incapable of begetting children (sterilization) by means of a surgical operation, provided it is established by scientific medical experience as very highly probable that any children he might beget would inherit some serious physical or mental defect."

Hereditary diseases in the meaning of the act are the nine cited above. Addiction to drugs also constitutes grounds for compulsory sterilization, according to one view, but this seems to be unclear.

An amendment to the law provides that sterilization by Roentgen-ray treatment is also permissible under certain circumstances.

The sterilization law applies to foreigners in the Reich as well as Germans, but foreigners may avoid having to submit to the operation by leaving the country.

All Germans over 10 years of age and suffering from any of the afflictions specified are, however, subject to compulsory sterilization, with only three exceptions:

1. Persons already incapable of begetting children due to advanced age or other reasons.

2. Persons whose condition is such that their lives would be endangered by the operation.

3. Persons already under full-time supervision in a state-approved, closed institution, or who agree to enter such an institution as an alternative to sterilization.

Voluntary sterilization is also provided for by the nazis. This is permissible, however, only "when a medical practitioner performs the operation in accordance with the recognized rules of medical practice in cases in which the life or health of the person so operated upon would otherwise be seriously endangered," in the words of the law.

Except under these circumstances, voluntary sterilization is prohibited in the Third Reich. For the nazis say that having children is not merely a right (for persons of whom the nazis approve, that is), but also a duty, and they forbid the German people to evade their "duty" by means of having themselves sterilized.

Nor is compulsory sterilization provided for by law on grounds other than those prescribed in the Hereditary Health Act. Even such a notoriously hereditary disease as haemophilia is not grounds for sterilization, for example. For only persons who themselves suffer from an affliction and who also are liable to hand it down to progeny may be sterilized. And whereas men (and only men) suffer from haemophilia, they cannot hand it down; and whereas women (and only women) hand it down, they themselves do not suffer from it.

Apart from the three exceptions already noted, on the other hand, no exemptions from the law are allowed. A plea for exemption was made in 1935 in Frankfurt in behalf of an unusually gifted musician whose sterilization had been ordered, for example. The man's gifts so far outweighed his affliction (which was not named in the reports of the case) that he should be allowed to hand down the gifts even at the risk of also handing down his affliction, it was argued. But the court rejected the plea and upheld the sterilization order.

The only qualities which are always handed down to descendants are diseases and other afflictions, two nazi officials asserted, commenting on this case in an official journal. Whether special gifts and talents are handed down depends on the operation of highly complicated biological laws, they said. Besides, the nation would suffer no great loss even if all the exceptionally talented should be prevented from having children, the writers asserted.

"WHO'S LOONY NOW?"

In examining supposedly feeble-minded persons to decide whether or not they are subject to compulsory sterilization, the nazis give them an intelligence test devised by the Reich government for this purpose. At least in Hamburg, however, and possibly elsewhere, too, this part of the examination has given rise to curious complications.

For some of the supposedly feeble-minded in Hamburg who first took the test copied out the questions and gave them afterwards to friends who were also supposed to be feeble-minded and who were due to be tested later, and the friends looked up and noted the answers, smuggled their notes into the examination, and in many cases passed the intelligence tests with flying colors.

Scoffers suggested that this scarcely showed deficiency of wit on the part of those who took the examinations, and some even asked unfriendly questions about the wits of those who gave the tests. "Who's loony now?" they asked, as John Armstrong Chaloner once asked his brother under not altogether dissimilar circumstances.

But the Hamburg authorities were little if any abashed. They soon detected the fraud, they said, because the cribbed answers were "too stereotyped" even when correctly given, and in some cases the "right" answers were given for the wrong questions. So the tests were revised and are still given, with precautions calculated to outwit the feeble-minded.

Intelligence tests make up only one part of the examinations for feeble-mindedness, in any event, moreover, and are not "slavishly" followed, nazis say. Character, as judged by the nazis, seems to play at least as important a part as intelligence in the diagnosis of feeble-mindedness. "The only criterion can be how the individual lives up to his position in life," Dr. Wagner once said.

In fact, "among the feeble-minded there is a large number who have a certain mental agility and who answer the usual easy questions quickly and apparently with assurance," says an official report on the enforcement of the sterilization law in

Hamburg, "and who only after a more searching examination betray the utter superficiality of their thinking, their inability to reason and their lack of moral judgment.

"This form of feeble-mindedness becomes especially clear when the disproportion is established between purely intellectual capacities—even if only superficial—on the one hand and the whole life conduct on the other," the Hamburg report declares.

All this places nazi sterilization for supposed feeble-mindedness in a curious light indeed. Do the nazis, of all men, judge "how the individual lives up to his position in life," in the words of the party boss of the entire German medical profession, and employ this judgment as "the sole criterion" in ordering sterilization? And do moral and intellectual disciples of Adolf Hitler decide what constitutes "utter superficiality of thinking," "inability to reason," and "lack of moral judgment," and regulate the breeding of 80,000,000 people in accordance with their decisions?

This sounds, in sober truth, like a program for breeding nazis, like an attempt by the party to breed a new people in its own image. Breeding for nazi conceptions of morals and intellect and character? The prospect is disconcerting.

How many of the more than 200,000 persons compulsorily sterilized for "feeble-mindedness" were forced to undergo the operation out of considerations like these? The nazis will not say, and there is no way of finding out.

ALCOHOLICS ARE SLOW TO AGREE

Diagnosis in the cases of other afflictions specified in the compulsory sterilization law, too, seems to depend more on the personal and political views of the nazi physicians who help to pick the unfit, and less on the criteria of science, than an unreconstructed citizen may find altogether comforting.

"The diagnosis of the group of manic-depressives . . . often presents special difficulties" also, for example, the Hamburg report says. "Fluid gradations are found, ranging from pronounced disease to fluctuations of temperament and spirits which psychiatry recognizes, but which still cannot be distinguished with absolute certainty."

How, then, do the nazis decide when to sterilize for manic-depressive insanity and when not? When the nazi doctor finds a condition of "pronounced disease," there is presumably no doubt. But what of the "fluid gradations"? How great do the fluctuations of temperament and spirits have to be, in the opinion of the official doctors, to warrant compulsory sterilization? The nazis give no indication of how they solve these problems.

It also seems to be difficult to diagnose alcoholism. In principle, acute alcoholics in the meaning of the act are only such persons as drink so much and so persistently over such a long period of time that they degenerate physically and mentally to a point at which they are repeatedly confined in prisons or other institutions because of acts committed under the influence of liquor. But these specifications are inexact at best.

And certainly the alleged alcoholics themselves are slow to agree to their sterilization, according to the Hamburg report: "The severe alcoholics make up the group with the least understanding of their disease," the report says. "At most they admit having been arrested a few times, having pawned a few things now and then, and having spent a few months in an institution taking a cure.

" 'But all in all it's not so bad' [they say]. 'The law is a fine thing and they applaud it in principle, but of course there is no question of its applying to them.' "

Although extremely careful examinations are necessary for diagnosing schizophrenia and epilepsy, other afflictions which constitute grounds for compulsory sterilization can be diagnosed with more certainty, the nazis say, except for the category "severe hereditary physical deformity." The closest to an official definition of this term it seems possible to obtain is a statement that it refers to deformities "of a sufficient degree to interfere with normal life and the capacity for earning a livelihood." Diagnosis and decision here, too, are "relatively difficult," the Hamburg report observes.

PERSONS LACKING IN UNDERSTANDING

Most of the approximately 375,000 persons the nazis sterilized up to the outbreak of the Second World War agreed to the operation before it was performed, the nazis say. In Hamburg, in fact (the only district for which a detailed study of compulsory sterilization has been published), 37.3 per cent of all applications for sterilization came from the persons to be operated upon, and 24.1 per cent from such persons' legal guardians, a total of 61.4 per cent, according to an official report.

Charges are often made in Germany, on the other hand, that an unknown but possibly large number of persons have not only been sterilized but even castrated because of hostility to the regime and on other grounds not recognized by law.

The nazis refuse to publish complete reports of their own on compulsory sterilization and castration, to say nothing of allowing any independent check to be made on their program, and they undoubtedly would arrest any German who openly accused them of abuses in this field. So the student can only suspend judgment on the claims of both the nazis and their critics.

The Hamburg report, however, does at least give a glimpse of some of the opposition and resistance to compulsory sterilization which have made themselves felt there, and other evidence seems to indicate that what has happened in Hamburg is probably typical of what has happened all over Germany.

"Persons lacking in understanding" try to evade appearing for sterilization hearings by fleeing from their homes and going into hiding, for example, the Hamburg report relates. Such conduct is silly and useless, however, the report adds, because sooner or later the police always find the fugitives and see to it that they appear for the hearings and, if the operation is ordered, that they submit to it.

Most of the opposition to sterilization seems to be based on one or more of six grounds:

1. The basic and perhaps instinctive desire to beget children (or more children) or at least to be physically able to do so.

2. Religious scruples, especially among Catholics.

3. Fear of death resulting from the operation.

4. Fear of the loss of all sexual powers and emotions.

5. Fear of changes in personality, appearance and other qualities, such as the voice.

6. Fear of ridicule and contempt.

OTHERS ARE DELIGHTED

Relatively little can be done to overcome opposition based on the first two of these grounds, although the nazis try, they say, to win over even those who oppose the operation for these reasons. Every effort is made to obtain the agreement of all those whose sterilization is ordered, party spokesmen say. But the nazis claim a good deal of success in overcoming other objections.

For the danger of death resulting from sterilization as it is carried out in the Reich is negligible, the nazis assert, and they say that most of the individuals affected are convinced of this, when the facts are explained. The regime refuses to give out any exact statistics on deaths following sterilization. A competent official estimates, however, that approximately 1 per cent of those operated upon die as a result; this would amount to a total of approximately 3,750 deaths in the period up to the outbreak of the war.

Nor does sterilization have any effect on the individual's sexual powers and desires beyond making it impossible for him to beget children, the nazis say, and still less does it cause any other changes in personality, appearance or other qualities. Most of those who have these fears confuse sterilization with castration, the nazis say, and when the difference between the two operations is made clear, most objections to sterilization are withdrawn, according to the nazis.

The regime takes elaborate pains to protect sterilized persons from contempt and ridicule. All officials and others concerned in sterilization proceedings are under an oath of secrecy, and violations of the oath are punishable by imprisonment up to 12 months. The courts also have imposed sentences of imprisonment on persons making ribald or otherwise unsympathetic remarks about those who have been sterilized.

But besides those who object to being sterilized there are

others who are delighted by the prospect. In Hamburg this group is described as consisting mostly of "girls, or more seldom men, who lead immoral lives and who see in sterilization a means of eliminating the dangers of parenthood and responsibility for support" of families, in the words of the official Hamburg report.

Welfare, religious and educational groups have protested that to sterilize such persons would only encourage them in unlimited immorality. To these protests, however, the authorities have replied that most of this category of persons are "morally feeble-minded," that their kind of immorality is hereditary, that fear of begetting children fails to deter such persons from immorality, and that the only effective way to deal with their vice is to stamp it out by sterilization. Perceiving that their protests were in vain, those who made them have now ceased to object, according to the Hamburg report.

15. Love Is a Paper Chase

Love is the fulfilling of the law.

ROMANS XIII, 10

For aught that I could ever read,
Could ever hear by tale or history,
The course of true love never did run smooth.

SHAKESPEARE

LOVE MAY STILL BE BLIND in the rest of the world, but it is not in Germany any more.

For the nazis are engaged in a program of selective human breeding and, like others before them, they regard love as an unreliable agent of selection. So they have made elaborate rules controlling marriage according to racial, physical, mental and moral principles, and they require lovers who want to marry to fill out questionnaires, produce documents and pass examinations to a point at which the only kind of blindness which might still be left to love would be blindness due to eyestrain and sheer fatigue. Love, it has been asserted, is like a red, red rose, but in the New Germany it is also a paper chase.

THE INDELICATE QUESTIONS

The nazis' measures for controlling marriage according to race have been described in a previous chapter. Their principal measures for marriage control according to physical, mental and moral standards are provided for in the "Law for the Protection of the Hereditary Health of the German People," often referred to as the "Marriage Health Law."

230

This law establishes two chief controls of marriage. First, persons are forbidden to marry who are afflicted with any one or more of four categories of physical, mental and moral diseases and disabilities. Second, all persons wishing to marry must obtain in advance a "Certificate of Marriage Fitness." These certificates are issued by public-health offices. They are given out only after applicants have passed thorough examinations and have satisfactorily answered a host of the most exhaustive and delicate—or indelicate—questions about themselves and their families.

Love blind? Here are some of the facts about doting couples that must be ascertained, scientifically verified, meticulously described and officially recorded before marriage licenses are issued in the New Germany:

Bony structure, distribution of fat, muscular development, bearing and other general physical characteristics;

Sex life, sex organs;

Number of times failed in school, and other aspects of mental development;

Ages at which learned to walk and talk;

Childhood and other diseases;

Character development;

Use of alcohol and tobacco;

Ability to beget children;

Adaptation to environment.

This and other information must be checked by the public-health office, recorded in an official form and accompanied by one full-face and one profile photograph of the citizen—"which, if they at all resemble the official passport variety, would provide ample cause for separation" in themselves, a student has said.

"What stature is she of?" asked Jaques of Orlando, and was told, "Just as high as my heart." But the nazi who tried such pretty answers would soon find himself disqualified for marriage fitness.

FOURTH-CLASS WOMEN WOULD BE POPULAR

The nazis, however, pay no more heed to pleasantries like these than they do to other criticisms of their policies. "Regeneration" of the German people by control of marriage has long been close to the hearts of party leaders and some of them have proposed controls which go far beyond even those provided for by the "Marriage Health Law."

R. Walther Darré, Minister of Agriculture and Reich "Leader of Peasants," once proposed that all German women should be divided into four classes in accordance with their biological virtues:

First-class women alone, he proposed, would be permitted under this plan to marry those whom Darré described as "the new [nazi] nobility." Second-class women would be permitted to marry nazi nobles if they successfully served a period of probation the nature of which was not altogether clear. Third-class women could marry "inferior" men, but the men would be sterilized to prevent them from begetting equally "inferior" children. And fourth-class women would be permitted neither to marry nor to have children. A disrespectful critic suggested that the popularity of fourth-class women would be overwhelming.

Another proposal by a nazi periodical called for marriage control based on fondness for the theater and sports, as well as on racial grounds:

"Every Aryan man should marry only a blonde Aryan woman with wide-open, blue eyes, a long, oval face, a pink and white skin, a narrow nose and a small mouth, and who under all circumstances must be a virgin," the periodical declared. "A blonde, blue-eyed man must not marry a brunette or Mediterranean-type woman with short legs, black hair, hooked nose, full lips, a large mouth and inclination to plumpness. [Also] a blonde, blue-eyed Aryan hero must not marry a negroid type of woman with the well-known negroid head and skinny body.

"The Aryan hero must marry only his equal," the periodical said, "an Aryan woman—but not one who goes out too much or likes theaters, entertainment or sport, or who wants to be seen outside her home."

The nazis have refrained, so far, at least, from adopting

these proposals as they stand. Close controls of other kinds, however, based on some of these same principles, have been established.

MARRIAGE: THE DUTY TO THE STATE

"Fitness to marry" is, in fact, subject to just as close checking and control as fitness for military service in the New Germany. Even some of the qualifications for fitness are similar—racial, physical, mental and moral—and the same word for "fitness" is used in both cases. Marriage in the Third Reich is, indeed, a form of service to the state, too. For it has been proclaimed on the highest authority that the state must have many children and that it is the function of marriage to provide them.

The "Marriage Health Law" lists four categories of persons as unfit to marry and therefore forbidden to do so:

1. Those suffering from a contagious disease which gives grounds for fearing serious harm to the health of persons they might marry and children they might beget.

2. Those who have been placed under guardianship or temporary trusteeship.

3. Persons who, although not under guardians or trustees, nevertheless suffer from "a mental disorder which causes marriage to appear undesirable from the viewpoint of the community of the people."

4. Persons suffering from hereditary diseases in the meaning of the compulsory sterilization law. (Such persons may, however, marry partners who are sterile.)

In interpreting this law, the courts have added a fifth category of persons whose marriage is held to be contrary to the spirit and intent of the law: no person who has been sterilized may marry a healthy, fertile partner who otherwise would be able to bear or beget healthy children.

The law allows a good deal of discretion to the officials who administer it (as almost all laws in the New Germany do), especially in the many borderline cases in Group 3. What is a "mental disorder which causes marriage to appear undesirable from the viewpoint of the community of the people"? Obviously the decisions in many cases are bound to be influenced by the ideas of the responsible officials.

So the nazis exercise their marriage control partly by compulsion and partly by advice. Persons in Groups 1, 2, 4 and 5 usually are forbidden to marry. In borderline cases in Group 3, officials may advise against marriage without flatly forbidding it.

Persons who persist in marrying contrary to official advice against their doing so must be allowed to wed anyway if there are no grounds for definitely refusing to issue licenses. At the same time, an official whose "advice" is ignored may always change his advice into an order forbidding marriage. Marriages contracted in defiance of official orders forbidding them are void, and contracting such a marriage or attempting to do so is punishable by imprisonment for not less than three months. The law fixes no maximum sentence.

Typical contagious diseases included in Group 1 are gonorrhea, syphilis, diphtheria, scarlet fever, smallpox, typhus, leprosy, spotted fever, yellow fever, plague—and tuberculosis if there is danger of infection of the other partner or of children the couple might have. Persons suffering from any of these and various other diseases are forbidden to marry in Germany until cured. Doubtful cases are rare in this category. Diagnosis is relatively easy, and once it has been made, the question of eligibility to marry is automatically determined.

Nor is there room for much, if any, doubt in cases in Group 2. Persons are placed under guardianship or trusteeship in the Reich most often after a court has declared them incompetent to administer their own affairs, owing usually to mental aberration, excessive drinking or an inveterate tendency to run into debt. Here, too, marriage control is relatively easy, and the question whether a license is to be granted or withheld is answered by reference to court records.

Marriage is always forbidden to persons in Groups 4 and 5. Sterilizations under nazi law are a matter of official record to which public-health offices have access, and sterilizations performed before 1933 are few in number and can also be medically established. Diagnosis in the cases of hereditary diseases as defined by the "Hereditary Health Law" is often difficult. Once the case has been diagnosed, however, whether well or badly, there are few difficulties in the practical administration of the "Marriage Health Law."

But both diagnosis and decision, in the cases of persons in Group 3, are necessarily at least as personal and political as they can possibly be scientific and dispassionate.

CRIME IS A LOOSE TERM

The nazis are so careless—or so deliberately vague—in their use of language that it is difficult here, as in most other phases of their policies, to be sure of what they mean. They have, however, given some indications as to how they define a "mental disorder which causes marriage to appear undesirable from the viewpoint of the community of the people."

Thus, pederasty and lesbianism are held to constitute such disorders. A distinction seems to be made, however, in the cases of persons suffering from these disabilities, between those considered to be hopelessly perverted, who are forbidden to marry, and those considered curable, who are advised (if they should wish to marry) to wait until it seems reasonably certain that a cure has been effected.

A second category of persons held to come under this heading consists of those whose mental or moral shortcomings are such that they would have caused the person concerned to be placed under a guardian or trustee except for special circumstances irrelevant to their fitness or unfitness to marry. A man may be mentally incompetent and yet be allowed to administer his own affairs if his affairs are so trivial that even a half-wit could manage them, for example. Or a man may be wildly extravagant and yet escape guardianship if he is extremely wealthy. Yet both of these men would be officially advised not to marry and, in especially grave cases, could be forbidden to do so.

A propensity for crime is also considered a "mental disorder which causes marriage to appear undesirable from the viewpoint of the community of the people," and so is a proclivity toward "conduct dangerous to the community of the people," and persons characterized by these qualities, too, the nazis forbid to marry.

The meaning of this view of the law is reasonably clear in the cases of persons found guilty by the courts of having committed acts that are considered crimes in most civilized communities: acts like robbery, or kidnapping, or murder. But "crime" is a loose term in the New Germany, and "conduct dangerous to the community of the people" is an even looser one. They are used to describe a multitude of acts and kinds of conduct that everybody else in the world considers harmless idiosyncrasies at worst, and positive virtues at best.

The lawgivers, the courts, and Hitler himself, have said that the profession of an orthodox Christian faith is conduct dangerous to the community of the people and that it is a crime, and that so is the championing of a liberal form of government, and membership in a Masonic lodge or a Rotary club, and the painting of impressionistic pictures, and the telling of funny stories at the expense of Dr. Goebbels. Persons who commit offenses like these in Germany are "criminals," the nazis say. Does this mean that the nazis forbid them to marry? If the language of the official commentators on the law means anything, it means precisely this.

BAD HUMOR AS A MARRIAGE BAN

Further interpretations of the law open up still broader vistas of marriage control:

For "conditions characterized by severe bad humor, depression, fear, disgust with life and inclination to suicide" are also held to constitute "mental disorders which make marriage appear undesirable from the viewpoint of the community of the people," and so are "grave spiritual shortcomings" of all sorts, in general. And these terms are so vague that they could well be interpreted to mean that the whole German people—and, above all, the nazis themselves—are unfit to marry. For most of them have been suffering from "mental disorders" like these for the past several years. "Severe bad humor" as a ban to marriage? Here, as elsewhere, there would seem to be no limits to the powers of nazi officials.

Even the official commentators themselves concede that the language of the law and its interpretations are not as clear as they might be. "There will be borderline cases," they say, ". . . whose judgment requires great expert knowledge and a strong sense of responsibility on the part of the examining physician."

Confronted by such arbitrary, far-reaching and ill-defined authority over his ability to marry, wielded by a regime which boasts of being a government of men—or of one man—and not of laws, the unreconstructed German may well feel uneasy.

Nor will he be reassured by the assertion that the "strong sense of responsibility" required of examining physicians must be a political, as well as a scientific (and, presumably, human) one; it is "self-evident" that official marriage advice may be given only by doctors who, to be sure, have had adequate medical training and experience, but who also must "stand fast on the basis of the national socialist movement," the late Dr. Arthur Guett, of the Ministry of the Interior, once said.

There is just one source of comfort for the individualist in all this, just one realistic reason for believing that in this phase of nazi population policy, as in others, the nazis prevent marriage and childbearing in a minimum of cases covered by the party's legislation. For the regime wants a high birth rate, and has succeeded extraordinarily well in inducing one. And the more people who are forbidden to marry and have children, the lower the birth rate is liable to be. The fact that the rate is high, therefore, seems to indicate that enforcement of the law is not unduly restrictive.

All of which, of course, might afford cold comfort to the individual in any given case. Especially since he has no way of knowing how much of the increase in the birth rate is due to the issuing of licenses to marry to persons who really should not have them but who are politically reliable, to make up for the withholding of licenses from persons who should have them but whose political philosophy—or religion or art or club life or sense of humor—is unsatisfactory.

16. Replenish the Earth

*And God blessed them, and God said unto them,
Be fruitful, and multiply, and replenish the earth,
and subdue it: and have dominion over the fish of
the sea, and over the fowl of the air, and over
every living thing that moveth upon the earth.*

GENESIS I, 28

APPROXIMATELY 800,000 more marriages took place in the
"Old Reich" (Germany exclusive of Austria, Czechoslovakia
and Memel) from the time the nazis seized power until the
Second World War began, and approximately 1,550,000 more
babies were born, than would have been the case if marriage
and birth rates had remained what they were before.

The marriage rate went up from 7.9 per 1,000 inhabitants
in 1932 to 9.4 in 1938 and living births from 15.1 per 1,000 inhabitants to 19.7 in 1938. There were 644,363 marriages in
Germany in 1938, which was 24,392 more than there were in
1937 and 127,570 more than in 1932. Living births totaled
1,346,911 in 1938 in the Old Reich. This was 69,865 more
than living births in 1937 and 375,737 more than in 1933.

Too few babies were still being born in Germany when the
war began (600 a day too few, according to one official calculation) to maintain the numbers of the German people in the
long run. The Nazis had been unable to wipe out altogether the
deficit in the national ledgers of life and death they had found
when they had taken over. The German people, like all the
other peoples of the Western world, will begin in time to de-

cline in numbers unless the birth rate can be raised still more, or the death rate lowered still more, or both.

But the Nazis' achievement is nevertheless an extraordinary one. The German birth rate, which had sunk the most catastrophically of all those of the white peoples in the period between wars, the nazis raised far above that of the others. The time when the German people would begin to shrink in numbers, the nazis postponed for 20 years. And given time, fewer general mobilizations and the prospect of a more certain future, the nazis might well succeed in raising the birth rate enough higher to guarantee an indefinite increase in the numbers of the Germans.

The increases in both the marriage and the birth rates in the Reich, furthermore, took place in spite of the enforcement of elaborate controls of the whole sex lives of the German people. Tens of thousands of marriages and births were prevented on grounds of race, health, intelligence and morals. Also at least 250,000 persons, and possibly many more, left Germany during this period because they found life too unpleasant—or impossible—to be borne. Thousands of others who remained endured economic hardships, were imprisoned and suffered other hindrances to their getting married and having children.

The increases in marriages and births which occurred in Germany therefore represent both a quantitative and a qualitative phenomenon (for better or for worse), possibly without parallel in history: they are the results of the greatest program of controlled, selective human breeding the world has ever seen.

How have the nazis been able to regulate the sex lives of the German people so closely and yet at the same time bring about such increases in marriages and births?

Both German and other experts disagree as to the relative effectiveness of the various measures the nazis have adopted. The experts agree at least to this extent, however: they concur in believing that the increases in marriages and births in Germany under nazi rule must be due to a combination of some or all of the policies the regime has adopted to bring about these results. The increases are not accidental, the experts agree, and the fact that they have occurred under nazi rule is not just a coincidence.

Some students give much of the credit for the increases to the economic boom the nazis brought about, and improved economic conditions probably did help raise the marriage rate in the Reich, while they lasted, as they have done in other countries. The increase in the birth rate, however, seems to be due primarily to other causes. For with a few minor exceptions, there were no increases in birth rates in other white Western European countries from 1933 to 1938. The rate and number of marriages went up elsewhere, but in general birth rates kept on going down, although at slower rates of decline in most cases than before.

The nazis, for their part, say that a "psychological revolution" took place in Germany, partly as cause and partly as result of the party's seizure of power, and that this has played an important part in causing the increases in marriages and births in the Reich. People in Germany are happier than they were before, the nazis say, and less selfish and they have more confidence in the future, and therefore they have bigger families.

It is doubtful if even the nazis who say this believe it themselves. And certainly no one in his right senses who lived in Germany throughout this era could subscribe to it. It is true enough that there was a "psychological revolution" in Germany in the years 1933 to 1939, but it was not the kind these nazis talk about: it was exactly the opposite kind. Most Germans are not more happy under nazi rule, but less happy; they are not less selfish, but more selfish; they do not have more confidence in the future, but less. To the extent that the "psychological revolution" helped cause an increase in births in Germany, it is because the "revolution" resulted in considerable measure from the shadow of death that steadily deepened in Germany as the specter of a new war grew more and more monstrously— a shadow in which the sexual expression of the life impulse habitually asserts itself with especial vigor.

But the Germans have bigger families also because of specific measures the nazis have taken to induce them to do so.

These measures consist of three main sorts: the nazis lighten the financial burdens of having big families; they favor fecundity by propaganda and by conferring special honors and privileges on parents of several children; and they make abortion extremely difficult.

PROCREATION PREMIUMS

As part of their campaign to raise the birth rate, the nazis have set out to equalize completely the economic burdens of raising big families.

The ideal which the regime hopes to realize is a system under which the man who earns $100 a month and has five children, for example, will be no worse off economically than the man who earns $100 a month and has no children. The childless man will be taxed so heavily and the man with five children will be taxed so lightly and subsidized so handsomely that the two will be equally well off—or equally badly off, depending on the point of view.

This system of adjusted burdens will be administered, the nazis intend, through a "Family Equalization Fund." Virtually all Germans will pay into this fund taxes and other levies, graduated according to the individual's earnings and the size of his family. The bigger the individual's income and the smaller his family, the heavier the payments he will have to make into the equalization fund. The sums so collected will then be paid out in bonuses, or procreation premiums, to big families, according to the families' sizes and incomes. The bigger the family and the smaller its income, the more it will receive in benefits from the fund.

No attempt will be made to provide a workman with five children with the same net income as a bank president with five, but the workman with five children will be no worse off than a workman who earns the same but who has no children, and the nazis even plan to do something about equalizing the burdens of bank presidents' families, too.

The war has made it necessary to postpone the establishment of the Family Equalization Fund as such. But even without such a formal fund the nazis do a great deal toward lightening the economic burdens of raising big families and thereby, the party hopes and believes, to encourage more couples to marry and have big families—at the expense, in considerable measure, of those who have small families or none at all.

The regime lends money on easy terms to help couples marry and set up homes of their own. It makes outright single, lump-sum payments and monthly grants to hundreds of thousands of families with three or more children each. It gives scholarships to such families, allows them big tax reductions, helps them obtain higher wages and salaries, and pays them extra social insurance benefits.

The law providing for the granting of special loans to help newly-married couples set up homes of their own was one of the first of these measures to be adopted. The law went into effect August 1, 1933. By May 1, 1939, approximately 1,200,-000 of these loans had been made, of a total value of approximately 750,000,000 marks, and further loans were being granted, as of that date, at a rate of approximately 25,000 a month.

Originally the marriage loan policy was intended to serve several purposes: to eliminate women from jobs that could be held by men, to encourage the employment of women in domestic service, and to create jobs by stimulating the household furnishings and allied trades, as well as to raise the marriage and birth rates. Loans therefore were granted only in cases in which the bride had had a job and quit and promised not to go back to work, or had been doing housework in her own home which a maid was hired to do when the bride left to be married.

But the chief purpose of the policy has always been to encourage the birth rate. So the nazis provided, at the outset, that one-fourth of the loan would be canceled for each of the first four children born to the couple.

The loans have served these purposes eminently well, the nazis claim. Approximately 650,000 women were eliminated from "men's" jobs, and approximately 150,000 new jobs were created in the household furnishings and allied trades, the nazis say, resulting, among other things, in savings of 375,000,000 marks a year in unemployment insurance benefits.

By 1937 the nazi boom had created a labor shortage in the

Reich, and from the economic point of view there was no longer any need or desire to eliminate women from the labor market. Since then, accordingly, loans have also been granted in cases in which the bride keeps a job or never had one or gets one after she is married.

BLESSINGS FALL ONLY ON NAZIS AND HYPOCRITES

Couples who obtain marriage loans have an average of twice as many babies as couples who marry without benefit of loans, according to official nazi statistics.

Approximately 1,000,000 children in all were born up to May 1, 1939, to couples marrying with the aid of loans. And since the nazis cancel one-fourth of the original debt for each of the first four children born, these 1,000,000 births resulted in cancellation of well over 150,000,000 marks of the total of 750,000,000 marks advanced.

There seems to be no particular reason to doubt the figures showing the high birth rate among couples marrying with the aid of loans. There is room for a difference of opinion, on the other hand, as to the extent to which the loans are responsible for the high rate.

Some students believe that the loans do not cause it at all. The loans are granted to couples who would have big families anyway, with or without loans, these students say. Couples already expecting the birth of a child and couples who strongly want and intend to have several children apply for and obtain loans to a greater extent than couples who want and intend to have few children or none at all, according to this view.

Data are lacking for a scientific judgment on the merits of this argument. Offhand, however, it appears reasonable to suppose that the loans are at least partly responsible for the high birth rate among couples obtaining them, although quite probably by no means altogether responsible.

At the very least, it seems to be the case that the loans make it possible for a fairly large number of babies to be born in wedlock who otherwise would be illegitimately born or whose births might conceivably be prevented altogether, by abortions, even in the New Germany. Among the couples who first obtained loans, at least, 8,123 had babies within three months after their marriages, and 29,498 had children between three and nine months after being married.

The loans probably also stimulate the birth rate in another way: by encouraging couples to marry at younger ages than they otherwise would. In general, the younger the age at which marriage occurs, the larger the family.

Marriage loans are limited to a maximum of 1,000 marks per couple. They bear no interest. The principal, minus deductions resulting from the birth of children, has to be repaid at the rate of 3 per cent per month of the original amount loaned if both wife and husband are gainfully employed and 1 per cent per month if only the husband has a job.

The loans are not intended to raise the birth rate indiscriminately, but to raise it only among such categories of the population as the nazis approve of. Here, too, the party's program of selective human breeding has been made effective. In general, the racial, physical, mental and moral conditions for obtaining loans are the same in principle as those which the nazis have laid down for all marriages in the Reich, but the conditions for obtaining loans are more severe in degree and more rigorously enforced.

Applicants and close blood relatives must be free of serious hereditary physical and spiritual defects and the couple themselves must not be suffering from any dangerous contagious disease. All four of each partner's grandparents must be of "German or similar blood," that is, Aryan. Persons of "pronounced a-social or anti-social tendencies" are ineligible for loans. And applicants must swear an oath of loyalty to the regime. "In the German state," as Kirkpatrick says, "blessings fall only on those supposedly loyal to the regime. Only hypocrites and national socialists receive marriage loans."

The funds for marriage loans, like those for the subsidies which the nazis pay outright for children in big families, are provided partly by the Reich Institute for Unemployment Insurance and for Providing Employment (that is, from payments made to the Institute by employed persons in Germany), partly from revenues from the income tax, and partly from repayments on the loans themselves.

IT PAYS TO BE PROLIFIC

The nazis pay such big subsidies for children that it is actually possible in the New Germany for a man to "earn" more by begetting babies than he does working for a living. It pays to be prolific in the Third Reich.

Several different kinds of premiums are paid for big families, but the most important are the "Child Subsidies"—the Kinderbeihilfen. These subsidies are of two kinds: single, lump-sum grants and continuing monthly payments.

Lump-sum grants are intended to help parents of large families and limited means to improve their homes. The grants may be spent for furniture, household implements, clothing and, in the cases of certain categories of rural and suburban families, for home building, home extensions and farm machinery and equipment.

These single subsidies are limited to a maximum of 100 marks per child and 1,000 marks per family.

To be eligible for them, a family must have at least four children, including adopted and step-children, who have not completed their sixteenth years. Widows, divorcees and unmarried mothers may obtain grants even if they have fewer than four children. The parents must be of "German or similar blood," they must be unable to provide a "suitable" home for their children out of their own resources and their conduct and reputation must be "unobjectionable." Parents and children alike must be free of serious hereditary defects.

The nazis began to grant these lump-sum subsidies in October, 1935. By May 1, 1939, they had paid out a total of approximately 255,000,000 marks for approximately 3,750,000 children, an average of 68 marks per child.

Since that time, the nazis have granted fewer lump-sum payments, on the theory that most of those who were entitled to grants of this sort had already received them, and the continuing monthly payments have played a relatively more important part in this phase of population policy.

To big families covered by the compulsory social insurance system, the nazis make monthly payments of 10 marks for the third child, 10 marks for the fourth and 20 marks for the fifth and further children. Families of government employees and others not included in the social insurance system receive 10 marks for the fifth and each subsequent child.

These continuing grants began August 1, 1936, at a flat rate of 10 marks per month for each of approximately 300,000 children, a total outlay of approximately 3,000,000 marks per month. October 1, 1937, the conditions for obtaining grants were liberalized and payments of 10 marks per month were made thereafter for approximately 500,000 children, a total of approximately 5,000,000 marks per month. Beginning April 1, 1938, the conditions were still further liberalized and the amount of the grants for fifth and subsequent children was raised from 10 marks to 20 marks for families in the social insurance system. Nazis said in the Summer of 1939 that monthly grants were then being made for approximately 2,500,000 children. The total sum then being granted amounted they said, to approximately 30,800,000 marks per month.

Conditions for obtaining monthly subsidies require that the family have an income of no more than 8,000 marks a year. There must be at least four children in the family under 16 (five in the case of families not included in the social insurance system). Step-children and adopted children count the same as the parents' own. Children between 16 and 21 are also counted if they are still being educated or are permanently unable to work or if they earn less than 30 marks per month. Other conditions are the same as those for obtaining lump-sum payments.

This system of child subsidies is the most important single measure the nazis have adopted in their program for equalizing the economic burdens of raising big families. Under this system it is possible for a man to obtain a larger sum every month in the form of child subsidies than he obtains in the form of wages or salary from his employer:

A German earning wages of 120 marks a month (and millions of Germans earn no more) and with 11 children, for example, and satisfying the conditions for obtaining continuing monthly grants, is eligible for child subsidies totaling 160 marks a month. He also probably has received a single lump-sum payment of at least 350 marks. And he is eligible for still further financial assistance provided for by other nazi laws.

THE DESIRE CANNOT BE BOUGHT

"The desire for a child cannot be bought," Dr. Gerhard Wagner, late "Leader of Reich Physicians," once said. "It is basically a question of spiritual and philosophical training, and not the result of a system of premiums and rewards for bringing children into the world."

Dr. Wagner here expressed the official "party line" on this phase of race and population policy. The party has set up an elaborate system of premiums and rewards for bringing children into the world, and the nazis hope and believe that the system encourages Germans to have big families. But the regime also says that its premiums and rewards are an attempt to do justice for its own sake to big families at least as much as to encourage more Germans to marry and have them. It agrees that "the desire for children cannot be bought," and it devotes much time, energy and thought to the "spiritual and philosophical training" for which Dr. Wagner called and to honoring parenthood and easing its other, non-economic burdens.

Special honors are conferred on big families, especially on mothers. Preferential treatment is accorded them in several respects. They are granted special protection against exploitation and abuse. Propaganda glorifies maternity. Censorship forbids criticism of the regime's policies and advocacy of any others that conflict with or diverge from those of the regime.

Hitler himself ordered the conferring of special "Orders of Merit" on mothers of several children: an iron decoration for mothers of four or five, a silver decoration for mothers of six or seven, and a gold one for mothers of eight or more. These orders are conferred in the name of the party on August 12 every year—Hitler's mother's birthday—and the day is a "Day of Honor" for all German mothers.

The nazi radio broadcasts congratulations upon the births of babies in big families, and various towns publish special citations in local newspapers on such occasions. Solingen's official congratulations are published under the heading, "The City of Solingen is Proud of Your Families-Rich-in-Children."

Other towns issue to mothers of three or more children "Honor Cards" which entitle the bearer to be attended to without waiting her turn in party and government offices and, in some cases, to go directly to the heads of lines and be waited on first in stores and other places.

The nazis also deal drastically with those who abuse or exploit mothers and expectant mothers. The criminal code provides severe penalties for overworking them, and when a man slapped the face of an expectant mother in a town in Bavaria—on what provocation, if any, is not recorded—a local court said he had "committed a crime against the whole German nation" and sentenced him to a term of imprisonment.

The criminal code also specifically penalizes anyone ridiculing marriage and maternity, and one article provides that:

"Whoever brings into public contempt measures of the Reich for the protection of sound heredity or of race, or whoever publicly incites or encourages opposition thereto, or whoever publicly and maliciously engages in activities hostile to the basic policies of the state for sound heredity and race, is punishable by imprisonment. In especially grave cases the punishment is penal servitude."

The official Chamber of the Arts, for its part, has forbidden artists to use the word "family" in the title of any picture showing fewer than four children, even when the picture portrays an actual family. Such a picture may be entitled "Herr und Frau Mueller and Their Two Children," for example, but it may not be called "The Mueller Family."

"The Race Policy Office of the party calls attention to the unfortunate fact that portrayals of the German family are being publicly displayed which show only one or two children," says an official statement issued in this connection.

"National socialism combats the two-children [family] system with vigor, as this system would inevitably lead to the decline of the German people. National Socialism stands for the encouragement of at least four children in every family, in order at least to maintain the present numerical strength of the population.

"Whenever artistic considerations permit—and this will be true in the majority of cases—the artist, and especially the painter and commercial artist, should set himself the goal, within the framework of the possibilities of representation, of showing at least four German children when a 'family' is portrayed.

"Measures will be announced which will increase interest in such portrayals among artists as well as among the public. The Race Policy Office urges the same view also with regard to advertising and similar representations whenever the family is shown."

THE REASON WAS NOT BIOLOGICAL

The German birth rate began to go up almost immediately after the nazis seized power, and when the increase continued through the first three months of party rule, a spokesman claimed that credit for this was due to national socialism.

Unsympathetic listeners scoffed. They said it was biologically improbable, to say the least, that a change in government could have any effect on the birth rate in three months. But the unsympathetic listeners were wrong and the party spokesman was right. Because the reason for the increase in the birth rate was not biological so much as it was legal, or political: One of the first things the party did in its campaign to raise the birth rate was to tighten up enforcement of the laws forbidding abortion, and this began to affect the number of births almost at once.

The nazis also set out to discourage the use of contraceptives. Soon after seizing power, the party closed down the birth control clinics that had been operating under the Republic, limited the giving of birth control information and forbade the advertisement and public display of contraceptive devices. Manufacture and sale of such devices has not, however, otherwise been limited, partly on hygienic grounds, and it would appear that this phase of the party's population policy has probably had much less effect on the birth rate than the campaign against abortion.

The regime has made only two changes in the anti-abortion laws already in effect under the Republic. On the one hand, the nazis require that a special commission of three physicians in each public health district must approve all abortions before they are performed, a measure of supervision and control lacking before. On the other hand, the nazis allow abortions in cases in which women are likely to give birth to hereditarily diseased children. The law requires that the consent of the woman be obtained in advance in such cases.

But much more important than these new laws is the grim determination with which the nazis enforce those already on the statute books when the party seized power.

Under the Republic, the authorities were relatively lax in enforcing anti-abortion laws. Prosecutions were rare, convictions even more rare and sentences light. Cases are on record in which Berlin courts did nothing more drastic than impose fines of only 30 and 40 marks on persons found guilty of abortion, for example. This all speedily changed when the nazis took over. Known or suspected abortionists were driven out of the medical profession. Several were sent to concentration camps without the formality of a trial. Others fled the country. Prosecutions and convictions multiplied and heavy sentences were imposed. In the space of a few weeks in the Summer of 1938, three offenders were sentenced to penal servitude for 5 years and 1 month, 6 years and 7 years, respectively.

The result has been a sharp decline in abortions in the Reich, and a corresponding increase in births.

Between 600,000 and 800,000 abortions were performed every year in Germany before the nazi revolution, according to what seems to be the best available estimate. Between 33 and 40 per cent of all pregnancies in the Reich were interrupted by abortions. In Berlin there were more miscarriages than normal births in some years, and most of the miscarriages were artificially induced, Dr. Friedrich Burgdoerfer believes.

But if this was the case, then the nazi campaign against abortion would only have had to be between 40 and 50 per cent effective to account for the entire increase in births that has taken place in Germany under nazi rule. And the burden of the available evidence seems to indicate that the campaign *has* been this effective. The rise in the German birth rate is probably due almost entirely to this single policy. Subsidies and propaganda help make the increased number of babies welcome and help support them, but the principal reason why the babies are born is that the nazis prevent the people from seeing to it that they are not born.

So much for "psychological revolutions."

17. The Big Battalions

It is said that God is always on the side of the heaviest battalions.

VOLTAIRE, LETTER TO M. LE RICHE

ONLY BIG FAMILIES provide the big battalions without which victories are not won," Mussolini once said to representatives of Italian Catholicism, and he asked them, for this reason, among others, to help him in his campaign to raise the Italian birth rate.

It is typical of Mussolini's cynicism that he used this argument in appealing to representatives of a Christian church. But the argument does at least have this much merit: that it reduces to its baldest and most essential terms the chief reason why both Mussolini and Hitler have moved heaven and earth to raise the birth rates in their countries, and the chief reason why it is vitally important to the rest of the world that Hitler, at least, has succeeded in raising the rate in Germany.

OSMOSIS AND WARS

For, other things being equal, the most numerous and most rapidly growing peoples will inherit the earth. Not necessarily at once, or even in one or two generations, and not just because they win battles. But over a period of several generations and because they will inevitably and inexorably seep through and across frontiers, by a kind of osmosis, and will crowd less vigorous peoples into smaller and smaller—and less desirable—space. Much and perhaps most of this process will take the form of wars, in which, as Mussolini said, and men much greater than Mussolini, the big battalions are necessary to victory. But even without wars a biologically vigorous people will triumph over a biologically weak one.

And if this is true "other things being equal," it is all the more true when the biologically vigorous people is one as gifted, as highly organized, as zealous, ambitious and as able in warfare, as the Germans. If the German birth rate can be still further increased and maintained, and if rates in other white countries continue to decline or remain at their low levels of the era between world wars, a day will inevitably come when the German people will surely inherit, if not the whole earth, at least a much larger and richer portion of it than they have ever had before. The balance of population power throughout the world will shift so far, and with it the balance of political power and cultures, that the whole map and the whole character of civilization will be changed.

Even in the few brief years the nazis were in power before the Second World War, the balance of population within Germany shifted, and the character of German society and of the German economic system altered in consequence. A country with many children is different from a country with few in somewhat the same sense as a family with many children is different from a family with few, and from 1933 to 1939 the Germans again became a country of relatively many children—while other western white nations still had relatively few.

The nazis' success in raising the German birth rate had moral consequences, too, as well as these other and, in the first instance, quantitative, results. For in raising the birth rate the nazis greatly reduced abortions on the one hand and made early marriage easier on the other hand. The value of these achievements in terms of health and happiness and morality is indisputable.

At the same time, however, of course, it is possible if not probable that tens of thousands of children were born during this period, owing to nazi policy, whose parents neither wanted them in spite of all the nazi propaganda nor could afford to care for them and bring them up properly in spite of all the nazi subsidies, and the unhappiness caused on this score must be balanced against the happiness caused on others.

WHAT WOULD HAVE HAPPENED

The compulsory sterilization of the unfit and the marriage controls which the nazis enforce as part of their program of selective human breeding reduced the number of congenitally feeble-minded babies born in Germany every year by approximately 20,000 by 1938, it has been estimated by Professor Dr. Reinhold Lentz, of the Reich Ministry of the Interior, a nazi specialist in this field.

Professor Dr. Lentz is an ardent champion of the nazi program, rather than a disinterested observer, and his estimate should be regarded as a partisan statement of the case for the defense, rather than a judicial summing up. Any estimate involving a conditional negative, furthermore—any statement of "what would have happened if something else had not happened"—must necessarily be only approximate, at least any such estimate based on the operation among human beings of the laws of heredity.

Even after applying these and other appropriate rules of evidence, however, the student cannot help being impressed by at least some aspects of the nazis' program for breeding out the unfit. It may well be that the number of congenitally feeble-minded babies born in Germany every year has fallen by less than 20,000. Perhaps it has fallen by only half that many, or even less. But it appears to be the case that it has fallen to at least some extent and that it will continue to fall as more and more feeble-minded and otherwise unfit persons are prevented from marrying and having children.

At the same time, the number of schizophrenic, epileptic, manic-depressive, deaf-mute and blind babies born, and of babies afflicted with St. Vitus' dance and with severe deformities, and of those susceptible to acute alcoholism (if such a propensity can be transmitted by heredity, which is extremely doubtful) should also decline, for persons with these afflictions, too, are forbidden to marry in Germany and are sterilized as rapidly as circumstances permit.

Experts disagree as to the extent to which these afflictions are transmitted by heredity, and the extent to which it is possible to eradicate them by sterilization and marriage controls. The discreet layman will, accordingly suspend judgment as long as this is the case. At the very least, however, the nazi program cuts down the number of children who, even if they would have been perfectly normal when born, nevertheless would have been subject to the disadvantage of growing up in homes cursed with these afflictions (or in institutions or in the care of guardians) and this in itself would appear to be a clear gain.

This is the first qualitative achievement of nazi population policy.

The second qualitative achievement is that it has reduced the number of babies born into criminal homes—into homes, that is, where the parents would be considered criminals in any civilized country, not parents called "criminals" in Germany but considered useful citizens elsewhere. For all habitual criminals are forbidden to marry in Germany, and certain categories of sex criminals are castrated—which also tends to reduce the number of sex crimes committed.

HOW CHANGED?

So far can the student go in recognizing the qualitative achievements of nazi population policy. The outsider will be more temperate than the nazi in his appraisal of these achievements. He may or may not believe that the achievements are worth the price that must be paid for them. But he at least will recognize that the nazis are reducing the number of babies born in Germany to physically, mentally and morally unfit parents.

So far can the student go—but little further. For besides these rules of physical, mental and moral selection which the nazis enforce in their population policy, and to which the outsider may subscribe in considerable measure, at least in principle, the nazis also enforce other rules to which, as the nazis explain and execute them, no fair-minded outsider can possibly subscribe, in principle or in practice.

For the nazis apply their own grotesque and often obscene standards of morality and even intelligence in deciding whether citizens ought to marry or not, and, in some cases, even whether they should be sterilized or not—the standards of morality and intellect, that is, of men like Hitler and Goering and Himmler and Ribbentrop and Goebbels and Julius Streicher and the murderers of Potempa and countless other men like these. It may be doubted—it is most devoutly to be doubted—that the qualities of mind and character these men exemplify can be transmitted by heredity. But even if they cannot, the attempt to breed according to such standards is a criminal one, and one bound to lead to a bitter and immeasurable unhappiness on the part of those who are made its victims.

As for the nazis' program of racially selective breeding, it is only on two points that the student can agree with the nazi claims: First, it is true that to all practical intents and purposes the nazis have put an end to "race mixture" between Jews and gentiles in Germany. Second, the ending of such "race mixture" may indeed have some effect on the character of the German people—although the outsider may well doubt that the direct, biological effect will be as great as the nazis say it will be.

But as to the kinds—and the desirability—of the effects all this will have, there can be little agreement or none whatever.

The nazis say that thanks to their "race purity" the German people will be vastly improved in virtually all things both great and small. They will be more honest, more brave, more beautiful, more generous and more intelligent, the nazis say. They will have better teeth, better livers, more freckles and bigger and better beards. Their women will use less makeup and will keep their legs together in street cars and railway trains, and their men will conquer the earth.

The outsider will have difficulty in discovering independent authority for accepting these claims. The character and appearance and manners of the German people may indeed be changed, after several generations or more, by the virtual disappearance of "Jewish blood" from their veins. But how changed? What will be the qualities which will disappear?

Will they be the sinister and vicious qualities the nazis attribute to "Jewish blood"? Only a Hitler, a Rosenberg or a Streicher could believe such madness. Other qualities might, however, really disappear: a touch of warmth and vivid color and grace; sensitiveness and adroitness and flashing insight and inspiration; a merciful gentleness and lightness of touch; a soaring, far-ranging inquisitiveness; a saving skepticism.

These qualities began to disappear after only a few years of nazi rule—but that was not genetic; it was political.

ERRORS AND OMISSIONS EXCEPTED

Trying to appraise the moral and biological costs of the nazis' program of selective human breeding is like trying to appraise the economic and financial costs of the regime's policies in other fields. In both cases the nazis refuse to reveal some of the facts necessary for estimating even the full extent of the programs themselves, to say nothing of the full price in blood and treasure and moral and biological values that the programs cost. In both cases, furthermore, some of the terms in which major items of cost are expressed have been debased and otherwise altered, deliberately in some instances and by the remorseless pressure of events in others, and now have different values at different times, in different places and under different circumstances. How much has the nazi program of public works cost? It depends partly on how much you think the mark is worth. How much has the nazi program of selective human breeding cost? It depends partly on how much you think personal liberty is worth. "Errors and omissions excepted" must be writ large over any attempt to audit balances like these.

Subject to these reservations, however, it is at least possible to indicate some of the respects in which the nazi program destroys moral and biological values to an extent that may outweigh its probable achievements.

The first and most easily verifiable item of cost consists of the killings of the (at least) 100,000 people the nazis have liquidated as "unfit."

The second item consists of the deaths following sterilizations. The nazis say these totaled approximately 3,750 up to the time the Second World War began.

Another item consists of the loss to the world of the normal, healthy human beings who would have been begotten, and the geniuses who might have been begotten, by the persons the nazis have castrated, sterilized and prevented from marrying.

Assume that there is absolute legal and medical certainty in identifying the crimes and afflictions for which the nazis castrate and sterilize and prevent from marrying. Assume that there is complete agreement that these criminal tendencies and afflictions are, in fact, transmitted by heredity. Assume that they warrant the stigma of unfitness. Assume that there are no blunders and no abuses in the nazis' administration of the laws. Make all these assumptions. But the fact still remains that some of the children who would have been born to some of the persons prevented from begetting them would have been normal and some might well have been geniuses.

THE NAZIS' NICE DISTINCTIONS

But actually how many of these assumptions is it safe to make?

Can law and medicine be sure in identifying feeble-minded-ness and acute alcoholism? What is a "severe physical malfor-mation"? Is a harelip? Is a clubfoot? What is "a mental dis-order making marriage appear undesirable from the viewpoint of the community of the people"?

Is there agreement among scientists that the criminal tend-encies and afflictions for which the nazis castrate and sterilize and prevent from marrying are, in fact, transmitted by heredity? And even if they are hereditary, do they all warrant the stigma of unfitness?

Actually, there is the most emphatic disagreement among scientists on the medical questions involved and among moral-ists, and all human beings, on the human questions involved, and so long as this is the case there will be room for innumer-able mistakes and abuses.

The nazis insist that they do not forbid political opponents to marry just because they are political opponents, nor sterilize nor castrate them. It is ridiculous, if not insulting, even to raise the question whether the regime does such things, they say. But why is it ridiculous or insulting? Men—and women and chil-dren, too—are deported and deprived of their citizenship and robbed of their property and arrested and jailed and sent to concentration camps and beaten and tortured to death every week in Germany for "crimes" no more heinous than being members of some certain "race" or voicing certain religious or political beliefs or painting certain kinds of pictures or telling certain kinds of funny stories.

Which is worse: to forbid the Reverend Martin Niemoeller to marry and have children, or even to sterilize or castrate him— or to send him to a concentration camp, tearing him away from the wife and children he had? The nazis do the one thing and boast of it, and they say it is ridiculous if not insulting to suspect that they do the other thing, too. Nice nazi distinctions like these are hard for the unreconstructed to appreciate.

How many perfectly normal men and women have been forbidden to marry in Germany because the nazis hated them on personal or political grounds? How many men and women of outstanding virtue and achievement? How many have been sterilized? How many castrated?

Until some impartial investigation is possible—if it ever is— the only real basis for answering questions like these must be the character of the nazis as revealed in other phases of their conduct. The suspicions which any such consideration must necessarily rouse are ugly ones.

18. The Suppression of Intelligence

> *Military discipline has its place as one of the component parts of society. If, instead of being contained in society, it contains society itself, then it is no longer military discipline but the suppression of intelligence. An artist with the face of a corporal, a scientist with that of a sergeant, or a politician waiting on a command in order to carry it out blindly—such are not really artists or scientists or politicians, but just imbeciles.*
>
> BENEDETTO CROCE

THE GERMANS have long excelled in the things of the mind and spirit. Centuries before Adolf Hitler—and Alfred Rosenberg—were born, and before there was any such thing as a national socialist party, the German intellect and feeling for truth and beauty had achievements to their credit that were the admiration of the civilized world. The nazis, however, weighed these achievements in the balance and found them wanting. Some, they conceded, were adequate. But German Kultur on the whole was, they announced, unsatisfactory, and they set about straightaway imposing their own notions of truth and beauty on the Germans and on anybody else who fell under their sway. They asserted the right of eminent domain, not only over the citizen's property and his body, but also over his soul as well. They set out to dictate, not only what the citizen might do, but also what he might think. They attempted to regulate, not only the people's sex lives, but also their intellectual and artistic lives.

These things the nazis have undertaken to do by propagating a new, national socialist "philosophy of life" which inspires and animates, they say, a new Kultur, and by suppressing all other philosophies of life and destroying all such other expressions of truth and beauty as do not satisfy nazi specifications.

These undertakings are all-important, the nazis say:

"The national socialist movement stands and falls with its philosophy of life," Rosenberg has said, and Hitler himself has proclaimed that "If the national socialist movement is to have a real revolutionary significance, it must strive to give tangible proof of this significance by authentic creative work in the cultural sphere. We can imagine no resurgence of the German people without a resurgence also of German Kultur and especially of German art."

What is this new Kultur that the nazis have set out to establish in a monopoly of the German mind and spirit?

It is first of all, of course, an authoritarian Kultur: it is revealed, promulgated and enforced by the regime.

Second, the new Kultur is also totalitarian: it takes within its purview every single conceivable manifestation of the human feeling for the true and the beautiful.

And third, the new Kultur is "ulterior": no art, no science, no discipline of learning, has any values or standards of its own or any reality or meaning in itself, but all must submit to and praise the name of the doctrines and dogmas of the national socialist party. The new Kultur, that is, is a form of propaganda.

"JUST AS THE SOLDIER"

"With the victory of national socialism," Hitler has said, "the play of free forces introduced by democracy came to an end" in German Kultur as in all other phases of the national life.

A more pithy summing up of one of the most important characteristics of the new nazi Kultur could not be asked for. Because in the New Germany culture, like everything else, is regimented within an inch of its life. To the unreconstructed, in fact, it appears that culture is regimented several inches beyond life.

The patterns to which the new Kultur must conform are fixed by the national socialist party. The artists, writers, musicians and others who may contribute to the new Kultur live and work on the sufferance of the party, and they must belong to and be licensed by the Chamber of Kultur of the party. The Kultur which they create is subject to the most piercing scrutiny by agents of the party. And it and they are judged, rewarded and punished by the party.

"Freedom of artistic creation is also guaranteed in the new state," Dr. Goebbels has remarked, using "freedom" in the nazi, or nonsensical, meaning of the term. "This artistic creation [however] takes place within the sharply limited field of our national necessity and responsibility. [And] these limits are fixed by politics, not by art."

"In the various sections of the Chamber of Kultur," the minister has explained, "the German artist of today is educated to consciousness of his profession, to discipline and to a sense of corps honor."

There is no nonsense about this discipline, either:

"All we national socialists are convinced that we are right," Dr. Goebbels has said, "and we cannot bear with anyone else who maintains that he is right. For if he is right, then he must be a national socialist, and if he is not a national socialist, then he is not right."

"Just as the soldier cannot be allowed to strike and shoot when and as he likes," Dr. Goebbels has explained, "and just as the peasant cannot be permitted to sow and reap what and where he wishes, so the author has no right to go beyond the limits of the people's welfare in living his individual life." Here again, of course, the nazis define the limits.

So, too, are all other agents of the new Kultur obliged to respect limits set by the regime. Even news dealers are included. They, too, must belong to the Chamber of Kultur, and they, too, are ordered "to reject everything in contradiction to national socialism." Scientists likewise have this same obligation. Some of them, at least, however, have lived up to it only imperfectly on occasion, it appears. For Julius Streicher, the sex-maniac Jew-baiter of Nuremberg, found it desirable some time ago to forbid all scientific lectures on race questions in his bailiwick. Such lectures, he explained, were having a "diluting and distorting effect on the national socialist philosophy of life" in Franconia.

These negative controls are supplemented by positive measures, although the nazis themselves admit that it is much harder to create what is good than to destroy what is bad, no matter what your standards of good and bad may be.

Hanns Johst, for some time president of the Reich Chamber of Literature, one of the sections of the Chamber of Kultur, has indicated one positive method of attack. The German people, he said in a speech at Weimar, are to be induced "by loving force" to read the works of nazi authors—which apparently were not being read, at the time, by virtue of any other inducements.

NO MARQUIS POSA

A good many Germans, in fact, have shown a regrettable distaste for what the nazis consider they should like and an even more regrettable fondness for what the nazis consider they should not like.

Production of Schiller's "Don Carlos" in the winter of 1936-1937 provided audiences all over Germany, for example, with the occasion for showing a partiality for freedom which, under the circumstances, could only be viewed as a distinct lack of enthusiasm for their own lot and for the regime that was responsible for it:

In Act III of "Don Carlos," King Philip II tells the Marquis Posa to look about him and observe the peace and well-being that obtain in Spain.

"The peace of a cemetery!" Posa retorts, and goes on:

"You alone in Europe wish to turn back the wheel of history? To seize and halt the irresistible spokes of destiny? You shall not do so.

"Already thousands flee, poor but happy, from your domain. The citizens you have lost were your best.

"You plant for eternity by sowing death? Such a work of violence will not outlast the life of its author. . . .

"Give up this deification of yourself which is destroying us! Become an example of the eternal and the true! Never had mortal so many means at his disposal . . . One stroke of the pen from this [the king's] hand and the earth is created anew. "Give us back freedom of thought!"

This speech struck a responsive chord in the hearts of German audiences. It described a situation which seemed somehow familiar, and it expressed sentiments they found admirable. Audience after audience burst into storms of applause that stopped performances for several minutes on end.

Earlier in nazi rule Berlin audiences had shown an equally regrettable fondness for quite completely non-nazi music. They had demanded repeated encores of music by Paul Hindemith, for example, just after an official anathema had been pronounced on all his works.

Nazi radio programs, on the other hand, were so widely and so heartily criticized for a time that Horst Dressler-Andress, president of the Chamber of the Radio in the Chamber of Kultur, said that the criticisms were "an insult to German Kultur," and film audiences in Berlin enthusiastically hissed a picture written and produced by Willi Krause, Reich Film Adviser in the Propaganda Ministry.

Still another audience, a predominantly Catholic one in Westphalia, interrupted the performance of a play about Widikind with angry shouts of, "No history faking!" The director appeared and explained that the play was being produced with the special approval of Dr. Goebbels, but the utterance of this name did anything but soothe the citizens, and the angry shouts were redoubled.

The authoritarian state, however, obviously cannot permit its authority to be flouted, and appropriate measures were taken for dealing with this recalcitrance:

Hindemith's music was banned altogether from Germany. An official organ of the Hitler Youth warned audiences that excessive enthusiasm for Posa's plea for liberty might have unpleasant consequences. In Westphalia, S. A. men removed the obstreperous Catholics from the galleries so that Dr. Goebbels' approved drama about Widikind could be played out in peace. Dressler-Andress announced that further criticism of nazi radio programs would not be tolerated. And Wilhelm Frick, Reich Minister of

the Interior, himself issued a warning against treasonable behavior on the part of motion picture audiences.

The public must not show disapproval of films passed by the
nazi censorship, he said. In some cases, Frick asserted, audiences
had even hissed pictures which had been approved by Hitler
himself. Demonstrations against such films constituted "express
defiance of the will of the Fuehrer," Frick said, and were "calculated in the highest degree to endanger the authority of the
state and cause unrest among the people."

The logic of authoritarianism as expounded by Dr. Frick is
unanswerable in a police—or secret police—state, and "express
defiance of the will of the Fuehrer" is no laughing matter in
the Third Reich. Up to the present, at least, there has been no
Marquis Posa in the New Germany. The demonstrations against
officially approved films ceased almost altogether. You never
know who may be sitting next to you in a theater.

PRINCE ADOLF AND THE SLEEPING BEAUTY

"The national socialist movement," says Alfred Rosenberg,
"strives for the totality of the national socialist philosophy of
life in all spheres." Dr. Rosenberg, for once in his life, at least,
is too modest. For the nazis not only strive for totality, but they
succeed in achieving it, to a degree that is almost incredible. The
process of achieving it is known as "education."

"The national socialist movement," Hitler himself has said,
"has given the state the directives for the education of our people. This education does not begin in one certain year and end
in another. The education of the individual never comes to an
end."

It hardly can come to an end, in fact, because it is totalitarian.
That is, it extends to every conceivable phase and aspect of life.
It extends to history, to geography, to philosophy, to art, music,
the theater and, of course, the schools. It also extends to religion,
science and mathematics. It extends to the homeliest, most intimate stuff of the everyday life of the people.

One ardent "educator" has held that the new Kultur policy
should even extend to wax models in store windows and to
children's dolls. The display of "Aryan style" wax models by

Jewish merchants is an insult to German womanhood, this patriot wrote at a time when Jews were still allowed to be merchants in the Third Reich, and Jewish children should not be allowed to play with "Aryan-appearing" dolls.

The nazis dealt with the first of these problems by wrecking and looting every Jewish place of business in Germany and forbidding Jews to open new ones, and with the second problem by impoverishing the Jews to such a degree that many of them could hardly afford dolls of any kind for their children—and by undertaking to drive them all out of Germany, men, women and children alike. These measures, however, were not primarily cultural in nature and purpose, as others have been and are:

Santa Claus, for example, was "co-ordinated," as early as 1936. He wore an S. A. uniform under his traditional costume when he appeared at the Berlin Christmas Fair that year, and he gave the nazi salute.

Dentists, also, have been subjected to the discipline of the new Kultur. They, too, are its agents. For do they not have waiting rooms where patients read and reflect? Do not they themselves talk to their patients under circumstances in which the patients are, perhaps, especially susceptible to suggestion, or at least cannot talk back?

This, in any event, was the argument a leading nazi dentist advanced at a professional convention. The dentist of the future, he said, must above all live in the spirit of the national socialist philosophy of life. The argument was persuasive, and it was provided that thenceforward students of dentistry must have four weeks' special training in such matters.

Fairy tales were among the first cultural treasure of the community of the people to be "co-ordinated." The national socialist *Teachers' Gazette* published nazi versions of "The Sleeping Beauty" and "Little Snow White" early in the history of the regime. The Sleeping Beauty, it informed teachers, is to be regarded as Germany, bewitched by alien powers, and the Prince who wakens her with a kiss is obviously Adolf Hitler. Similarly, Snow White is also clearly an allegorical personification of Germany. For is she not described as "white as the snow, red as blood and black as ebony"? And are these not indisputably the Reich's national colors? No attempt was made, apparently, to decide who the seven dwarfs were supposed to be.

One party office even wanted to co-ordinate the Grimm Brothers in person. Shortly after a publisher in Mainz had brought out a new edition of the Grimms' fairy tales, he received the following letter from the official nazi association of authors:

"Your firm has published a work by the Brothers Grimm. These authors are not yet registered with our office, as required by law. We request you to furnish us with their addresses within one week and at the same time to inform us whether the Brothers Grimm are foreign citizens or German authors residing abroad.   "—Heil Hitler!"

MYSTERY OF BLOOD

"It is the eternal power-currents of our blood which find formative expression in German Kultur," Fritz Moraller, a director of the Reich Chamber of Kultur, has said, and another only slightly lesser authority, Wilhelm Westecker, has expressed his essential agreement: in a book entitled, "Kultur in the Service of The Nation," Westecker has written, "A people creates art out of the dark urging of its blood."

If this is so—and the most exalted nazi authorities agree that it is so—then obviously an authoritarian and totalitarian regime will enforce in every sphere of the national culture the dogma of what Rosenberg has called "The Mystery of Blood." And this the nazis do.

The nazi dogma of blood and race asserts that the Nordic race has created all culture worthy of the name since the swirling mists of pre-history were dispelled. The great philosophers of India were Nordics, according to this dogma. So were the great religious mystics of Persia, the architects, sculptors and thinkers of Periclean Athens, the soldiers and statesmen of Rome and virtually all great creative human spirits since.

As long as this Nordic race maintains the purity of its blood and culture, nazi dogma says, the race establishes and maintains powerful, enlightened communities and creates great Kulturs. But when it allows alien and inferior races to mingle their blood and cultures with its own, it is undone both politically and culturally. Obviously, therefore, the Nordic strain in Germany must be safeguarded with the holiest zeal against the "corrupting" influence of Jews and other "enemies."

This is the dogma which has been set up as the first of all standards of judgment for Kultur in the New Germany. Is a work of art, a musical composition, a theory of physics, a novel, a play, "Nordic"? If it is not, it is not merely alien to Germany but also dangerous to the German soul.

Other dogmas of the national socialist philosophy of life have also been set up as cultural standards, less important, perhaps, than the dogma of blood and race, but more important, certainly, than any other standards that western civilization may apply to the arts and sciences as such.

In the Third Reich there is no such thing as what liberals mean by abstract truth, or art for art's sake, or freedom of intellectual inquiry, or individual critical judgment. There is only "truth" as it is revealed in nazi dogma, "art" only for the sake of the national socialist philosophy of life, "freedom" only to corroborate the principles of this philosophy of life, and "individual critical judgment" only of what lies outside that philosophy of life—which is not much.

"We do not know of or recognize truth for truth's sake or science for science's sake," Dr. Ernst Krieck proclaimed early in the history of the regime, and the nazis appointed him rector of the University of Heidelberg. (They appointed a veterinary surgeon rector of the University of Berlin.)

NO MORE HURRAHS

To make the dogma of blood and race effective as a standard of Kultur it was, of course, essential to determine who the bearers of the best blood were. This did not present as many difficulties to the nazis as it might to other men. Rosenberg solved the problem readily in his book, "Blood and Honor": The S. A., he wrote, are the chief custodians of the racial ichor. In the veins of the Storm Troopers, he said, courses the best German blood.

Logically enough, if this is the case, Viktor Lutze, chief of staff of the S. A., proclaimed that the Storm Troopers did indeed have a special responsibility in the cultural development of the New Germany:

"The S. A.," he announced, "has the task of being the champion of the new style [in art] which will transmit the spirit of our era to the future," and he established three prizes for the S. A. for poetry and literature, for music and for art.

The S. A. does not have a monopoly of the new Kultur, not as these lines are written, in any event. But "persons of German or similar blood" do. For to engage in any cultural occupation in Germany (including that of news dealer), it is necessary to belong to the Chamber of Kultur, and to belong to the Chamber of Kultur it is necessary to be Aryan.

It is "the proudest achievement" of the nazi Kultur program, Dr. Goebbels once said, to have created a Chamber of Kultur which is "one of the very few organizations in Germany, outside the party itself, to which no Jew, no half-Jew and no person with any Jewish blood at all belongs."

The Mystery of Blood holds sway, however, even if less mysteriously, in other organs of the new Kultur as well, among them the Reich Institute for the Advancement of German Literature. Controlled by Rosenberg, this Institute is a colossal censorship bureau, with a staff of 900 censors, whose approval is necessary for the publication of all books in Germany.

The censors are drawn from every walk of life, Hans Hagermeyer, director of the Institute, has explained; they number "ministers of state as well as labor foremen." "We are trying the experiment," Hagermeyer said, "of working not only with literary critics but also with those who approach a book from the viewpoint of the common man."

"The results of the experiment," he added, "are not altogether clear."

But whatever the literary capacities of the Institute's censors may be, their racial qualities are above reproach:

"When one looks through the file of our censors and sees their photographs," Hagermeyer exclaimed, "one is enraptured by the wonderful racial selection they represent!"

Nothing is too exalted and nothing too humble to be judged by the racial standard. At the one extreme, artists have been "advised" to represent Christ as a blonde, blue-eyed Nordic. And at the other extreme even ejaculations of pleasure and approbation should take the form, according to some enthusiasts, not of the Italianate "Bravo!" (this was before the Axis was forged and the fascists found that they, too, were Nordics) or of the Anglican "Hurrah!" but of the pure Nordic cry of the Walkyries: "Hojoto! Hejaha!"

THE LIMITS OF A GERMAN ARTISTIC FEELING

The belief that art and culture are international is regarded by the nazis as one of the most fallacious and dangerous of all the heresies which, they say, threaten civilization.

To at least one comrade, Wilhelm Westecker, in fact, the false doctrine of the international character of art and culture is insidious French propaganda, designed to establish Gallic supremacy. For what are called international art and culture, Westecker maintains, are really French art and culture, employed by the French for the corruption of the cultural traditions of other peoples. Other nazis regard this doctrine as a Jewish, rather than a French, deception. The claim that art and culture are international was used as the entering wedge, or jimmy, with which world Jewry broke into German cultural life, they say.

This French and/or Jewish plot almost succeeded in Germany, nazis say:

"It finally got to the point, not only of preaching the international character of art, but even of claiming that science in its origin was in no way connected with nationality!" Rosenberg once exclaimed, and Hitler himself has said that "the idle talk of an 'internationalism' of art is as stupid as it is dangerous."

In reality, the nazis say, true art and culture are peculiarly national and must serve national interests. The new Kultur which the nazis have undertaken to create is peculiarly "German" just as it is peculiarly "Nordic," before it is anything else. Only Germans are allowed to have a hand in it. Only "German" means of expression may be used. Only Kultur that testifies to the greatness of the German people is tolerated.

"For," as Hitler himself has proclaimed, "art is more effective than any other means which might be employed for the purpose of bringing home to the consciousness of a people the truth that their individual sufferings are only transitory, whereas the creative powers and therewith the greatness of the nation are everlasting. Art is the great mainstay of a people, because it raises them above the petty cares of the moment and shows them that their individual woes are not of such great importance after all."

It follows from this nationalistic theory of Kultur that history, for example, must not question the noble virtues of the race nor the heroic character of the national development. And music, too, must be, above all, "German."

"Freedom of research," Rosenberg has said, "is not to be confused with freedom to insult German history, the great German past, the great German race."

As for music: "Let youth seek new ways of musical expression—naturally within the limits of a German artistic feeling," Professor Dr. Paul Groener, vice-president of the Reich Chamber of Music and head of the Association of German Composers, has urged. "Far too much foreign music is still being played in Germany."

NATIONAL SOCIALIST PURITY OF HEART

Kultur in the Third Reich is national socialist as well as Nordic and German.

"In future," Dr. Goebbels has said apropos of art criticism, "the only persons who will be allowed to discuss the achievements of art will be those who understand this task with the purity of heart and the conviction of national socialists." Or, as Ministerial-direktor Dr. Alfred-Ingemar Berndt, former chief of the official government news agency, has put it: "Judgment

of works of art in the national socialist state can be based only
on the national socialist conception of Kultur. Only the party
and state are in a position to determine artistic values by reference to the national socialist artistic viewpoint."

What is this "national socialist viewpoint"? In addition to
race and nationalism it includes a bewildering variety of dogmas
and doctrines. Five of these, however, are especially important:

First, the new Kultur must be what the nazis call "healthy."
It is to shun what the regime considers morbid and ugly. It is
not to concern itself with deliberate attempts to express the subconscious. (Although the unwitting revelations it affords of the
nazi subconscious would provide a field day for a college of
psychiatrists.) As defined by the nazis, "healthy" also means
anti-modernistic. The regime damns most of the schools of art
that have developed since 1860.

"We love the healthy," Hitler has said. "Art must be a herald
of the sublime and the beautiful and the expositor of a natural
and healthy way of living. . . . It is not the purpose of art to
record symptoms of degeneracy, but rather to strive to overcome
such symptoms by directing the imagination to what is eternally
good and beautiful."

Much if not most modern art is morbid and diseased, according to Hitler:

"Indeed," he said on one occasion, "we considered most of
the activities among these cultural protagonists as criminal. If
we had entered into a public discussion with such people we
should have ended by sending them to some mental asylum or
to a prison, according to whether they believed in these fictions
of a morbid fancy as real inner experiences or merely offered
their deplorable lucubrations as a means of pandering to an
equally deplorable tendency of the times."

Second, the new Kultur must also be "heroic." There is to be
no sympathy for pacifism, no defeatism, no nonsense about turn-
ing the other cheek:

"The ideal of a new creative German art stands clear and
uncompromising before our eyes," Dr. Goebbels once declared.
"It will be manly and heroic and free from all effeminate senti-
mentalism."

Third, the new Kultur is to glorify fecundity and thus, it is hoped, stimulate the birth rate.

Fourth, the new Kultur must glorify life on the soil and ennoble the farmer.

And fifth, the workman, too, is to be exalted.

19. Worst Tyranny

Of all the tyrannies on human kind
The worst is that which persecutes the mind.

JOHN DRYDEN, "THE HIND
AND THE PANTHER"

A Demosthenes can be silenced in a meeting if only
fifty idiots, using their mouths and their fists, do
not wish to let him speak.

ADOLF HITLER, "MEIN KAMPF"

The greatest of spirits can be liquidated if its bearer
is beaten to death with a rubber truncheon.

ADOLF HITLER, "MEIN KAMPF"

THE SIMPLE, monumental character of the national socialist philosophy of life will require a certain period of time to produce in the spheres of art and philosophy really creative work corresponding to the greatness of the times," Rosenberg said early in the history of the regime. "What a revolution really signifies in its innermost meaning is never revealed in the days of its first breaking out, but only in the later years of its development."

Nevertheless, Rosenberg added, "The first ten steps which are taken along the road toward the goal are decisive."

By this time the nazis have had "a certain period of time" to achieve something positive in matters of culture. They have taken, not only "the first ten steps," but many more than that.

They themselves, in fact, proclaim that, in certain spheres, at least, they have revealed the true "innermost meaning" of the new Kultur. What is this true innermost meaning? What is the new Kultur like? What do the nazis offer in the place of what they destroy? Let us seek the answers to these questions in four different fields: in science, in music, in education and in art.

THE PLOT AGAINST NORDIC SCIENCE

"Everywhere in Germany it is clear that efforts are being made to direct scientific research in accordance with the national socialist spirit," Rosenberg announced in the third year of nazi rule. The nature of this national socialist spirit has been considered. But how is scientific research to be conducted in accordance with it? And what are the results of doing so? The utterances of nazi scientists provide the answers: they reveal what science has become, and the kind of men who are called scientists, and the kind of "thinking" these men do, in the New Germany:

"Modern physics," says Professor Rudolph Tomaschek, director of the Institute of Physics in Dresden, "is an instrument of [world] Jewry for the destruction of Nordic science."

Professor Wilhelm Mueller, of the Technical College of Aachen, goes beyond this. In a book entitled, "Jewry and Science," he reports that not only modern physics but all the other sciences are being used as implements for destroying civilization. This is how he describes the sinister plot:

The Jews, says Professor Mueller, are over-intellectual, excessively abstract in their thinking, remote from perception and reality, and at the same time materialistic. Applying these qualities of mind to the exploitation of science, says Professor Mueller, the Jews have deliberately set out to reduce all human experience to infinitesimal, artificial and meaningless units. These units, he says, the Jews then re-form and express in mathematical-chemical formulas which pretend to represent truth but which deny spiritual, moral and racial values.

These formulas, according to Professor Mueller, the Jews employ to undermine and destroy, first, all organic structures of thought and morals, and, second, and as a result, the peoples of the earth themselves, and most especially the Nordic people, who must have organic structures of thought and morals to live. Once this work of destruction has been accomplished, says Professor Mueller, the Jews will set up a world dictatorship.

This plot, according to Professor Mueller, reached a high point with Einstein's formulation of the theory of relativity and its dissemination throughout the world. The theory of relativity, Professor Mueller writes, "is directed from beginning to end toward the goal of transforming the living—that is, however, the non-Jewish—world of living essence, born from a mother earth and bound up with blood, and bewitching it into spectral abstractions in which all individual differences of peoples and nations, and all inner limits of the races are lost in unreality, and in which only an unsubstantial diversity of geometric dimensions survives which produces all events out of the compulsion of its godless subjection to laws."

The acclamation which seemed to pay tribute to the theory of relativity when it was first formulated was really rejoicing over "the approach of Jewish world rule which was to force down German manhood irrevocably and eternally to the level of the lifeless slave," Professor Mueller explains.

Other nazi scientists share Professor Mueller's views of Einstein's theory:

Professor Ludwig Bieberbach of Berlin has described Einstein as an "alien mountebank," and B. Thuering asserts that the theory of relativity is a declaration of war on Nordic man's conception of the world. Basically, says Thuering, it is a form of scientific Marxism, and therefore not a scientific theory at all, but a political one.

ARYAN PHYSICS

But alas for Nordic man: Einstein is not the only plotter against his soul whom nazi scientists have discovered. The whole field of science, they say, is riddled with concepts repugnant to the true Nordic spirit.

Even such apparently innocent subjects as statistics, and the concept of force in physics, must be studied "in accordance with the national socialist spirit," Professor Tomaschek reports. "Statistical laws in physics," he writes, "must be racially understood." Thuering, in turn, finds that the whole concept of force is alien to the Jews.

"It is no coincidence," Thuering writes, "that the half-Jew Heinrich Hertz and the full-Jew Einstein sought to construct a system of mechanics from which the concept of force entirely disappeared. The Jewish philosopher Spinoza likewise ignores this concept. It seems to be alien to the world-sense of the Jew. He therefore seeks to exclude it from the study of nature. . . . Einstein's theory of relativity disposed of the concept of force by a violent distortion of the concepts of time and space."

"German science" is, of course, vastly different in nazi eyes from the "Jewish" variety. Not only is it true, as opposed to the falseness of non-Aryan science, in fact, but it is the source of all truth in this field: True science is almost an exclusively Nordic German achievement, the nazis say.

"True physics is the creation of the German spirit," Professor Tomaschek proclaims, and, in fact, all "European science is the fruit of Aryan, or, better, German, thought."

This is also true of "German mathematics," in the considered judgment of Professor Bieberbach: "German mathematics," he says, "like all science in its present form, is most particularly the creation of Aryans. Only during the last century did some non-Aryans make contributions. These contributions were considerable in extent but . . . they were characterized by a lack of a sense of proportion and of intuition and by a destructive, critical logic and a fondness for denying perception."

The founding father of "German" or "Aryan" physics is, however, none of these gentlemen, but Professor Phillip Lenard of Heidelberg, and he has been appropriately honored by the nazis by means of a research institute at the University, named for him. In the introduction to his four volume work, "German Physics," Lenard writes:

"The question will be asked, Why 'German Physics'? I could have said, 'Aryan Physics' or 'The Physics of Nordic and Similar Men' just as well, or 'The Physics of Those Who Seek the Truth and Fathom It,' 'The Physics of Those Who Founded Natural Research.' 'Science is international and will always remain so,' it will be objected. A mistake always lies at the roots of this viewpoint, however. In reality, science, like everything else that mankind creates, is conditioned by race and blood. . . . The peoples of different countries who have handed down science of the same or a similar kind, like the German people, were able to do so only because and to the extent that they are or were equally a predominantly Nordic racial mixture. Peoples of another racial mixture have another way of engaging in science.

"Absolutely no people has ever begun natural research without basing its work on the fertile soil of the already existing achievements of Aryans. . . .

"A unique kind of Jewish physics has developed very extensively. . . .

"The Jew conspicuously lacks understanding for the truth, and for anything more than a merely apparent conformity with the reality which exists independently of human thought, being in this respect in contrast to the Aryan research scientist with his careful and serious will to truth. . . .

"Jewish physics is thus a phantom and a phenomenon of degeneration of fundamental German physics. . . ."

So much for the ten German Jews who won Nobel prizes for scientific achievement between 1905 and 1931.

THE RHYTHM OF GERMAN BLOOD

"The whole a-tonal movement [in music] in repugnant to the rhythm of the blood and soul of the German people, and precisely for that reason was encouraged by those in political power before," Rosenberg writes in his book, "Gestaltung der Idee."

"We reject all political thought of the past 150 years," he adds. "We also feel, moreover, a deep inner repudiation of the corresponding distorted imagery of the last several decades in the field of art and many of the musical structures which are repugnant to the German life rhythm."

This assertion that the encouragement of a certain kind of music is part of a world plot against the German nation is typical of the processes and products of the nazi mind. Made by a man as important as Rosenberg, it strikes a keynote for nazi Kultur policy.

The nazis have, in fact, silenced a-tonal music in Germany, frustrated the dark designs "those in political power before" had in encouraging it, and, in general, have done a thorough job of stamping out those musical patterns which are "repugnant to the German life rhythm."

Not only has music itself been "co-ordinated," but the composers who write it, too, the artists who play and sing it, the words which accompany it, the directors who conduct it, and the managers who try to make it pay.

Nazi music policy regulates everything from Mendelssohn's music—and his statues—and the titles and texts of Handel's oratorios and Mozart's operas to jazz. Music by modern composers like Paul Hindemith and Alban Berg has been, of course, the object of special attention. Some of Stravinsky's music, on the other hand, curiously enough, may be played in the New Germany.

The attack on Handel's oratorios opened in real earnest when it was announced that special ceremonies would be held in 1935 to commemorate the 250th anniversary of the composer's birth. No record can be found of official hostility toward Handel himself or toward his music as such, but the Old Testament, that is, non-Aryan, titles and themes of several of his works were bitterly denounced. Devout nazis found strongly repugnant to the German life rhythm such chorals as "Esther," "Israel in Egypt," "Deborah," and "Judas Maccabeus," and they demanded that these compositions be either purged of their non-Aryan content or suppressed.

Disconcerted, those responsible for the anniversary celebrations asked the nazi Chamber of Kultur for official "advice" as to how, if at all, they might honor the composer. The Chamber considered the problem at length. Finally it announced that the oratorios could be given as they were.

But the matter was not allowed to rest there. The nazi Kultur Community, controlled by Rosenberg, found the combination of Nordic music and Old Testament titles and themes intolerable in spite of what Dr. Goebbels' Chamber of Kultur had said, and it commissioned a guaranteed pure Aryan author to write new texts suitable to the times.

Two years later the first of these new texts was completed. The choral which the rest of the world still knows as "Judas Maccabeus" became in the New Germany, "Hero and Work for Peace." It describes "the distress and resurgence of the German people."

Four of Mozart's operas have been similarly purged. The standard German texts of "Figaro," "Don Giovanni," "Cosi Fan Tutte" and "Die Gaertnerin aus Liebe" were translated by a Jew, Hermann Levi, from original Italian texts written by Lorenzo da Ponte, another Jew, and were thus doubly accursed in nazi eyes. Something obviously had to be done. So new and Aryan texts were written by Dr. Siegfried Anheisser, whose given name alone surely testifies to his Aryan qualities.

The case against Mendelssohn required more drastic treatment, from the nazi viewpoint, for Mendelssohn was a Jew, and his music, according to nazi dogma, is therefore necessarily bad for the German soul. So the music was banned altogether and Aryan composers were summoned to provide new music for the "Midsummer Night's Dream."

To silence Mendelssohn's music was not, however, enough. For a statue of the composer stood before the Gewandhaus in Leipzig, and nazi logic required that the statue disappear, too. And so, accordingly, it did disappear. It was removed and smashed. Carl Goerdeler, lord mayor of Leipzig at the time, resigned in protest, but that did not restore the statue—nor the music. Mendelssohn's compositions are heard no more in the Third and Aryan Reich.

THE GERMAN SOUL IS SAVED

The fate of living composers, conductors and artists has been just as ineluctable in the New Germany as that of the dead. Some of those who offended against the rhythm of the German blood and soul repented and recanted and were allowed to stay. Others—especially "persons of alien blood"—were banished. The cases of Wilhelm Furtwaengler and Richard Strauss are typical of those who repented and recanted.

Furtwaengler, who was chief director of the Berlin Philharmonic and conductor at the State Opera, first got into serious difficulties late in 1934, when he wrote a signed article in a newspaper defending Hindemith and his music. Hindemith seems to be considered satisfactorily Aryan, but his music had been officially damned, even then, as "as bolshevistic as Stravinsky's." The nazis later changed their minds about at least some of Stravinsky's music, but Furtwaengler's defense of Hindemith set off an explosion that blew Furtwaengler out of both the Philharmonic and the State Opera for more than two years. Furtwaengler later made his peace with the nazis. Hindemith, however, never did. His music is still banned in the New Germany.

Richard Strauss was reported in the nazi press at the time of the Hindemith controversy to have telegraphed his support of the nazi viewpoint to Dr. Goebbels. Strauss, too, however, soon had troubles of his own with the authorities to deal with. He composed an opera based on Ben Jonson's "The Silent Woman" and had Stefan Zweig write the text. But Zweig was not Aryan and the nazis were outraged at this flouting of the dogma of blood and race. They violently attacked composer and author alike, and the onslaught finally became so savage that Strauss resigned from the presidency of the Chamber of Music and from the "Leadership" of the Association of German Composers, giving, as his grounds, ill health. After time had been allowed to heal the wounds, however, Strauss, too, made his peace with the nazis.

For others, though, peace was impossible. Hindemith left Germany. So did Alban Berg. So did Ernst Silberstein, cellist of the Klingler quartette, the best in the Reich, and the quartette disbanded. Two successive concert masters of the Berlin Philharmonic "resigned." So did Bruno Walter and Otto Klemperer and Fritz Busch and Erich Kleiber and Hans Knappertsbusch (although Knappertsbusch, too, later came to terms with the nazis). Leo Blech "retired because of reaching the age limit."

Insofar as it was menaced by music repugnant to its rhythm, the German soul has, presumably, been saved.

A STRIKING INABILITY TO THINK LOGICALLY

In the first five years of their rule, the nazis dismissed approximately 2,800 professors and teachers of lower ranks from German universities, or approximately one third the total number, and replaced them by others considered more "reliable" politically, according to Dr. Otto Wacker, Minister of Education in Baden.

During this same period the number of students attending colleges and universities in the Reich fell from just under 200,000 to just over 70,000, or by 65 per cent.

Students who still did attend institutions of higher learning in Germany, after five years of nazi rule, entered them with a preparatory education which the nazis had reduced by three years below pre-nazi standard requirements, furthermore.

Courses taught in German colleges and universities, moreover, from statistics to art and from physics to history, were permeated by the national socialist philosophy of life.

And in both the lower and the higher schools the time left after the subtraction of three years altogether was devoted to a considerably greater extent than had been the case before to sports and political activities.

The students, finally, had acquired the habit of exercising a censorship over their teachers and of engaging in demonstrations and making threats against them when they were displeased. This habit assumed such proportions that Bernhard Rust, Reich Minister of Education, warned the students to leave their professors alone so they could get the research and other work accomplished that was necessary to the regime. The students, however, defied Rust and continued their demonstrations and threats.

Thus fewer students, less well prepared, attend German colleges and universities than before the nazi revolution; they spend more of their time in non-academic pursuits and less time studying; and the courses they do study have been "co-ordinated" and are taught by less-experienced instructors who also have been "co-ordinated." Coming at a time when the nazi armaments program and economic boom increased the demand for trained men, the effects of nazi Kultur policy on German institutions of higher learning, once the strongholds of science and the training schools for men who led the world in physics, chemistry, physiology, medicine and mathematics, were disastrous.

By 1937 there were grave shortages of teachers, engineers and other trained men. The proficiency of apprentices declined. The army complained of defects in character and training among newly entering classes of student officers:

"Cadets show a striking inability to think logically," the *Militaer-Wochenblatt* declared late in 1938. "Important though it is to cultivate an ideal attitude toward life in the home, the school and the Hitler Youth, in the sphere of logical thinking there is no room for ideal wishes and hopes and dreams. . . . An absolutely indescribable passion for phrase-making is also conspicuous in recent classes. The men themselves concede that they are only interested in covering as many as possible sheets of paper with writing."

Almost, if not quite, as serious, were the effects on science and industry of the nazi attack on intelligence. By the Winter of 1938-1939, Germany was losing the leadership it had held for many years in the field of chemistry, for example, according to *Die Chemische Industrie*, organ of the nazis' own compulsory national organization of the chemical industry. Standards in German chemistry were jeopardized to an extent that the national economy and national defense would soon be affected, *Die Chemische Industrie* said. The technical colleges were short of teachers, it declared, teachers who were available were overworked, classes were too large and colleges were unable to keep up with new scientific developments. There were also too few students to provide the number of trained chemists the nation required and standards of work were declining even among these. Laboratory equipment in the Reich was outdated and otherwise inadequate, *Die Chemische Industrie* asserted.

These, then, are some of the logical implications of the efforts Rosenberg reported to conduct scientific research in the spirit of the national socialist philosophy of life.

THE PURGE OF THE ART GALLERIES

Perhaps the most ambitious claims the nazis have put forward in behalf of their new Kultur are those they make in the field of art. On the one hand, the nazis have suppressed art of which they disapprove on a scale and with a thoroughness that are noteworthy even by their standards. And on the other hand they have produced, or least exhibited, examples of their own conceptions of the true, the beautiful and the good in such numbers that it is possible here, as it is not in most other fields, to judge nazi performance as well as nazi threats and promises.

The nazis began by assailing most modern artists, both German and foreign—virtually all those whom so able a critic as C. J. Bulliet has called "The Significant Moderns." Cezanne, Van Gogh, Gauguin, Matisse, Picasso; Nolde, Barlach, Liebermann, Feuerbach, Boecklin, Kokoschka, Corinth, Dix, Pechstein, Hofer, Grosz, Chagall: they are all decadent, degenerate and quite probably even criminal, too, said Hitler and Rosenberg and the other apostles of the new and truly German-Nordic art.

Works by the offending artists were purged from galleries and museums, and so were the directors and others who had exhibited them. Goering ordered the greatest of the purges. Acting as Prime Minister of Prussia, he directed Rust in the latter part of July, 1937, to apply nazi principles of art to all public collections of works of art in Prussia "without regard to legal forms and questions of ownership."

More than 6,500 works of art were removed from Prussian galleries and museums in the purge that followed this order. Most of them were turned over to a big moving and storage company in Berlin, which put them in one of its warehouses. Some were kept in a damp cellar, where they rotted. A special collection of outstanding examples of the "degenerate" art was made up and exhibited in Munich, Berlin and elsewhere. It proved enormously popular. Later, leading nazis helped themselves to some of the most famous of the pictures and such others as could be sold abroad for foreign exchange were disposed of in that way.

In the end, the nazis decided that some of the artists originally anathematized as "degenerate" were not so bad, perhaps, after all. Nolde, Corinth and Marc, among others, were rehabilitated. None of these men's works was restored to its original owner, of course, and no compensation was paid for the seizure of the works and the other losses incurred. The rehabilitation did serve one immediately practical purpose, however: it raised to very high levels the value of the works of art that the nazis had appropriated for themselves.

HITLER KICKS SOME HOLES

In the Summer of 1937 the nazis showed for the first time on a large scale what the new Kultur was supposed to mean in terms of art. They opened a great new gallery in Munich, "The House of German Art," built under the personal supervision of Hitler himself, and they exhibited in it works of contemporary art which they said exemplified the new ideals of the true, the beautiful and the good.

"The representative exhibit in the new House of German Art will show clearly what national socialism requires of true art," said Adolf Ziegler, president of the Reich Chamber of Art, at the opening ceremonies. "It will point the way and provide a model for all those who have been unable up to the present to free themselves from false conceptions."

Ziegler himself had had to free himself from some false conceptions, too, as it happened. For a time, he had dabbled and daubed in various modern styles of painting. But he had seen the light and been saved. By a happy happenstance, Ziegler had once painted a portrait of Hitler's niece "Geli," to whom the Chancellor was deeply and romantically attached. Hitler had liked the portrait, and when "Geli" committed suicide some time later, he cherished the picture all the more. He decided that Ziegler was a great artist, and he saw to it that he became president of the Chamber of Art.

This first exhibit of the new national socialist art consisted of approximately 900 works, chosen from almost 15,000 submitted. Hitler himself, attended by Heinrich Hoffmann, the chief official party photographer, made the final selection, re-

jecting several works which had originally been accepted by
a nazi jury presided over by Ziegler. Hitler was so annoyed
with some of the paintings the jury had accepted that he not
only rejected them but kicked holes in several.

There was room for differences of opinion as to the artistic
merit of the works finally exhibited. There could be no question, however, but that they satisfied the nazi terms of reference for true art: They were "Nordic," they were "German,"
and they were "nazi." They were "healthy," as the nazis understand the term, they were "heroic" in the same sense, they
glorified fecundity, they ennobled the peasant and they exalted
the workman.

There were 52 works of art dealing with party subjects—
all, naturally, in a highly flattering (by nazi standards) manner. There was a bust of Julius Streicher, four busts and six
oil paintings of Hitler, and two paintings of the house where
the Chancellor was born. The first painting the visitor saw was
a portrait of Hitler and almost the last was a huge symbolic
picture of him clad in shining armor, mounted on a white
charger and bearing aloft a swastika banner. Another picture
showed Hitler addressing a small political meeting, apparently
in a beer hall and presumably in the early history of the party.
It was entitled, "In the Beginning Was the Word." The S. A.
and S. S. men portrayed in the exhibit were all without exception heroically tall and slender, idealistic figures, dazzlingly
blonde and blue-eyed.

Franz Eichhorst's were almost the only convincing war pictures, notably a "Reconnaissance Patrol" and a "Guard on the
Yser." But Eichhorst had been an artist of repute long before
Hitler, Hoffmann and Ziegler had conferred their approval on
him. It was Ferdinand Spiegel's ethereal, blue-eyed, yellow-
haired figures of soldiers, sailors and fliers, and a collar-ad
wounded officer, that seemed to represent the truly new school.

A whole series of landscapes and farm scenes glorified German blood and soil. Hans Voelcker portrayed a gardener with
highly polished fingernails; George Ehmig, among others,
an immaculate barnyard; and Julius Paul Junghanns a selection
of goats so sublimated, so celestial, that it was impossible to

imagine that any of them could have smelled bad. Rudolf
Werner portrayed asphalt workers busy at their ennobling work
with every hair in place and not a drop of perspiration apparent
among them.

Ziegler himself was represented by a still life, a symbolic
female nude, "Terpsichore," a group of four more nudes por-
traying "The Four Elements" and two head studies. One of
these studies, "Liselotte," turned out, on close examination, to
be the element air in a blue polo shirt. The other, "Hertha,"
was the element earth in a white shirtwaist. The symbolic nudes
seemed both uncomfortable and uneasy. To paraphrase Hay-
don's comment on West's neo-classical paintings, they looked
as if they had never been naked before.

All in all, the true, healthy new German art was nothing
startlingly novel. The worst of it was candy-box cover, "pin-up"
and calendar art. And as for even the best, as one critic with
a boldness that was unusual in Germany said:

"What is offered in the place of what characterizes the past
is less a new friend than an old one of long standing. Especially
as regards the paintings, it is essentially the style of the declining 19th century. It is a return to ways of painting which ex-
cited attention and were considered revolutionary in the days
of our fathers."

20. The Three-Year Plan

*The best laid schemes o' mice and men
Gang aft a-gley.*

ROBERT BURNS, "TO A MOUSE"

THE NAZIS have a plan for the Germans' economic life, just as they do for everything else: the so-called Four-Year Plan. Hitler promulgated it at the 1936 party congress at Nuremberg. The Reich, he said, must be made as independent as possible of foreign commodities, and he appointed Goering to accomplish this task and gave him four years in which to do it.

The Four-Year Plan was a Three-Year Plan in reality, however. For it was above all a plan for war, a plan to make Germany as strong as possible against British—and, in the last analysis, American—sea power and the blockade which is sea power's most terrible weapon. And Goering did not have four years to carry out his plan. He only had three years. It was almost exactly 36 months to the day from the promulgation of the plan that Germany went to war against Britain again.

MALADY

It was a grievously stricken national economy that the Four-Year Plan was designed to strengthen and invigorate, an economy that had been sick for more than 20 years. Its fundamental character was this:

Despite a natural poverty in raw materials, the Reich had built up a highly developed industry. Raw materials and semi-finished goods were imported. Skilled craftsmanship, technique and science and able management fashioned these raw materials and semi-finished goods into finished products. Aggressive and intelligent merchandising sold the finished products to the outside world at a good and sufficient profit. A great merchant fleet bore the goods to all the corners of the earth.

For a time, this economy thrived. Capital was accumulated both at home and abroad. Population increased rapidly. The standard of living was one of the highest in the world.

But the First World War shattered this economic system. The Reich consumed its capital at home and lost its capital abroad, its colonies, its merchant fleet and its markets. The German national economy has been insolvent vis-a-vis the rest of the world ever since: It has not been able to finance the purchase abroad, not only of the raw materials and semi-finished goods that are necessary to keep the national industry operating, but also of those that are necessary to feed and clothe and house the German people.

Successive governments—and the outside world—have kept the Reich national economy functioning by resort to a series of desperate expedients. In the years 1919 to 1923, as Douglas Miller points out, Germany financed itself by selling paper marks. From 1924 to 1929 it kept itself going by selling long-term bonds. Then it lived on short-term bank advances. And then Germany "borrowed commodities"; it imported goods, that is, against promises to pay, and then either did not pay at all or paid in German goods its creditors may or may not have wanted, in quantities they may or may not have been able to use, at prices the commodities may or may not have been worth.

Neither the German boom of 1924 to 1929 nor the German depression that followed was essentially like the booms and depressions in other countries at those same times. The German boom was even more artificial and senseless than the others, because it depended entirely on foreign loans the Reich could not repay, and the German depression was a relapse into a condition of chronic sickness to which other nations were relatively immune.

CURE?

The nazis began by treating the national economic sickness symptomatically: They spent billions of marks to reduce the unemployment which was one of the chief outward and visible signs of the inner malady. They went on to spend billions more to build up armaments. They spent still further billions to subsidize German exports in order to obtain foreign exchange at almost any cost.

Production increased and unemployment declined. But the more the nazis spent, the higher German prices rose. Outraged by nazi policies, a host of enemies organized to boycott German goods. The balance of international payments (or at least the balance of obligations to pay) went from bad to worse. It became harder and harder to finance imports. The export subsidies were not enough to overcome the price differentials between the Reich and foreign markets, and even if they had been enough, they could not be kept up forever.

Preliminary, tentative attempts to make the country independent in respect of foodstuffs had no real, appreciable effect. Raw material shortages became chronic and increasingly severe. In the given political situation, the arms that Germany was accumulating could not be expected to solve the problem soon enough by winning a war that would be sufficiently rich in booty to solve it.

Economically, Germany was in an exposed position even in peacetime. In a war, its weaknesses might speedily prove fatal. Something drastic had to be done.

There were two principal possibilities:

One would have been to abjure the persecutions of the Jews, the Christian churches, the liberals, the socialists and the other helpless minorities and to abandon the gigantic arms program and to rely, in foreign policy, on the relatively peaceable means that the Republic had employed with considerable success.

But this, in view of the character and purposes of the nazis, was only a theoretical possibility. The nazis had not the slightest intention of abjuring their domestic savageries nor of abandoning their plans for foreign conquests or their preparations for them.

Practically, therefore, only one course of action was possible, the course adopted under the name of the Four-Year Plan. The essence of the Plan was this:

First, domestic production of essential raw materials and other commodities was to be increased as much as possible. But since this could not be enough by any means to satisfy German needs, artificial substitutes were also to be developed and produced in the largest possible quantities and consumption was to be reduced to a minimum and waste utilized to the maximum. Thus fewer products would have to be imported from abroad. At the same time, German exports would be maintained and if possible increased. The balance of payments would become "favorable," or at least less "unfavorable." A margin would be available for buying abroad such commodities as the Reich had to have and was unable or did not choose to produce at home. And Germany would be better provisioned and armored against blockade.

These, at least, were the hopes that inspired the promulgation of the Four-Year Plan.

MODEL

The most convenient way to study the Four-Year Plan in operation is to study it in a regional economy that is a miniature model, a microcosm, of the national economy as a whole. Saxony is such a microcosm. The basic characteristics, the basic strengths and weaknesses of the German economic system in its entirety are also the basic characteristics and strengths and weaknesses of the Saxon regional economic system. And in Saxony these fundamental features, being both smaller in scale and at the same time sharper in outline and accentuated in degree, are more clearly to be seen and comprehended.

A combination of poverty in raw materials, a highly developed industry, a dense population and a lack of profitable foreign markets (plus, of course, nazi policies) created the problems that the nazis tried to solve by means of the Four-Year Plan. These are precisely the outstanding characteristics of the Saxon regional economy. Saxony is even poorer in raw materials, even more highly industrialized and even more densely populated, and has been even worse hit by the loss of foreign markets, than the Reich as a whole.

One twelfth of the total population of Germany, one ninth of all persons in the Reich engaged in industry and the handicrafts and one fourth of all German textile workers live and work and have their beings in a Saxony that is only one thirtieth of the nation's total area.

In the Reich as a whole, the density of population is 139.1 inhabitants per square kilometer. In Saxony it is 346.8. In only one other region in Germany is the density of population greater: the Saar Territory, with 423.9 inhabitants per square kilometer.

In the Reich as a whole before the war, 40.4 per cent of all gainfully employed persons were engaged in industry and the handicrafts. In the highly industrialized Rhineland the corresponding figure was 48.5 per cent. In Westphalia it was 52 per cent. In Saxony it was 56.5 per cent.

A fine-mesh network of railways and a high percentage of automobile ownership bear witness to, and form part of, Saxony's highly developed industry, dense population and high standard of living. In Germany as a whole there are 124 kilometers of railway line for every 1,000 square kilometers of territory. In Saxony there are 219. In Germany as a whole there is one automobile for every 27 inhabitants. In Saxony there is one for every 22.

Saxony is primarily a producer of consumers' goods. In the Reich as a whole, 50 per cent of all industry was engaged in producing consumers' goods before the war, whereas in Saxony the figure was 60 per cent, according to one official Saxon estimate, and even higher, according to others.

The overwhelming proportion of the raw and semi-finished goods used in Saxon industry in times of peace is imported from elsewhere and the overwhelming proportion of the manufactured products is shipped elsewhere when they are finished.

IDEAL INDUSTRY

From the point of view of the Four-Year Plan, the ideal German industry is one with three outstanding characteristics:

First, it uses the highest possible proportion of domestic materials and, accordingly, the lowest possible proportion of materials that must be imported.

Second, it makes of these preponderantly domestic materials a product that can be sold at a price appreciably higher than the cost of the materials.

And third, the product is suitable for export.

Two industries that flourish in Saxony come as close as any industry can to being such ideal Four-Year Plan industries. One is the tourist trade: It attracts foreign visitors to Saxony, where they spend foreign currency for what are overwhelmingly German "products" and, to the extent that foreign "products" are involved at all, mostly on such as were paid for long ago if they are going to be paid for at all: art galleries, the opera, and the scenery, the railways and the hotels.

The other ideal Four-Year Plan industry in Saxony is the porcelain industry in Meissen, where "Dresden china" is made just outside Dresden itself.

Only one minor ingredient in Meissen porcelain must be imported, a special earth that is bought in Norway. All the other materials are found near the plant itself.

German artistry and technical and scientific skill make of these raw materials one of the most highly finished of all products. By far the greatest part of the sale price of the product goes into wages and salaries and interest and dividends to support the German workmen and artisans and chemists and engineers who produce it, the German laborers and contractors who erected the plant and the German lenders who advance the liquid capital to finance them.

And, finally, Meissen porcelain is sold all over the world for precious foreign exchange which can be used to pay for imports of foodstuffs and other commodities that Germany cannot obtain at home.

From the first scientific purifying and mixing operations with which the clays are treated to the last deft painting of the bud of a flower on a teacup or of the complexion of a shepherdess in a group of tiny figures, skill and artistry mean everything at Meissen. The requirement of a five year apprenticeship for all workers in the art departments testifies to the appreciation by the industry of the importance of this skill and artistry, and the respect which the Meissen trademark, the slender, curving, conventionalized crossed swords in cobalt blue, inspires all over the world, testifies to the success with which this appreciation has been translated into fact.

The skill and artistry that Meissen brings to the porcelain industry are typical of German skill and artistry at their best, and the triumphs that they have won in world markets are typical of the triumphs on which the Reich has built a great and prosperous national industry. But Meissen is also typical of German industry in another and less happy respect: it suffers disastrously from a loss of markets (and did so long before the Second World War).

The nazi state-financed boom did something to restore the domestic German market. Officers' clubs, especially, bought porcelain for their quarters. But the foreign market for porcelain never really recovered from the First World War, the overthrow of the princely houses that had formerly bought one-third of Meissen's entire production, the changes in the ways of living and styles of interior decorating that took place in the first two decades of the twentieth century and the development of porcelain industries and their protection by tariff barriers in other countries.

And the porcelain industry is, unhappily for Germany, anything but typical of the Reich national economy in its virtual independence of foreign raw materials. On the contrary, it is precisely Germany's dependence on foreign commodities that is one of the principal causes of the adoption of the Four-Year Plan.

TINKLING VALLEYS

Tucked away in the peaceful little "tinkling valleys" of Saxony in the "music nook" of Germany is an industry that provides a perfect example of one of the chief problems that

confront the German national economy. The industry is the
musical instrument industry and the problem that confronts
it is that of obtaining the foreign materials it requires. In
Markneukirchen, Klingenthal and Schoeneck, and to an only
slightly lesser extent in Zwota, Erlbach, Brunndobra and
Georgenthal, all lying near each other in Saxony, 80 per cent
of the entire German musical instrument and instrument string
industry is concentrated.

Just as in the case of Meissen porcelain, it is the craftsmanship of the artisan that gives precious value to the finished
product. The cost of the woods and tortoise shell and of the
sheep and cat entrails used is only a small fraction of the price
of the finished instrument. But most of the materials must be
imported from the outside world, and there's the rub. For Germany has found it harder and harder, ever since the First
World War, to pay for the materials it must buy abroad if it
is to maintain its economic existence. And as a consequence Germany has lived precariously, in what amounts to national bank-
ruptcy, ever since 1918, and Saxony even more precariously
than Germany as a whole, and the tinkling valleys of the music
nook even more precariously than Saxony as a whole.

In almost every house in some of these towns, highly skilled
artisans fashion violins or clarinets or accordions. Approximately
9,000 persons, a majority of the whole population of the region, many of them working in their own homes, earn their
livings by making instruments. From these simple houses, little
shops and occasional big factories, artistic and commercial relationships extend out all over the world. More than one modest
home in Markneukirchen, for example, has dealings with more
than 100 foreign firms.

But both artistic and commercial connections are as fragile
as threads of gossamer. For exactly the precisely correct type
of wood or tortoise shell of exactly the precisely correct age and
condition must be used for each part of an instrument, or the
quality of the instrument is inferior at the outset or speedily
deteriorates and the musician knows what has happened and he
and his fellow artists buy elsewhere. And although a log is the

most natural of natural products, the logs that make the best musical instruments must be bought in a score of out-of-the-way parts of the world and paid for in a dozen different currencies which Germany must somehow obtain unless it can get the woods by barter:

Jacaranda from Bahia and Rio, ebony from Mauritius and Zanzibar and Madagascar and Ceylon, zebra wood from Cayenne, mahogany from Santo Domingo and Jamaica and Cuba, grenadill from South Africa and pernambuco wood and coco wood and satinwood and rosewood and ailanthus, and especially pine and maple from the Siebenbuergen in Rumania and the Carpathians. Tortoise shell must be imported from Africa and South America, and even most of the sheep gut is bought in England, Scotland and Australia.

Celluloid, which Germany produces at home, can be used instead of tortoise shell for some purposes. More sheep are being raised in the Reich, as part of the Four-Year Plan, and therefore more gut can be bought in the home market. But not even the Germans have been able so far to invent synthetic substitutes for jacaranda and ebony and satinwood and ailanthus. And unless and until German scientists can produce substitutes out of test tubes, the German government has to find, somewhere, somehow, the means to buy the natural products abroad.

It was largely to obtain the foreign exchange with which to buy foodstuffs and the natural products abroad for such industries as this one—and, above all, for armaments, of course—which absolutely must have them that the nazis adopted the Four-Year Plan.

The artificial textile mills in Plauen, the lignite gasoline plants in the countryside near Bautzen, the collection of meat bones by school children and the lowering of the amount of tobacco in cigars and cigarettes—these and a hundred other plants and processes and privations, semicomic and altogether tragic in their ineluctable implication of war, are intended to reduce the amount of foreign exchange Germany has to use for products that are not absolutely indispensable, so that it will have more foreign exchange for products that are absolutely indispensable—like zebra wood and mahogany and pernambuco wood and coco and grenadill and rosewood for the tinkling valleys of the music nook.

THE PETTICOAT DISAPPEARED

The most dangerous malady from which the German national economy suffered in the era between World Wars was a lack of foreign markets. The rest of the world did not buy enough German goods at a good enough price to keep the Reich's business organism functioning in health and vigor.

And in this respect, too, Saxony is the best place to study the ills of the national economy as a whole and the Four-Year Plan for treating them. Because the Saxon regional economy is even more dependent on foreign markets than the national economy as a whole, it has lost an even greater proportion of its foreign markets than the national economy as a whole, the causes of the losses are even clearer, the effects even more disastrous—and the progress of the "treatment" prescribed in the Four-Year Plan can, consequently, be more readily observed.

Of all Saxon industries to be stricken by the loss of foreign markets, the textile industry of the Vogtland, centering in Plauen, is the one where the ravages of the disease are most clearly to be perceived. The Saxon textile industry fell sick in 1910 and has never been really healthy at any time since. The nature and causes of the sickness are typical, in kind, although acute in degree, of the nature and causes of the sickness of the whole national economic system.

It was something as apparently frivolous (to most men, at least) as a change in women's fashions that first struck at the textile industry of the Vogtland. For two of its most important products were lace and embroidery, and women simply stopped wearing lace and embroidery. The petticoat disappeared, the shirtwaist was seen no more, and an entire industry was brought face to face with ruin. It was the least predictable, the least preventable, the least reversible of revolutions, a revolution in women's styles of dress. It was also typical of the disasters that now broke over the heads of other industries, and over the head of German industry as a whole.

A whole world changed its ways of living, and the industrial consequences were at least as far-reaching as the social implications: More and more dwellings were built without generous fireplaces and mantelpieces, for example, dining room plate rails and parlor whatnots fell into disfavor, people began to live in small apartments and to move often—and the porcelain industry was stricken. For porcelain is hard to move and there was no room for it in the dwellings of the new era even if people were willing to cart it around with them and even if they did succeed in moving it intact from place to place every May 1. Again, the hanging garden style of hat disappeared with the shirtwaist, the petticoat and the whatnot—and the artificial flower industry was stricken, too. There were scores and hundreds and thousands of changes like these—changes in styles and habits and morals and diet and methods of heating and transportation and bringing up children—and each change meant something for industry, something good or something bad. For the textile industry in the Vogtland and the porcelain industry in Meissen it meant mostly something bad.

German industry as a whole suffered less than Saxon industry did from these first changes. But at about that same time there began to make itself felt a tendency which in the long run was to have far worse consequences for the Vogtland and Saxony and all Germany than changes of fashion and ways of living could ever have: The United States and other countries began to make for themselves the products they had been buying from Germany.

It was part of a trend by which the Reich had profited earlier. The Germans, for example, had begun by importing English textiles. Then they had imported English machines and had made their own textiles. And they had ended by making machines and textiles alike and exporting both.

The rest of the world now followed suit. Other countries began by importing German (as well as English) goods, went on to import the machines and make their own goods, and ended by making machines and goods alike, and selling both in markets where they competed with the German goods and machines.

Then came a catastrophe that hastened this process and

brought a thousand other disasters in its train: four years of war and blockade throttled Germany and shut it off almost entirely from its markets. Anything and everything the rest of the world could make for itself it speedily began to produce at home, and it erected tariff barriers to protect its own new industries, just as Germany had done earlier and continued to do.

The catastrophe of the war itself was followed by the catastrophe of the peace. The victorious allies treated Germany something as a victorious Germany had earlier treated some of its conquered foes.

In order to recover its national economic health, the Reich would have had to forswear its dreams and plans of aggrandizement. This the Germans refused to do. The Reich national economy, accordingly, has never been on a sound basis at any time since 1918—or 1914.

BONANZAS AT A LOSS

The School of Mines in Freiberg, in Saxony, is the oldest technical college in the world, its local admirers say. For 200 years it has studied and discovered ways to make mining more scientific and more profitable. Under the Four-Year Plan, the Lignite Research Institute of the School was pressed into service in one of the principal phases of the attempt to make Germany as independent as possible of foreign imports: it became a center for research in the production of gasoline, which Germany lacked, from lignite, which Germany had in abundance.

Thus in respect of the new synthetic substitutes, as well as in so many other respects, Saxony is again a miniature model by means of which the nature and causes and effects of the Four-Year Plan can conveniently be studied. For the application of the genius of German research to the production of domestic substitutes to replace foreign natural products is one of the chief phases of the Plan.

Research in production of gasoline from lignite is the most important Four-Year Plan task carried out by the Freiberg School of Mines, but the School's activities cover the whole range of mining, and its studies of other problems also play parts in the plan.

Almost all metals except gold and platinum are found in Saxony: lead, zinc, tin, tungsten, bismuth, cobalt, nickel, iron, molybdenum and silver. At several periods of history, mining has been the leading industry of various parts of Saxony. Silver once made Annaberg one of the richest towns in Europe. Saxon mines employed 12,000 men as recently as 1860.

But the mines petered out, richer deposits were found elsewhere, the Saxon mines could be worked only at a heavy loss, and Germany bought its minerals from other countries.

The Reich could do this, however, only as long as it could obtain the foreign exchange with which to finance imports. And then a time came when Germany could no longer do this—and wished to be independent of foreign supplies for the event of war, too. Hence the Four-Year Plan. The nazis reopened Germany's old mines and worked them again, even at a heavy loss when necessary.

As part of the Four-Year Plan, the nazis ordered a survey of the mining possibilities in Saxony. Research at Freiberg and elsewhere was intensified. (The Freiberg School found ways of doubling the amount of metal that could be extracted from certain low grade ores.) Hopes of new "silver rushes" and other mining "bonanzas" reawakened in towns whose exhausted mines had lain idle for generations and in some cases for centuries: bitter-sweet hopes based on prospects of "silver rushes" and "bonanzas" at a loss: of the revival of an industry which might help a few towns and countrysides but which would be a debit on the national economic ledgers—but which had to be revived as a counsel of semi-despair because that was part of the only hope of world empire and world rule.

THE PLAN WITHOUT ANY END

So much for the miniature model. So much for the Four-Year Plan in Saxony. But what of the greater problem, the problem of the national economy as a whole, its sickness and the attempts, by means of the Plan, to cure it?

No plan could, in itself, cure the German national economy, of course. The only thing that could do that would be a reorganization of Europe or a redistribution of the world's goods or the devising of a new system for obtaining access to them, or all of these things. But the Four-Year Plan could at least, the nazis hoped, do this much: it could keep the German national economy going well enough and long enough for the Reich to be able to fight and win a war which *would* cure the fundamental illness, by enabling Germany to "divide up the world anew," as Dr. Goebbels said: to take away from the vanquished the things that Germany needed—and, over and above these, all the things it wanted.

There is no precise way of measuring the success of the Plan, because there has never been a program of precise objectives, stated in statistics, that the Plan was expected to achieve. Even the time limit for the Plan was never as definite as the name implied. A German newspaper called it the "Plan Without Any End" as early as January, 1938, and when the first four years elapsed, in September, 1940, Hitler extended the Plan for another four.

The extent to which Germany is independent of foreign commodities, furthermore, depends on a variety of circumstances which cannot be determined in advance—or, in some cases, determined at all.

How much gasoline does Germany need to wage a war? It depends, obviously, both on how much civilian consumption can be reduced and on how much military needs increase. But nobody can know in advance how much the armed forces will need, because nobody can be sure what kind of a war the war will be or how long it will last. The nazis might think they know, and they might make their plans accordingly, but their plans also might gang a-gley, as plans have a way of doing.

And in addition to the questions of demand there are also the questions of supply. Sources oversea are bound to be cut off in a war with Britain. That much, at least, is definite. But how much can be seized in the form of booty from other countries? How much can be counted on from Rumania? From Russia? How much damage will bombers do to wells? To synthetic gasoline-producing plants? Nobody can know the answers in advance.

Subject to these reservations, however, the following data,

provided by Douglas Miller, on Germany's deficiencies in the most vital of raw materials, give some indication of the difficulties that have confronted Goering in his attempts to make the Reich "blockade proof." Failing victory in a world war, any such attempts will indeed have to go on "without any end":

Rubber

Consumption in a "normal" year	65,000 tons in 1935
Imports in a "normal" year	63,900 tons in 1935
Principal substitute	"Buna," made from coal and lime
Estimated production of the substitute for the most recent year for which data are available	rate of 20,000-25,000 tons per year at the end of 1938
Cost of substitute compared with that of natural product	Four times as great

Textile Fibers

Consumption in a "normal" year	969,000 tons in 1937
Imports in a "normal" year	684,000 tons in 1937
Principal substitutes	cell wool and rayon, made from cellulose
Estimated production of the substitutes for the most recent year for which data are available	cell wool 300,000-325,000 tons and rayon 100,000 tons in 1940
Cost of substitute compared with that of natural product	cell wool costs 1.60 marks per kilogram compared with 1.10 marks for cotton

Motor Fuel and Oils

Consumption in a "normal" year	5,150,000 tons in 1937
Imports in a "normal" year	gasoline and Diesel oil alone: 2,406,000 tons in 1936
Synthetic product produced from lignite and bituminous coal	
Estimated production for most recent year for which data are available	1,850,000 tons in 1937
Cost of substitute compared with that of natural product	Three times as great

Foodstuffs

No significant improvement in degree of independence of foreign imports has proven possible. Apparent improvements are for the most part unreal. An increase in the proportion obtained at home of needs of edible fats which the nazi statistics claim is due primarily to the fact that the Reich organized a huge whale-fishing fleet which brought in 91,800 tons of whale oil in the Spring of 1938, for example. But the whaling fleet cannot operate during a war with Britain, and it therefore contributes nothing toward achieving the Reich's wartime autarchy aims. Dairy and poultry farming, similarly, are largely dependent on fodders which must be imported from overseas.

The following table is taken from a report of the Institute for Business Research, a semi-official nazi agency, and gives the Institute's estimates of the percentage of the German consumption of key foodstuffs supplied by domestic agriculture in 1936:

Foodstuff	*Percentage of consumption supplied by German agriculture*
Bread, cereals, potatoes, sugar, coarse vegetables (cabbage), veal, mutton, milk, fresh-water fish	95-100 per cent
Total meat, total vegetables	90-94 per cent
Eggs, honey, total fruit	80-89 per cent
Total dairy products	80 per cent
Butter and cheese	75-80 per cent
Bacon and lard	60-69 per cent
Margarine (raw products used in production)	5-10 per cent
Total fats	50-55 per cent

Iron and Steel:

Consumption in a "normal" year	22,000,000 tons
Imports in a "normal" year (ore plus scrap)	11,200,000 tons

Non-ferrous metals:

Zinc: "Normal" needs covered by domestic production of approximately 200,000 tons

Aluminum: All the bauxite ore must be imported, but it is readily accessible, mostly in Hungary, Jugoslavia and Italy; the ore costs only a small fraction of the value of the finished aluminum

Copper: "Normal" needs average 200,000 tons per year; production of copper from domestic ore was only 25,000 tons in 1936; limited supplies are available in Finland and Jugoslavia

Lead: Consumption averages 220,000 tons; production from domestic ore was 60,000 tons in 1937

Manganese: The Reich is almost altogether dependent on imports, most of which come in "normal" times from Russia

The Reich's dependence on imports of foreign non-ferrous metals is one of the weakest points in its whole armor for war. Little can be done to increase domestic production of most of them. The principal means for dealing with this problem under the Four-Year Plan are these:

1. More intensive exploitation of German deposits of copper, lead and zinc.

2. Greater economy in the use of the metals.

3. Greater use of domestically produced light metals, notably aluminum and magnesium.

4. Development of other substitutes, such as plastics, glass and porcelain.

21. Bread—

Formerly the soldier received 20 pfennigs. By this was clearly meant, "Your work as a soldier I cannot pay you for, nor does the Fatherland attempt to pay you for it. What it does do is provide you your nourishment, clothing and physical well being. Precisely in this sense are you a soldier!" And a soldier has honor. Does the officer seek to drive a bargain with the soldiers, and the soldiers with him? Unthinkable! But the power of command is not enough. The greater the power of command, the greater must be the responsibility you bear. It is not easy to be an officer. It does not mean to be sole master in one's own house in accordance with civil ideas of arbitrary power, but it means to be a leader, to see to it that one knows and cares for every individual, molds the human beings, leads every individual in a truly inner sense. The question who will pay for it is ridiculous and irrelevant. The question is, "Is the principle right?" Do you want to be a business commodity or a soldier with honor? I ask the business man, does he want to be a calculator and a financier, or an officer? Then everything is clear and there are no more questions.

DR. ROBERT LEY

FROM THE DEPRESSION LOW of 1932, just before the nazis seized power, until July of 1939, just before they went to war, the number of wage earners and salaried employees gainfully employed in Germany rose from 12,580,000 to 22,050,000, an increase of 9,470,000, or 75.2 per cent. The average number of hours worked per week per person for all industries rose from 41.46 to 47.04 during this same period. Average hourly earnings per person rose by 14 per cent from the depression low to December, 1938, and weekly earnings by 31 per cent. Total wages and salaries paid, including the Army, the Labor Service and pensions, rose from 26,000,000,000 marks in 1932 to 36,690,000,000 marks in 1937. (The figure for 1938, the last full peacetime year, does not seem to have been published.)

Reduced to its barest statistical skeleton, this is the story of what is the nazis' greatest single achievement. No other regime has ever accomplished so much in these respects in modern times. There is nothing to be gained by trying to ignore it.

There is, however, a great deal to be gained by trying to understand it. How did the nazis do it? What was the price that was paid for it? Could the gains it represented have been long maintained if there had been no war? And what did it mean in terms of the lives of the human beings involved?

The questions of how the nazis did it and whether or not the gains it represented could have been maintained will be considered in a later chapter. The price that was paid for this extraordinary achievement has already been reported. It is plain for every eye to see except those that prefer not to see. It consists, morally, of the destruction of human decency and individual liberty of every kind and, to the extent that such a thing is possible, the destruction of the very individual soul; and it consists, both morally and materially, of this: that the principal motive power and purpose of the measures that created all this "prosperity" was the creation of armed forces destined for the destruction of a whole civilization and a whole way of life and the literal enslavement of literally a score of peoples.

But what of the more immediate effects of this achievement in terms of the everyday lives of the German people?

BOOM WITHOUT PROSPERITY

The nazis themselves were the first to say that the results of their state-financed boom left much to be desired in respect of the standard of living. It was, some nazis said, a boom without prosperity.

"We must recognize that we live in an era of poverty," said Dr. Hjalmar Schacht in February, 1935, "and that we must renounce for another decade the comforts of life we knew before the [First World] War."

Dr. Robert Ley fixed this period of relative poverty at 20 years.

Neither Dr. Schacht nor Dr. Ley has suffered notably during this period. Their "poverty" has indeed been relative. The common man in Germany, however, *has* suffered, as usual. It is seldom that the nazis publish figures from which it is possible to form an adequate conception of the German standard of living, but for the period 1932 to 1936 such figures are available. These are some of the uncompromising facts that emerge from the figures:

Earnings per employed person rose by 10.7 per cent during this period, but this represented an increase from only $336.75 per year to only $372.78 per year. (All dollar figures are calculated at the pre-nazi rate of exchange of 25 cents to the mark.) The cost of living, furthermore, rose from 1932 to 1936, while the government actually forced *rates* of pay down.

Money wages barely kept up with the rise in prices, if they kept up at all, and earnings rose only if, as and when the laborer and employee worked longer hours or at more difficult, more skilled or otherwise more valuable tasks. The average official tariff rate of pay for all skilled German workers in 1932 was 20.4 cents an hour, according to the Reich Statistical Office. Four and one half years later it was 19.5 cents per hour. Average tariff pay for unskilled workers fell during this same period —or rather, was forced down by the nazis—from 16.1 cents to 13 cents an hour.

The Germans disputed among themselves as to whether the cost of living rose more than money earnings during this period. The Reich Statistical Office claimed that wages and salaries rose more than prices. A nazi economic review asserted that there was an increase of between 1 and 2 per cent in real earnings. The Labor Front challenged these views and undertook a detailed study of 3,000 workingmen's family budgets which, preliminary reports said, showed there had been an appreciable decline in real earnings.

No matter who was right about real earnings, though, money earnings remained very low indeed by American standards. Dr. Ley declared at the 1936 party congress at Nuremberg that the earnings of full-time employed members of the Labor Front averaged $6.95 per week, and the Reich Statistical Office put average weekly earnings for all German workers at $6.29 for that year.

"Money wages are too low," said the *Frankfurter Zeitung* shortly after Dr. Ley made his statement about earnings. "Many opportunities of earning money are restricted as a result of raw material shortages, and tasks of national importance set by the regime require sacrifices which also reduce income. As a result of these conditions, during the past year, in spite of the reduction in unemployment figures, 12.9 million Germans were so hard pressed they had to be helped by the Winter Relief Fund. . . . Out of every 10 Germans, two were dependent on this 'Organization to Combat Want' for the essentials of life."

Die Deutsche Volkswirtschaft, a nazi economic review, also spoke out frankly in March, 1937, about wages in Germany:

"The profit situation in many businesses is such," it said, "that a certain increase in the real income [of labor] would be desired by and welcome to business on all possible grounds, for an increase in prices would not necessarily follow. That an increase in the real income of the masses at the lower income levels is desirable is apparent from the fact that there has been an increase in real income of only 1 to 2 per cent since 1933. This is all the more noteworthy because some skilled laborers are in a position to have obtained two or three times their present wages as a result of the strong demand for trained, experienced men, which [however] would have led to exaggerated differences in income."

Not only were money wages too low, in the words of the *Frankfurter Zeitung,* furthermore, but the nazis took, for purposes of their own, a constantly increasing share of such wages

—and salaries—as the little man in Germany did earn. The little man never even saw a relatively high proportion of his earnings; the nazis deducted it at source in the form of "voluntary" contributions to party causes and of taxes and insurance.

THE USUAL CONTRIBUTION

A workman in Cologne was discharged without notice in the Fall of 1936 because he declined to contribute to the nazi party's Winter Relief Fund. The workman appealed to a Labor Court against his dismissal, but the court upheld the employer.

"Even if there is no legal obligation to contribute to the Winter Relief Fund," the court said, "the unequivocal refusal of an employee to make the usual contribution to the national socialist welfare organization representatives constitutes conduct hostile to the community of the people and is to be most strongly condemned."

This pronouncement is typical of nazi logic and nazi playing with words. "There is no legal obligation to contribute." The nazis insist on calling these donations "voluntary." But the citizen who fails to make a "voluntary" donation can be dismissed from his job.

Not only does the citizen have to contribute, furthermore, but he has to contribute as much as the nazis think he should. The party, not the individual himself, decides what is the proper amount.

A factory foreman, also, as it happens, in Cologne, found this out. He offered to contribute 25 cents a month to the Winter Relief Fund, but was discharged by his employer on the grounds that this was not enough.

The foreman, like the workman, appealed to a Labor Court. He had a big family, he said, and could not afford to contribute any more. His employer, however, retorted that the foreman was earning $92 a month, that he had just bought a car, and that he could well afford to give a greater amount, and the court sided with the employer. The dismissal, it ruled, was justified.

There was only one way out, and the foreman took it: he offered to contribute between $2.50 and $5 per month to the

Winter Relief Fund. He was thereupon reinstated in his job.

The experiences of the workman and the foreman in Cologne are unusual in that they ended in courts and that the courts expressly affirmed the obligation of the citizens to contribute, and to do so on a scale considered adequate by the nazi collectors, to the party. In substance, however, all the courts did in these cases was to state explicitly what has been the case from the outset of nazi rule. If relatively few cases have reached the courts, it is because workmen and employees have known that the courts would affirm their obligation to pay.

Nor is the Winter Relief Fund by any means the only party cause to which the citizen is obliged to contribute. He also must belong to the Labor Front, and pay dues to that. And there are a host of other party organizations, funds, causes, and purposes that the people are required to support. One modestly paid citizen once confided to an American friend that he had to make donations to 32 different party causes every month, and there are doubtless millions of other Germans in almost equally difficult predicaments. The miscellaneous donations include a wide variety of items: subscriptions to party publications, levies for party celebrations, payments for setting up radio sets and loudspeakers in shops and factories, dues to nazi sport, youth and other organizations and purchase of calendars, memorial tablets, flags and portraits of Hitler and other leading nazis.

It is an exceptional day that at least one nazi collector does not come a-knocking at the door in the name of some party cause that requires cash support it can be embarrassing to refuse. The "usual contribution" is very usual indeed.

Contributions to the Winter Relief Fund are supposed to amount to at least 10 per cent of the wage tax for each of the six months from October to March, inclusive, with a minimum of 6¼ cents per month. Dues to the Labor Front range from 15 cents to $1.10 per month, depending on the individual's earnings. These two plus the other contributions the citizen is obliged to make to the party average 5 per cent of the gross earnings of the man in the street, according to the Reich Statistical Office—and to 9.1 per cent of gross earnings, according to the British Labor Research Bureau.

Besides these "voluntary" contributions, further sums are deducted from wages and salaries at source for insurance and taxes. Unemployment insurance averages 4.5 to 5 per cent of gross earnings, health insurance and pension contributions 5 to 5.5 per cent and wage and poll taxes 3.5 per cent, according to the Reich Statistical Office. Deductions for taxes and insurance combined thus amount on the average to 13.5 per cent of gross earnings. And these plus the "voluntary" contributions make a total of 18.5 per cent of the citizen's gross earnings, if you take the nazis' own word for it, and of 22.6 per cent, if you believe the British Labor Research Bureau, that the nazis siphon off and spend as they, not the citizen, see fit.

What does the common man in Germany do—what can he do—with what he has left?

PRICE OF GLORY: FIRST INSTALLMENT

Germany starved itself into greatness once, under Frederick. The nazis set out to repeat the performance. That is the essential meaning of the phrase, "Guns or butter." That was the first installment of the price of glory.

Every nation has to choose between guns and butter, and every nation chooses less butter in order to have more guns. Every nation must make the choice, if it is to survive; if it fails to make the choice, and make it in time, and make it in the proper proportions, it is destroyed, and then it has neither guns nor butter. But Germany's choice was more dramatic than those that most others make, because Germany had fewer guns and wanted many more in a greater hurry than is usually the case, and therefore had to give up more butter all at once.

In order to be able to buy as many guns as possible and at the same time as much butter as possible—to get the most possible greatness out of the least possible starvation—and to divide the available butter as evenly as possible among all those who wanted it and could afford it, the nazis have closely controlled consumption along with everything else in Germany. Two of the principal phases of this control, apart from direct rationing, have consisted of price and wage regulation.

The nazis decided they had to keep wage rates at the low

point of the depression if they were to put the 6,000,000 men and women back to work who were unemployed when the party seized power, and if possible, to employ two or three million more as well, and to carry out their political-military program too.

But even at the prevailing low rates of pay, the total earnings of labor and employees were bound to increase as more and more people began to work longer and longer hours. And since the supply of purchasable commodities would be limited, there were bound to be shortages, and prices were bound to go up as people began to spend their greater earnings. Rationing and price control were thus essential.

One notable exception to this policy of low fixed prices was deliberately allowed: foodstuffs. The nazis wanted to build up a stronger farming class, and one of the ways they chose to do this was to make farming more profitable. They raised the prices of domestic farm products.

Increases in world prices forced other exceptions. The Reich has to buy many necessities abroad, and these necessities cost more and more with the passage of time.

These have been the principal factors that have determined price changes under nazi rule.

One of the few comprehensive reports of variations in retail prices to be published in Germany the last few years before the war was issued by the semi-official Institute for Business Research for the period March, 1933, to March, 1937. These are the changes recorded:

Item	Price Change in Per Cent
Bread and rolls, total of all kinds	− 2
Peas	+ 52
Beans	+ 31
Sugar	+ 2
Potatoes	+ 22
Other vegetables	+ 4
Meat, meat products and fish, total	+ 18
Beef	+ 18
Pork	+ 11

Item	Price Change in Per Cent
Veal	+ 40
Mutton	+ 41
Milk, dairy products, total	+ 15
Milk	+ 7
Butter	+ 35
Margarine	+ 44
Eggs	+ 31
Coal	− 1
Gas and electric current	− 1
Clothing	+ 24
Linen	+ 17
Household equipment	+ 6

MORE POTATOES

By the Summer of 1937, retail prices in Berlin for most necessities were roughly equivalent to those in Chicago (using the rate of exchange of 25 cents to the mark), although somewhat lower than prices in New York City and Washington. Yet the Berliner had much less money to spend than the Chicagoan and New Yorker and Washingtonian. The earnings of insured workmen in Berlin averaged $8.16 per week in 1936 and those of insured employees $13.72 per week, according to the Reich Statistical Office. Then how did Berliners live on their earnings at all, to say nothing of keeping up the appearance of decency they did?

They kept up appearances partly, if not largely, because they wanted very much to do so. Germans attach a great deal of importance to outward appearances, and spend a higher proportion of their earnings and devote more time and effort and attention to keeping them up than Americans think it is worth while doing. It is a question of scales of values. The German will shave every day, have his hair cut frequently, shine his shoes often and wear a well-kept dark suit when he goes out, even if he is hungry. The American, on the other hand, thinks it is more important than the German does to eat well and less important than the German does to look well, and often enough actually prefers looking as shabby as possible.

But apart from the question of scales of values, of what people prefer to do with their money, there is the question of scales of wages and prices, of what people are able to do with their money. And the solution of the essential mystery of the German standard of living, the mystery of how the German masses live as well as they do on the very small wages and salaries they earn, is to be found precisely here, in the nazis' manipulation of prices.

It is true that most foodstuffs cost as much in Germany as in the United States. In October, 1936, wheat flour, wheat bread, white granulated sugar, second quality mutton and coffee, for example, cost more in Berlin than they did in Chicago. Margarine cost almost exactly the same. Butter and eggs cost only 10 per cent less.

But this did not matter a great deal to the German man in the street, because he did not eat these expensive foodstuffs. He ate only 68 per cent as much beef and veal, only 57 per cent as much white bread, 51 per cent as much sugar, 47 per cent as many eggs and 18 per cent as much mutton as the average American, according to figures published by the International Labor Office in Geneva.

The German ate other foodstuffs instead. He was accustomed to eating these others, and he preferred them. The average German ate 1¾ as much cabbage as the average American, almost twice as many potatoes, more than four times as much rye bread and 7⅓ times as much margarine, according to the International Labor Office.

And the nazis kept the prices of these other items down. Second quality beef cost only three-fourths as much in Berlin as in Chicago in October, 1936, second quality pork only three-fifths as much, rye and black bread less than one-half as much and potatoes less than one-third as much.

Not only were the regular retail market prices of these and certain other basis foodstuffs kept low, furthermore, but the nazis made still further far-reaching concessions to the low wages and salaries earned by the German masses. They did this by a system of cards. The cards were of two kinds. One guaranteed the bearer a minimum quantity of the cheaper grade of table margarine at the regular market price. This was intended to make sure that those who could not afford butter and other more expensive fats and "spreads" would have first chance at the available supplies—which were limited—of the cheaper fat. The other kind of card guaranteed the bearer a minimum quantity of margarine, butter and other fats, cheese, sausage and bacon at prices ranging from 27 to 50 per cent below the market price. Between 22,000,000 and 24,000,000 persons received these reduced price cards.

So it was that the German masses could eat, if not luxuriously, at least adequately, in spite of their low earnings.

"But how could you live on $7 a week?" a baffled American asked a German workman who had kept a whole family alive on that amount in Berlin during the depression.

"Oh, we just ate more potatoes," said the workman matter-of-factly.

THE NOT-SO-FULL PERSON

But other factors besides price manipulation have helped determine what, and how much, the man in the street in the Reich has had to eat under nazi rule. The "boom without prosperity" did curious things to the German diet.

The Germans had more money to spend the last two or three years before the war than they had had previously. So, like most other peoples under such circumstances, they bought more of most things that were available, and especially they bought things they had had to give up during the preceding depression: luxuries, above all, like white bread, butter, coffee, beer, wine, brandy and tobacco. On the other hand, they bought less of some things they had relied on to a relatively great extent during hard times because they were cheap: things like rye bread and potatoes.

But here the changes in the German diet that came with the nazi boom ceased to follow the normal pattern for such changes in times of prosperity. For this "prosperity" was not normal.

It was not normal, first, because the increased industrial activity was deliberately concentrated to an extraordinary degree in production of armaments and producers', not consumers', goods. It was not normal, second, because the nazis were neither able nor willing to make available to the German people some of the foodstuffs (and other consumers' goods) that the people would have liked to have and could have afforded to buy. They were not able to do so because they could not obtain enough foreign exchange to finance the purchase of both guns and butter abroad, and because they could not produce enough of both guns and butter at home, and they had chosen guns. They were not willing to do so because they wanted to make the Reich as blockade-proof as possible—as independent as possible of commodities which had to be imported from overseas and which therefore could not be imported at all during the war with England the nazis were preparing for.

The nazis set out, accordingly, to induce the Germans to eat things that could be obtained by barter agreements and other methods that required the expenditure of no foreign exchange, and of things that could be obtained from neighboring and near-by countries on the continent of Europe, and to induce the Germans not to eat things which had to be obtained from overseas and which had to be paid for in foreign currencies.

The Germans would have liked, and could have afforded to buy, more eggs, cheese, margarine, other fats and meats. But considerable proportions of these foodstuffs—or the fodders that were necessary for the cattle and poultry that provided them—came either from countries that would be inaccessible in a war with England or from countries that required payment in foreign exchange, or from countries that fell into both these categories. So the nazis held consumption of these things to a minimum. Honey and jam and fish, on the other hand, could be obtained at home or at least without having to spend foreign currencies for them, and the nazis therefore encouraged the Germans to eat more of these things.

The effect on the German diet of this combination of economic and political influences was a bizarre one. The most detailed study to be published of the changes in what the Germans ate during these years was one issued in 1937 by the Reich Statistical Office comparing consumption of certain foodstuffs for the years 1932 and 1936 per "full person," that is, for that mythical but convenient creature, half human and half statistical,

that represents an average adult male. The Statistical Office's
study reported the following changes:

Item	Percentage of Change
Meats	+ 2.8
Margarine and other vegetable oils and fats	− 20.5
Raw pork fat	− 5.
Butter	+ 15.6
Cheese	− 10.
Sea fish	+ 38.3
Eggs	− 15.3
Sugar	+ 10.6
Potatoes	− 10.8
Rye flour	− .3
Wheat flour	+ 14.9
Coffee	+ 15.3
Cocoa	− 2.1
Tea	− 10.4
Beer	+ 20.1
Wine	+ 66.
Brandy	+ 66.6
Tobacco	+ 15.

"Tell me what you eat, and I will tell you what you are,"
Brillat-Savarin said. He would have had a hard time telling
what the Germans are. The "full person" has not been as full
as he would have liked to be, under nazi rule, and still less has
he been full of the things he would have liked to have and
could have afforded to buy, but that the nazis saw to it simply
were not there to buy.

22. —and Circuses

Socialism is affirmation of life, socialism is com-
munity, socialism is struggle, socialism is comrade-
ship and loyalty, socialism is honor, my friend, is
blood and race, the holy, deep, earnest belief in a
God.
                                    DR. ROBERT LEY

FORCED DOWN to depression levels, the German standard of living was low when the nazis seized power, and the nazis neither could nor would do a great deal toward raising it.

Again and again Dr. Ley promised that wage rates would be raised or prices would be lowered, or both, but there was always some excellent reason—there was, in fact, a whole series of different but equally excellent reasons—why neither of these things could be done. First it was because "we are only just beginning." Then it was because men were still out of work. Later it was because wage increases "would cause inflation." Finally, it was because of the war.

These explanations were all very well in their way, but they were not enough, and Dr. Ley knew that they were not enough. A diversion was indicated.

"We had to divert the attention of the masses from material to moral values," Ley later explained. "It is more important to feed the souls of men than it is to fill their stomachs."

So Dr. Ley set about diverting the attention of the masses and feeding their souls. He used three principal soul foods. The first consisted of a colossal program of low-cost recreation and education and improvement of working conditions. The second consisted of a system of Courts of Social Honor to protect the dignity, the self-respect, the glory—and the political reliability—of labor. The third consisted of a program to break down the social barriers between employers and employees and to bring them together on a "comradely" basis.

STRANGE SHIPS

The *Wilhelm Gustloff* and the *Robert Ley* are two of the most extraordinary ships that ever sailed the seas.

They have no class distinctions. Their accommodations and their crews' quarters are as alike as human ingenuity can make them. They are deliberately designed to operate at a loss. They were built with the pennies of German workmen and white-collar employees. Their only passengers, apart from guests of honor, have been these same workmen and employees (until the war, that is, when they were converted into hospital ships).

The building of these ships is one of the proudest achievements of the nazis, and, more specifically, of Dr. Ley and the Strength Through Joy organization of the Labor Front. The *Wilhelm Gustloff* and the *Robert Ley* represent the high point of the regime's efforts to provide recreation and vacations for the German masses at costs low enough for their exceedingly flat purses.

The little man in the Reich earns so little that it is sometimes hard to see how he keeps body and soul together. The nazis, furthermore, have robbed him of every liberty ever written into a bill of rights and a good many more besides. At first glance, life seems scarcely worth living for most Germans, even in times of so-called "peace." Even at second and subsequent glances few Americans in their right senses could see any reason for wanting to change places with the Germans.

But the German standard of living is not quite as excruciatingly low as it appears to be. And one of the chief reasons why it is not, one of the biggest buffers between the German and the stark mathematics of his pay-check, is the Strength Through Joy organization. Something like the Dopolavoro of the Italian fascists except that the nazi organization is much bigger and more elaborate and operates on a much more lavish scale,

Strength Through Joy engages in a wide variety of activities intended to instruct, strengthen and amuse the masses of the people, to provide them recreation, sports and vacations at low costs.

Apart from the idealistic motives for this program, there are at least two highly practical reasons for it: first, healthy, happy, busy people are easier to govern than sickly, unhappy, idle ones are; and second, they get more work done.

Membership in the Labor Front, which is, in effect, compulsory for most German workmen and white-collar employees, automatically confers eligibility for the benefits of Strength Through Joy. There were more than 25,000,000 members in the Front just before the war.

Organizing cheap vacation trips both on land and at sea is the most spectacular single activity in which Strength Through Joy engages. In addition to the *Wilhelm Gustloff* and the *Robert Ley,* the organization had a fleet of ten ships it leased for cruises before the war. Five of these were in more or less regular service: the *Sierra Cordoba* of 11,430 tons, *Der Deutsche* of 11,470 tons, and the *Oceana,* the *Monte Olivia* and the *Monte Sarmiento* of 14,000 tons each.

The *Wilhelm Gustloff* and the *Robert Ley* were, however, the pride of the Labor Front fleet. Of 25,000 tons, they were tied for fifth place in size in the entire German merchant marine. Each had 248 two-bed and 241 four-bed cabins and could accommodate 1,460 passengers; each had a sports deck, a sun deck and two promenade decks, a swimming pool and two dining rooms big enough so that all the passengers could be served at two sittings.

Strength Through Joy began its cruises in the Summer of 1934 with trips down the English Channel to the Isle of Wight and up the Norwegian and Baltic coasts. The next year cruises to Madeira and the Azores, with stops at Lisbon, were begun. Later, trips to the Mediterranean were added, and cruises to the Far East were scheduled for 1939 and 1940 but had to be canceled because of the war.

A round trip ticket to Madeira from a member's home anywhere in Germany and return, with landings at Lisbon and Madeira, cost only $25. Other cruises were correspondingly cheap.

THE SOCIALIZATION OF SKIING

Winter sports, too, as well as cruises, were socialized:

A Berlin workman or white-collar employee could go to a winter sports resort in the Bavarian Alps and spend a week there skiing, with the help of an instructor, if he wanted one, for a total cost of $11, including transportation, as part of the program of low-cost recreation organized by Strength Through Joy before the war.

The average cost of a week's skiing was even less, because the trip from Berlin to the Bavarian Alps is longer than most journeys to winter sports resorts, and amounted to only $8.75.

If the workman or employee had no skiing outfit he could buy skis for $4 and ski boots for $4.75. An average of 22,000 outfits at these prices were sold in Germany annually each of the last few years before the war.

The workman or employee could do these things at such low costs, that is, if he belonged to the nazi Labor Front and could satisfy officials that he could not afford to pay full prices for his vacation and vacation equipment. No fixed wage and salary limits were used in determining who could and who could not afford to pay full prices. Officials exercised their own discretion.

The nazis also set out to make other sports accessible to the German masses, and they succeeded notably. More than 7,500,-000 persons took part in sports organized by Strength Through Joy each of the last few years before the war.

The program for the future calls for even more spectacular achievements: When the war broke out, the Labor Front was engaged in building a special bathing resort for its members at Ruegen, on the Baltic Sea, which would accommodate 20,000 persons at a time, when completed. It was intended to make it possible for Labor Front members to spend a week end at Ruegen for $4.50, including round trip transportation. Three other similar bathing resorts on the Baltic are also planned.

MICHAEL GOES TO THE THEATER

When the Strength Through Joy organization was planning its program, it "analyzed the market": among other things, it circulated a questionnaire among the 50,000 workmen and employees of the Berlin works of the Siemens Company to see to what extent these people had attended theaters and operas in the past. Answers to the questionnaires showed that 87.6 per cent of the men and 81.3 per cent of the women had never heard an opera, and that 63.8 per cent of the men and 74.2 per cent of the women had never been inside a theater.

No check seems to have been made among these same workmen and employees since then. But the Strength Through Joy organization certainly has done much in general toward introducing the German masses to the music and the drama. The German Michael now goes to the theater and the opera as the little man in few other countries does. In a "normal" year (1936) Strength Through Joy made it possible, by arranging for greatly reduced rates, for 4,500,000 Germans to attend theaters. It organized concerts at low admission prices which 1,600,000 persons heard that same year, and it arranged 450 special art exhibits in factories and stores which 2,500,000 workmen and employees visited.

The Feierabend office of the organization is in charge of this phase of its program. It arranges concerts, plays, operas, operettas, vaudeville and motion picture performances, art exhibits, special conducted tours through museums and galleries and other educational and recreational programs at greatly reduced rates for Labor Front members. During 1934, the first year that the office functioned, 9,000,000 persons attended programs and other events the office arranged. By 1936 this number had risen to 31,000,000. Figures for later years do not seem to be available.

The Strength Through Joy organization even has its own symphony orchestra of 90 pieces that travels all over the Reich giving concerts in factories, stores and regular auditoriums, most often in communities that have little or no good music of their own.

Another office in Strength Through Joy conducts a program of adult education. It has 200 centers throughout the country where it gives courses for Labor Front members in languages, vocational training, painting, wood-carving, model-making and a dozen other subjects.

LIKE SOME OTHER MISSIONARIES

The liberal will have fewer reservations about the activities of the Strength Through Joy organization than he will about most other phases of nazi policy. Yet he will have a few about even this phase.

On the credit side of the ledger, for fees roughly equivalent to union dues, German workmen and white-collar employees receive, at strikingly low costs, opportunities to travel, to hear concerts and operas, to attend the theater and to learn languages and handicrafts and trades and other subjects of enrichment and profit to their lives.

On the debit side, first, certain of the organizations and facilities that make the whole program possible the nazis seized from or denied to others who had been doing the same sorts of things or could have done them as well or better.

Also, the Labor Front has never made any but the vaguest accountings of its funds. It refuses to reveal either its total revenues or its total disbursements, either the sources of the one or the objects of the other. For this and other reasons there is grave doubt, to put it mildly, as to what happens to the sums collected from the masses of the people.

Then there is the intangible, imponderable price paid for the benefits of the program:

The individual has little or no freedom of choice or conduct in the Strength Through Joy program. His behavior is almost as closely regimented as that of a soldier in the ranks.

Like some missionaries of other faiths, moreover, the nazis heal only on condition that the patient become at least outwardly a convert. The plays and films the Labor Front members see, the concerts and operas they hear, the history they are taught—all are "co-ordinated" with the national socialist philosophy of life. And it is a rare person indeed whose political reliability is in serious doubt who is able to benefit by the facilities of the program.

And there is, finally, the price paid in terms of the loss of almost all the liberties the Germans enjoyed before. Among other things, the Germans have lost every iota of collective bargaining power. Their wages and salaries are fixed by politicians, and are fixed at rates lower per unit and hour of work performed, even at the peak of the nazi boom, than they had been at the very nadir of the depression.

DISILLUSIONMENT OF A JUNKER

The Junkers of Pomerania have the reputation of being the most feudal, in both the good and bad senses of the word, of the land-owning, officer-class nobility of all Germany. So when one of their number thought he had caught his master forester in double-dealing and embezzlement, nothing seemed more natural and desirable to the Junker than to tell the forester exactly what he thought of him, and this he did.

But the master forester was not feudal. He was, on the contrary, very much of the New Order. He accused the landowner of "wounding the sense of honor of a member of his following" and brought suit against him on this charge before the Court of Social Honor in Stettin.

The Court upheld the forester (the land-owner could not prove his accusations), found the Junker guilty of the charge preferred against him, and fined him $250.

Apparently still unrepentant, the land-owner appealed to the Reich Court of Social Honor, the court of last resort for such cases. But the Reich Court not only upheld the lower tribunal —it increased the fine to $750.

This history of the disillusionment of the Pomeranian Junker is typical of one phase of the work of the Courts of Social Honor the nazis have established. It is typical both for its definition and its defense of what the nazis call the "social honor" of the employee.

The nazis have set out, they say, to develop a whole new conception of social relationships. One of the most important aspects of this attempt has to do with relations between em-

ployers on the one hand and workmen and white-collar employees on the other.

The old relationship between master and man is to be destroyed in the New Germany, the nazis say. So is the more recent relationship between relatively freely organized capital
and relatively freely organized labor, bargaining and battling
for power and earnings with the government acting as referee.

Instead, in the Third Reich, the nazis have all the power and
control all the organizations—and all the earnings—and employer, workman and employee alike are supposed to be servants
of the common weal, setting their hands and minds in differing
but equally honorable capacities to the national tasks. Emphasis
on personal and class interests is Marxistic and sordid, the nazis
say, and harmful to the national interests.

Since the New Germany is above all authoritarian and totalitarian, the nazis give all the orders, define the common weal,
determine the national tasks and the manner of performing
them, and forbid real debate of these matters, as of others.
There are, therefore, difficulties in the way of appraising the
new social policy—especially for a liberal who is prone to think
sordidly in terms of making a living anyway, and of who
profits, and how much, in this brave new world where there is
so much talk of the brotherhood of man and so little explanation of who goes to concentration camps, for how long, and
why.

The avowed ideals of the nazis can, however, be reported,
and evidence is available that gives some indication, within
limits, of how these ideals are being realized in fact.

GRIM FOLLOW-THE-LEADER

Three of the principal concepts in the new ideal of labor
relationships the nazis have set out to realize are "the community," "loyalty" and "social honor."

The nation as a whole is supposed to be the great, all-
inclusive "community of the people." Within this greater community, each factory and store and other business enterprise
is supposed to constitute a smaller but equally real "plant community."

In both the greater and smaller communities, the "leadership principle" is supreme. That is, orders come from the top and obedience from the bottom. This obedience must be "loyal."

The owner or manager of the enterprise is the "leader" of the "plant community," just as Hitler is the leader of the nation as a whole, and the workmen and employees are the "followers" in the establishment, just as the whole German people are the followers in the nation at large. In both cases the collective totality of followers constitutes the "following." It is all a sort of great, grim follow-the-leader.

The Weimar Republic enacted enlightened labor legislation (as Bismarck's Second Reich had done before) and established Labor Courts to interpret and apply it. These courts and some of this legislation have survived under nazi rule, although the legal department of the Labor Front has steadily encroached on the competence and authority of the courts.

But to interpret and apply the newer social philosophy the nazis set up their own Courts of Social Honor beside the Labor Courts. These new tribunals were provided for by the Act for the Organization of National Labor, which also defined the new social relationships.

"Every member of a plant community," Article 35 of the Act provides, "shall be responsible for the conscientious performance of the duties incumbent upon him in consequence of his position in the said community.

"He shall conduct himself in such manner as to show himself worthy of the respect due his position in the plant community.

"In particular, he shall devote his powers to the service of the establishment and serve the common good, always bearing in mind his responsibility."

The Courts of Social Honor deal with cases of alleged delinquency in the performance of these duties, in this worthy conduct and in this devotion to the service of the establishment and the common good. Article 36 of the Act attempts to define these terms more specifically:

"(1) Gross breaches of the social duties based on the plant

community shall be dealt with by the Courts of Social Honor as offenses against social honor," this article provides. "Such offenses shall be deemed to have been committed in the following cases:

"1. When the owner of an undertaking, the leader of an establishment or any other person in a position of supervision abuses his authority in the establishment by maliciously exploiting the labor of any of his followers or wounding their sense of honor;

"2. When a follower endangers industrial peace in the establishment by maliciously provoking other followers, and in particular when a member of the Council of Confidential Advisers in the establishment knowingly interferes unduly in the conduct of the establishment or continually and maliciously disturbs the community spirit within the enterprise;

"3. When a member of the plant community repeatedly makes frivolous and unjustified complaints or petitions to the Labor Trustee or obstinately disobeys instructions given by him in writing;

"4. When a member of the Confidential Council reveals without authority any confidential information or technical or business secrets which have become known to him in the performance of his duties and have been specified to be confidential matters.

"(2) Public officials and soldiers shall not be subject to the jurisdiction of the Courts of Social Honor."

The Act for the Organization of National Labor provides for six different kinds of penalties for infractions of these provisions: (1) warning; (2) reprimand; (3) fine not to exceed $2,500; (4) deprival of an owner or manager of the right to conduct his own or any other business; (5) deprival of a member of a Confidential Council of the right to serve in such a position; and (6) dismissal of a workman or employee from his position.

The case of the Pomeranian Junker typifies one kind of decision the Courts of Social Honor hand down. Other cases exemplify other kinds of decisions less agreeable to workmen and employees. And still others bear witness to a point of view on the part of the courts disagreeable to employers. workmen and employees alike.

NEW DIGNITY AND HONOR

A factory foreman in an industrial town in central Germany set up a racketeering tyranny that held all the workmen in his department in its grip. How he was able to do it is not clear, but what he did is clear enough: He "borrowed" money from his men and never paid it back. Sometimes he even "borrowed" food from them on the same terms. He opened a special account for himself at an inn near the factory; each week the workmen paid money over to the innkeeper for the account of the foreman, who then drew against it for tobacco and drinks. Some weeks the total amount paid in was as much as $100. Workmen who refused to contribute were dismissed.

But somebody finally rebelled. And, characteristically in the New Germany, the rebellion took the form of an appeal for redress, not merely to the foreman's superiors in the plant, but to the local Court of Social Honor.

The foreman evidently saw what would happen. In any event, he quit his job.

The Court, after hearing the evidence against the foreman, expressed regret that he had already left the plant. If he had not, the court said, it would have taken pleasure in ordering his dismissal. But the Court could still fine the foreman, and this it did, in the amount of $75, which is probably as much as the man earned in a month.

For the foreman was found guilty of three of the worst offenses specified in the Act for the Organization of National Labor: of "abusing his authority in the establishment by maliciously exploiting the labor of his followers," of "maliciously wounding their sense of honor" and of "maliciously disturbing the community spirit within the plant community."

In other cases, too, nazi Courts of Social Honor have defended the rights and dignity of German workmen and employees against insults and abuse from above, and thus upheld the new nazi concept of the dignity and honor of labor.

The Reich Supreme Court of Social Honor in Berlin, for example, gave short shrift to the daughter of a factory owner who had "maliciously wounded the sense of honor" of "followers" in her father's plant. The daughter, who helped in the management of the factory, was accused of repeatedly insulting the laborers. One expression she was charged with using especially often was "filthy workmen."

Some of the "filthy workmen" brought suit against the daughter before the Berlin Court of Social Honor. The court found the daughter guilty and fined her $1,250. She appealed the case to the Reich Court, but her appeal was rejected and the fine upheld.

The Court of Social Honor for the judicial district of central Germany added still another interpretation to the law protecting the rights and dignity of workmen and employees. A land-owner in the district was obligated to provide living quarters as part of the compensation for a married farm hand with several children. The farm hand found the quarters that the employer placed at his disposal inadequate. He also accused the land-owner of using abusive language to him. He took his grievances to the court, and the court found the land-owner guilty on both counts and fined him heavily.

The Berlin Court of Social Honor invoked the most drastic of all penalties against a factory owner in the Berlin-Brandenburg district. It found him guilty of failure, despite repeated warnings, to improve sanitary conditions in his plant, of failure to pay his workmen and employees promptly although the factory was fully occupied with orders, of making arbitrary deductions from wages and salaries, of mistreating those who protested against these abuses, and of trying to stir up dissension among the men ("disturbing the community spirit within the plant community") and deprived him of the right to operate his plant.

A wholesale news dealer in Breslau met with the same fate at the hands of the Court of Social Honor there. The court ordered that he be deprived of control of his business on the grounds that he had persistently paid wages and salaries below the officially fixed minimums, had grossly insulted his workmen and employees, and had forced minors to work 59 hours a week without overtime pay.

PRIMACY OF POLITICS

One of the fundamental principles of national socialism is the principle of "the primacy of politics." This means that the politicians and policies of the party take precedence over everything and everybody else in the country. This principle applies with perhaps especial force to labor questions in the Third Reich, and, more particularly, to the functioning of the Courts of Social Honor. There is a fly—there are several flies—in the ointment of the new dignity and honor of labor.

The whole concept of "social honor" is a political—or moral—rather than an economic or a legal one. Recourse to the Courts of Social Honor is possible only with the permission of the Labor Trustees appointed by the nazis, and the Trustees are neither lawyers nor workmen nor employees, but politicians. The Labor Trustee can also attend hearings and "make recommendations" as to decisions and sentences. The Courts can decide certain types of cases without hearings, merely on the recommendation of the Labor Trustee, and impose sentences against which there is no apeal. They can find defendants guilty even though they have been declared innocent of any violation of the law by the ordinary courts. The judges of the Courts of Social Honor are political appointees and are not required to have served previously in any judicial capacity. And, finally, the decisions and sentences of the Courts seem to be determined just as often and just as much by political considerations as by those of law, economic welfare or what the rest of the world calls justice.

These same implications of the primacy of politics are also to be discovered in the functioning of the Labor Courts under nazi rule.

A Labor Court in Leipzig, for example, on one occasion upheld the dismissal of a workman from his job because he had failed to attend a mass-meeting of the men in his plant to hear a radio broadcast of an important speech by Hitler. In handing down its decision, the court said:

"The group radio reception of a speech by the Fuehrer is an occasion on which the sense of belonging to a great community of the people, on the part of every single business establishment and every single one of its leaders and followers, is brought home to the consciousness, not only symbolically and figuratively, but also actually and directly, through the physically-perceived fact that millions are gathered around a single Fuehrer and that all, without class distinctions, are members of the same community who have to march toward the same goal and not to quarrel among themselves. Therefore it is an especially important duty of every employer to see to it that so far as possible no one in the company he commands is absent."

So it is that the terms of the new nazi legislation—terms like "community" and "loyalty" and "social honor"—are often interpreted by Labor Courts and Courts of Social Honor to the disadvantage of German workmen and employees, as well as to their advantage. Sentences are reported with especial frequency in which the courts seem to be much more concerned with the defendants' politics than with their workmanship, their welfare, or their dignity and honor. Courts have upheld the dismissals of workmen and employees for uttering criticism of the regime, for failure to give the nazi salute, for remaining away from official May Day celebrations, and for "conduct unworthy of a true German workman" on a trip organized by the Strength Through Joy organization of the Labor Front.

A court in the town of Hindenburg, for one, upheld the dismissal without notice of a workman who had criticized the regime. Labor Courts in Kassel and Beuthen, among other places, upheld dismissals without notice for failure to give the nazi salute and say, "Heil Hitler!"

"Discharge without notice is justified of anyone who fails to conduct himself in the manner called for today," said the court in Kassel, and the court in Beuthen based its decision on the argument that failure to give the salute and say "Heil Hitler!" damages the reputation of the whole "following" of the plant where the offender is employed.

VOLUNTARY SOCIAL GATHERING

But the nazis have not relied exclusively on the courts to develop their new social ideal of the "community" in each business enterprise. They have undertaken also to educate the citizen by other means. Each enterprise should be like one big, happy family, the nazis say, and they have set out to teach "leaders" and "followers" alike to live in accordance with this idea. One of their educational devices for teaching this new idea consists of what the nazis call "industrial family schools."

The school of this type the nazis operated for some time in Hamburg seems to be typical of these institutions. The Labor Front took over a large house in a suburb of the city and gave what the nazis called "courses in comradeship" and other subjects lasting eight days.

"Students" in the school were organized in units called "industrial families." Each "family" consisted of three persons: an employer, a workman or white-collar employee and a minor nazi boss, who played the part of teacher.

The "family" lived together in the school, sharing meals and always shaking hands before sitting down at the table. "Middle-class" habits such as wearing collars and ties were outlawed. The "students" were expected in general to act like old friends, using the familiar "du" in speaking to each other.

"Comradeship evenings" for workmen and employees and their employers in the same establishment or industry were also organized on a large scale before the war with the same social end in view.

Attendance at both "industrial family schools" and "comradeship evenings" is theoretically voluntary, but actually compulsory.

All workmen and employees in a certain big business establishment in Berlin, for example, were once handed the following notice, signed by the manager of the business and countersigned by the owner—both of whom were nazis and therefore not to be trifled with in either their business or their political capacities:

"Our plant leader [that is, in this case, the owner] has summoned all the working comrades of the company and the members of their immediate families to a comradeship evening at 4 o'clock on [here the date was given] in the rooms at ——. In the case of a married man, members of his immediate family are to include his wife and children, in the case of a single man, his fiancée or sister or brother.

"In doing this, our leader has given us the opportunity for a voluntary social gathering at the small admission fee of 20 pfennigs per person, of which, however, 10 pfennigs are for tax.

"Our leader offers us a few enjoyable hours at a free three-hour program of entertainment by professional artists, and in addition presents to each member of the following four coupons of a total value of 1 mark which will be accepted by waiters in payment for drinks (coffee and beer). There will also be a lottery.

"With this announcement, which will be handed today in printed form to every working comrade without exception, I appeal to all members of the following to attend this comradeship evening unconditionally from beginning to end, and not to remain a mere two or three hours.

"It is the duty of every working comrade without exception to appear with his wife. Exceptions can be allowed only if his wife is actually sick, a fact which must be proved in advance by presentation of a doctor's certificate when possible.

"Whoever does not appear at this comradeship evening, or tries to cloak non-appearance in invalid excuses, places himself beyond the pale of the working community of —— and thereby beyond the pale of the present order of things in general, for this company stands with both feet firmly on the foundation of the national socialist state."

23. The Tired Business Man

The manager practices his functions primarily as a representative of the state, only secondarily for his own sake.

WALTER E. KINKEL, QUOTED BY GUENTER REIMANN, "THE VAMPIRE ECONOMY"

The sovereign is completely discharged from a duty, in the attempting to perform which he must always be exposed to innumerable delusions, and for the proper performance of which no human wisdom or knowledge could ever be sufficient; the duty of superintending the industry of private people, and of directing it towards the employments most suitable to the interest of the society.

ADAM SMITH, "THE WEALTH OF NATIONS"

THE TIRED BUSINESS MAN is a legendary figure out of what Westbrook Pegler has called The Era of Wonderful Nonsense in the United States. He was Babbitt, a brother of the butter and egg man, or perhaps the butter and egg man himself, a dull fellow who was so tired from making money that he was a bore even when he was awake and was very apt to fall asleep.

The Third Reich has its Tired Business Man, too, and he is just as tired and just as much of a bore as his American cousin was. But he is tired for different reasons. He is tired, not so much from making money, or even from actually engaging in business, as from struggling with the nazis for the privilege of being allowed to engage in business at all, for the myriad permits that are necessary for the carrying out of each transaction in his business, and for the "right" to keep some share of his profits, if any, for himself. The business man in the Third Reich is not a butter and egg man; he is a permit and priorities man.

Under the new dispensation in Germany the business man is subject to a degree of political supervision and interference such as the most violent of New Dealers never imagined in his wildest deliriums:

He must belong to a fantastic number and variety of official and semi-official business organizations.

He must take orders from a number and variety of party and government offices so bewildering that the party and government themselves do not know what they all are or where the authority of one ends and the next begins. He must be prepared for reversals without notice of policy and orders from any or all of these offices. He must hire a certain proportion of party members for jobs in his organization whether they are qualified for the jobs or not. He must take on party men as members of his board of directors if he has one, or in other important capacities if he does not, and he must hire at least one nazi as a political contact man and protector.

He must reorganize and restaff his company, not only on this immediately political basis, but also in order to do business under these conditions: he needs extra lawyers and stenographers and telephone operators and file clerks, for example, and he gets along with smaller sales and advertising forces.

And finally the tired business man must pay tribute to the party in the form of outright graft, "voluntary" contributions to party causes and heavy taxes, as well as in the other forms implicit in hiring party men for posts where they are economically inefficient or worse, in restaffing and reorganizing, in expanded paper work and in membership dues in compulsory organizations.

The business man in the Third Reich is busy. He has orders. But these are the conditions subject to which he gets and fills his orders, subject to which he is busy. This is how he is busy, and with what. His lot is not a happy one.

THE BUSINESS MAN AS A CAMEL

The nazis have a low opinion of the business man. He is, in fact, like a camel, in the nazi view: a useful beast of burden for bearing the party wherever it wants to go, but hardly to be consulted as to the destination, the route, the burden, or even the amount of provender it receives. The driver has to provide enough food and water to enable the beast to do what is expected of it, of course, but that is the only respect in which the camel's welfare is a matter of concern or even interest to the driver.

"If we fall into the political inconsistency of eliminating the inclination to acquire, to create and to possess, by an all-too-rigorous restriction of reserves, and thus eliminate the possibility of development under private initiative, we may be in the position of the rider in the desert who allows his mount to carry him by instinct to a water hole but who then laps up all the precious drops himself and does not give the camel, who found the water for him, anything to drink," said Rudolf Brinkmann, Undersecretary in the Ministry of Economics, in a speech to bankers and insurance men convened at Duesseldorf, October 21, 1938. "What is the probable reaction of the camel? Greater diligence in finding water? That could not be expected even of a camel."

Brinkmann lost his mind some time after making this speech, and a bitter jest was made: It was not surprising that a man in a position of responsibility in the nazi economic and financial system should go mad, an American banker said; the surprising thing about it was that anybody should have noticed that he was mad.

But Brinkmann was sane enough when he made this speech— all too sane. And his metaphor is a perfect description of the status of business in the New Germany: the business man is the camel, the party is the driver, the Third Reich is the economic and financial desert; the camel finds the water and the driver drinks most of it up. "Even a camel" became increasingly disgruntled with the passage of time. There was, however, little that he could do about it.

The camel became increasingly disgruntled especially because he was subject to the orders, "most of them in an insulting tone," not merely of one driver, but of a number so large and so constantly changing and of such conflicting aims and uncertain authority that he never knew who they all were, what they wanted, or whom to obey. The drivers agreed among themselves only in their common low regard for the camel and in their conviction that the only way to treat him was to beat him frequently and hard.

It is impossible to give a clearly outlined account of the system of political authority to which business is subject in the Third Reich because the political authority itself is not clearly outlined, nor is it, accordingly, a system at all.

The nazis set out originally to establish a corporative state similar to that which Mussolini had undertaken to organize in Italy. But the attempt broke down. Mussolini got as far as organizing his corporative state on paper. He even created a Ministry of Corporations and built a reasonably imposing building to house it, a sort of Temple to the Unknown God. But that is as far as he ever got. Hitler did not even get that far. Urgent current demands on the national economy outdistanced even the German ability to devise an organization that could accommodate the demands.

The nazis, accordingly, took to creating a new organization and establishing a new authority to deal with each specific problem as it arose. And since the problems that arose were almost infinite in number and complexity, so were the organizations and authorities that the nazis established. In the end, there were —and are—loose odds and ends left over from the beginnings of the "corporative state," functional organizations of business and geographical organizations of business and both functional and geographical organizations of business: offices that control the labor supply, offices that control foreign exchange, offices that control raw materials, offices that fix prices, offices that supervise the exploitation of the soil, offices that supervise the collection and use of garbage and other waste—and others almost literally without end.

There is only one formula the nazis seem to know for dealing with this confusion: whenever the situation threatens to get completely out of hand, they set up a new office to co-ordinate and rationalize the ones already in existence. In time, even the co-ordinators and rationalizers become so numerous and so confusing—and confused—that co-ordinators of the co-ordinators have to be appointed to rationalize the rationalizers.

A study made of the political controls of certain heavy industries in January, 1939, showed that seven different categories of such controls had been imposed and superimposed on them, one on top of another, seven different degrees of political supervision and regulation, each established in its turn, to supervise the ones below it.

There is one paramount authority over business in the New Germany—Goering's office for the Four-Year Plan. But there is conflict and confusion between this office and others that still survive, and even within this office itself.

The result of all this is, of course, that the individual business man is involved in a confusion of organizations, regulations, restrictions, authorizations, correspondence and red tape in general that it is almost impossible to conceive of until you actually experience it and extremely difficult to survive when you do.

WHAT HAPPENED TO THE CHIMNEY SWEEPS

The *Deutsche Reichsanzeiger und Preussische Staatsanzeiger*, an official gazette, published the following item, among others, in its number (101) of May 5, 1937:

"On the grounds of Section IV of the order of the Herr Reich Minister of Finance concerning the constitution of a Special Group 'Beer Conduit Cleaners' of the Reich Group Handicrafts of October 19, 1936 (*Deutscher Reichsanzeiger und Preussischer Staatsanzeiger* No. 247 of October 22, 1936), the following is hereby ordered:

"All enterprises (natural as well as legal persons) which are engaged independently and professionally in the cleaning of beer conduits are to report themselves in writing not later than May 20, 1937, to the Special Group Beer Conduit Cleaners, Hamburg 26, Wackerhagen 10.

"Hamburg, April 26, 1937.

"Leader of the Special Group Beer Conduit Cleaners of the
Reich Group Handicrafts (m. d. G. b.).
Kurt Stiedl."

History does not record what happened to the German beer
conduit cleaners when they reported themselves to Herr Stiedl.
It is to be presumed, however, that they were satisfactorily
organized—or rather, reorganized, because they had already
been organized at least once before. The cleaning of beer conduits was doubtless taken in hand and regulated some more.

But history does record another aspect of the incredible degree of the political regulation of German business that was
brought up to date at about this same time: the regulation of
all chimney sweeping in the Reich. For the *Reichsgezetsblatt*,
in which the texts of laws are published, came out on July 30,
1937 (No. 88), with a special section giving the texts of two
new orders regulating chimney sweeping. The orders filled 24
pages of fine type.

What has happened to beer conduit cleaners and chimney
sweeps in the New Germany might not matter much, in itself,
to business as a whole in the Reich. But what has happened to
beer conduit cleaning and chimney sweeping is typical of what
has happened to every other business—typical, that is, in kind,
but not typical in degree, for these two businesses are, after all,
relatively simple compared with many others, and the more
complicated the business, the more complicated the organization
and regulation to which it is subjected.

Consider the house-wrecking business. It finds its place in
the nazi organization and regulation of the national economy
under this title: "Special-Sub-Group-for-Businesses-Engaged-
in-Wrecking-and-Tearing-Down of the Special-Group-for-
Businesses-Engaged-in-Dealing-in-Old-and-Waste-Materials in
the Group-for-Businesses-Engaged-in-the-Wholesale-Import-
and-Export-Trade." And the *Frànkfurter Zeitung* of September
26, 1937, published a report of a meeting of representatives of
the "Special-Sub-Group-for-Businesses-Engaged-in-Producing-
and-Dealing-in-Technical-Chemicals-and-Technical-Raw-Ma-
terials" with representatives of the "Special-Sub-Group-for-

Businesses-Engaged-in-Producing-and-Dealing-in-Vegetable-Drugs" of the "Special-Group-for-Businesses-Engaged-in-Producing-and-Dealing-in-Technical-Oils-and-Fat-Drugs-and-Rubber" of the "Group-for-Businesses-Engaged-in-the-Wholesale-Import-and-Export-Trade."

This kind of political organization of business would be bad enough even if the organizations were only "social": if they only required business men to go out to lunch and call their fellow business men by their first names and sing songs and listen to speeches. But the organizations are by no means content with these relatively harmless activities. They exist to regulate business, and regulate business they do.

The head of one small business who shall remain nameless for obvious reasons confided to a friend that he was subject to orders from 328 different organizations and other government agencies.

In a case cited by Guillebaud, the manager of a small sugar refinery wanted to build a new boiler room with an electrical power connection. In order to do so he had to obtain the permission of 12 different offices, all of which demanded multiple copies of specifications and drawings.

Approval of 15 different offices had to be obtained to erect a new factory and of 24 to build a new house, according to the *Voelkischer Beobachter*. Laid end to end, the permits to build a house stretched for 45 feet, Dr. Ley once asserted. Peter Drucker writes that permission to execute one export order requires up to 120 different forms and permits.

"Official communications now make up more than one-half of a German manufacturer's entire correspondence," Walther Funk, Reich Minister of Economics and President of the Reichsbank, has said. And as Douglas Miller reports, the fast trains from the provinces to Berlin came to be known some time ago as "permit trains" because "they were principally occupied by legal gentlemen coming to government offices in search of these indispensable documents."

Firms engaged in foreign trade are even worse involved in red tape than others, because of the particularly exhaustive—and exhausting—regulations governing commodity shipments over frontiers and foreign exchange transactions the nazis have established. Stephen H. Roberts cites a statement that 237 different values have been officially assigned to the German mark in relation to other currencies at various times, and Funk himself has said, "The German export trade involves 40,000 separate transactions daily; yet for a single transaction as many as 40 different forms must be filled out."

It is impossible, of course, for many business men even to know what all the offices are that have authority over them, to say nothing of knowing all the regulations these offices issue.

Der Deutsche Volkswirt, an economic review that for several years voiced as much as it was possible to voice of the views of Dr. Schacht, published in June, 1937, a report of an investigation into the extent to which the retail textile trade in one district in western Germany was adhering to the nazi price regulations which had shown that 80 per cent of the firms investigated had been found guilty of violations.

"As there is no reason to believe that the number of offenders should be especially large in this one district," the *Volkswirt* said, "it must be assumed that a careful investigation in other districts would have disclosed a similar state of affairs.

"The question arises," the *Volkswirt* went on, "how it was possible that legal regulations which had been in force for several years could be violated on such a large scale. Most of the merchants detected in violations declared that they did not know exactly what the regulations were. Some had misunderstood them or had observed only the especially easy ones, which actually were intended only for exceptional circumstances. In this case, it may also be noted, a branch of business is concerned in which the competent compulsory organization tries with special zeal to keep its members informed and in which there is a numerous and effective trade press.

"It is by no means to be supposed that, in a state whose strict authority everyone knows and in principle affirms there is a special inclination to frivolous violations of the law. We have rather observed again and again that merchants whose attention has been called to mistakes they have made have been anxious to make amends. There is no lack of good will.

"The question arises," the *Volkswirt* said with the caution appropriate in criticizing the government, "whether it is literally possible for the business man to know all the regulations which apply to him, and to understand and obey them. Anyone who considers the mass of regulations which apply today to every branch of business, even the most insignificant, will be unable to answer this question in every case with a flat affirmative. . . .

"It is necessary to limit the number of regulations to a minimum. Otherwise the danger arises that an excess of regulation reduces even the man of good will to resignation or indifference, so that, feeling that he cannot satisfy all the regulations, he does not even observe those of vital importance."

As Brinkmann said, certain things cannot even be expected of a camel.

CORRUPTION IS AN ECONOMIC NECESSITY

"Under such circumstances, corruption is not merely a vice but an economic necessity," as Guenter Reimann has pointed out.

The state interferes in everything. Its action is arbitrary; there is no check on its powers, no appeal against its decisions. And there simply are not enough human beings in Germany (or in any other country) to exercise so much and such arbitrary authority both virtuously and wisely. There are not enough to exercise it at all. Yet by the very definition of the authoritarian, totalitarian state, the authority must be exercised. The permission of the "competent" politicians must be obtained, or business cannot function at all. To obtain these permissions, therefore, and to obtain them in time, the business man must bribe whether he wants to or not.

And the politicians in the New Germany, for their part, are more insistent upon being bribed than politicians anywhere else in modern times have probably ever been. The corruption in the Third Reich makes New York City and Chicago—and Paris—at their worst look like the purest alabaster Cities of God in comparison.

This corruption takes several forms. The most primitive consists of cash payments for favors received or anticipated, or simple thievery of funds. These go on in the New Germany in much the same way that they do everywhere else, except for the colossal scale on which they go on in the Reich and except for the fact that they are complicated by the degree of sincerity of the official to be bought. The more sincere some nazis are, the more it costs to buy them. "It depends on what kind of a party member you have to deal with," in the words of a story told by Reimann. "If he no longer believes in national socialism, it will cost you 100 marks. If he still does, 500 marks. But if he is a fanatic, you will have to pay 1,000 marks."

Some nazis, however, cannot be bribed quite so openly. In dealing with these other party members, business men, or, more often, whole business organizations or industries, make "free will gifts" consisting of villas or yachts or private planes or cars or some other form of contributions in kind.

In still a third form of corruption, the seeker after favors— or simple justice—contributes nothing at all directly to the politician, but asks him to recommend a good lawyer or political agent and pays the person so recommended handsome fees which the recipient then splits with the politician.

Corruption in these forms exists in the New Germany on a staggering scale and to an extent and in a detail and with a thoroughness that are almost incredible, even to one who knows the worst there is to know about corruption elsewhere. In kind, however, as distinct from degree, they are essentially like similar forms of corruption in other times and places.

But there is still another kind of racketeering that characterizes the Third Reich that is almost unique in anything like the scale on which it exists in Germany. This consists of the putting of politicians on business pay rolls and of giving them preference for all jobs.

There are three main criteria which the German business man uses in deciding how many party men he must put on his pay roll and which jobs he must give them.

First, there are certain functions that only a party member in good standing can ordinarily fulfill with any degree of success. Generally speaking these consist of the tasks of obtaining the myriad permissions from party and government offices which are necessary for the conduct of virtually all business in Germany.

Second, apart from the nature of the duties of an office, the German business man usually finds it necessary to have at least one relative or friend of some particularly powerful party leader on his pay roll on general principles. If he does not, he may have trouble obtaining his permits no matter how irreproachable the political standing of his "permit officer" may be.

And third, the German business man ordinarily has to hire worthy party members for a certain number and proportion of all jobs throughout his whole enterprise, on the grounds that the party members, having saved the Reich from a fate worse than death, deserve well of their country and, more specifically, of their country's business men.

PARTY MEMBERS PREFERRED

The nazi boom created an actual labor shortage in Germany after it got well under way, and in the end there were jobs for everybody, nazis and non-nazis alike. When the party seized power, however, there were between 6,000,000 and 7,000,000 unemployed. And while the regime set out to find work for as many of these millions as possible (except, of course, for Jews and political enemies), it undertook most particularly to find jobs for its own party members.

So much pressure did the nazis exert on employers, in fact, that the practice soon developed of specifying "Party Members Preferred" in advertising for men. This tendency became so marked that even the party's own press began to have misgivings:

"Is a new party caste system being built up in Germany?" the *Niedersaechsische Tageszeitung* asked, and it warned against the dangers of giving too much preference to party members for jobs. National socialists have special responsibilities, it declared, but no special privileges.

This appeared at first sight a singularly unworldly position for a party paper to take. The *Tageszeitung* went on, however, in a different vein:

"For us," it said, "the question cannot be, 'Party member or not party member?' but only, 'National socialist or not national socialist?' It is no more than right and fair that Old Fighters should be preferred in every way. [An Old Fighter is a member who was active in the party in the lean years before it paid to be a nazi.]

"This, however, is not merely a question of providing for the Old Fighters. It is desirable to keep alive the fighting spirit of these men and, in doing this, to train up our youth.

"Thus for us also in the community of the people is the natural order of rank fixed by character and achievement alone," the *Tageszeitung* concluded with a triumphant non sequitur characteristic of nazi utterances.

A considerably more important party journal, the *Westdeutscher Beobachter,* took a similar position. Under the heading, "The Right of Old Fighters to Jobs; a Self-Evident Duty of Gratitude," it said that deserving party members had suffered economically as a result of devoting themselves to the cause and it was therefore "no more than a duty of decency and gratitude to the Old Fighters" to provide them with satisfactory positions.

Much had already been done in this respect, the *Westdeutscher Beobachter* reported, and generally speaking the recognition by the country of this "self-evident duty of gratitude" had been satisfactory. "In almost all sections of the German people," the paper said, "there is full understanding for the position of the Old Fighters. Cases in which the hiring of Old Fighters has been refused or agreed to only with aversion have been exceptional."

And no wonder. For the campaign to provide adequate jobs for deserving party members was conducted by three such powerful agencies as the national leadership of the party, the high command of the S. A. and the Reich Institute for Providing Employment and for Unemployment Insurance, which has almost unlimited authority over hiring and firing in Germany.

As part of this campaign, party headquarters for the district of Southern Hannover-Brunswick, for one, issued a statement announcing:

"A considerable number of old and deserving national socialists are still without work. Every business man conscious of his responsibilities must do all that is possible to support the party by hiring these Old Fighters. The Chamber of Commerce and Industry has requested all member firms to see, whenever a post is to be filled, if it cannot be given to an Old Fighter."

Party headquarters in Delmenhorst County took more active measures. It announced in the Spring of 1937 that there were still deserving Old Fighters in the county in need of jobs and it informed employers that they were to attend a meeting with local party leaders every fortnight until jobs were found for every worthy Old Fighter of the S. A.

Preferment extended even to the theater. When contracts for the theatrical season 1936-1937 were being drawn up, Alfred Frauenfeld, vice-president of the Reich Chamber of the Theater, issued a statement in behalf of the president saying, among other things:

"I have been obliged, to my regret, to recognize the fact that negotiations for the approaching theatrical season are almost concluded and that a large number of party members and veterans who saw active service in the war have not been engaged. All theater directors are obliged to give preference to party members and such war veterans for all openings that still exist. Actors and actresses engaged on these grounds for the past season are to be retained in companies whenever possible and their contracts are to be renewed except under very special circumstances."

THE LITTLE MAN IS EATEN

Revolutions proverbially eat their own children, and the national socialist revolution is no exception. For the nazi movement was primarily a revolt of the little man, in the beginning, of the lower middle class, of the shop keepers. The party, furthermore, made glittering promises to the shop keepers. The department and chain stores and the mail order houses were to be handed over to the small retail merchant. The power of the "money interests" was to be broken. Little business was to come into its own.

But in the event the election promises have tarnished, and tarnished badly. It has been the lower middle class that has profited least and suffered most under national socialist rule. It has been the small shop keeper above all others who has been destroyed. It is precisely the little man who has been eaten. Not only has he not received what was promised him, but he is worse off than he was before.

There are several reasons for this:

For one thing, as Guillebaud puts it, "The recovery measures, based as they have been on great national works and rearmament, have inevitably favored the big firms, which alone were in a position to carry out orders on so large a scale."

For another thing, the elaborate organization and regulation the nazis have imposed on all business entail an amount of red tape, legal knowledge and advice and other costs of operation that the small business man simply cannot afford.

Nazi price policy has also imposed special hardships on retail trade, and particularly on independent shop keepers. For on the one hand the nazis have forbidden most retail price increases and on the other hand they have been unable to prevent wholesale price increases nearly as effectively, and have actually encouraged certain increases. Retail trade, consequently, has been ground between the upper and nether millstones—precisely as it was during the Bruening deflation in the years before the nazis came to power.

By a peculiarly bitter irony, even the nazi boom harmed small businesses in the Reich almost as much as it helped. For not only did big business get most of the orders and not only was the little man strangled in red tape and caught in the price shears, but when labor shortages began to develop the nazis adopted the policy, among others, of shutting down tens of thousands of small businesses out of hand and forcing the shop keepers, handicraft workers and employees to take jobs as day laborers in factories instead.

The *Frankfurter Zeitung* reported as early as October 17, 1936, that 18,000 persons had already then been purged from the hotel and restaurant business on the grounds that they were "incompetent," and the purge continued. On March 24, 1939,

the same newspaper reported that the authorities had closed
150 of a total of 900 wholesale radio firms in the Reich. The
Voelkischer Beobachter of April 15, 1939, reported the issuing
of a decree by the nazi czar for the electrical power and light
industry ordering 1,200 electrical firms to go out of business.
The *Deutsche Allgemeine Zeitung* reported in its evening edition of July 29, 1939, that the total number of handicraft business enterprises had been reduced by 180,000 since 1936. Within the preceding year alone, 76,000 such businesses had been
closed by the authorities, the paper said.

In all these purges and other policies the nazis claimed publicly, of course, that they were motivated exclusively by a desire
to serve the common weal. Privately, on the other hand, they
were, as usual, more candid:

"How do you decide which businesses to close and which to
leave open?" an American once asked one of Funk's bright
young party men.

"Oh, we ask the local trade organization to give us a list,"
the bright young man said.

Then he grinned.

"Of course our special pals don't suffer any," he added, "and
neither do the local party bosses' pals!"

Funk himself once provided a simple but vivid example of
the psychology of the purgers: A small band of street musicians,
a sort of "Hungry Five," thought to do the Minister a special
honor by playing under his office windows one day. The instant
the first note of music sounded, Funk got up from his desk and
looked out the window. "Call a cop," he said to an aide who
happened to be in the room, "and have those birds shipped off
to work in a factory."

24. The Economic "Miracle"

They see nothing wrong in the rule that to the victors belong the spoils of the enemy.

WILLIAM LEARNED MARCY, SPEECH IN
THE UNITED STATES SENATE, 1832

OTHER THINGS BEING EQUAL, if you expand credit on a large scale in a text-book specimen of a free, capitalistic national economy in a world of other free capitalistic national economies, you are supposed to produce a fairly standardized kind of results:

Production increases. Unemployment declines. Prices, wages, dividends and interest rates go up. The national income rises. Imports tend to increase and exports to fall.

If you expand credit too far under these circumstances you are liable to cause an uncontrollable inflation, with panic flights from the national currency into goods and other currencies, runs on banks, bank failures and soaring prices.

The nazis, though, have expanded credit on an enormous scale and, temporarily, at least, they have produced the results they needed and wanted to produce but at the same time they have been able to prevent most of the results of credit expansion they have neither wanted nor been able to afford.

They have increased production, employment and the national income. But they have kept prices, wages, dividends and interest rates within limits which, considering the circumstances, are remarkably narrow. Up to the outbreak of the war, they maintained exports extraordinarily well. And they kept down imports and limited them for the most part to commodities that served the purposes they themselves designated, notably armaments.

When the nazis began their enormous spending program, critics said the regime could not possibly keep it up any length of time without causing disaster. When the nazis continued year after year to spend without causing the kind of disaster to the kind of people the critics had in mind, the critics proclaimed that the regime had performed a miracle.

The critics were, of course, wrong both times. They were wrong because they made two major miscalculations:

First, they failed to realize how very far the German national economy was—and could be made to be—from being the kind of a text-book, free, capitalistic economy to which classical precepts of public finance apply. More specifically, they failed to realize how well the nazis could insulate Germany from the influences of the outside world, and they could not believe that the German people would accept the restrictions on their lives, their liberties and their pursuit of happiness that would have to be imposed on them if the program was to be possible.

And second, the critics did not allow for the colossal booty that the nazis were to seize from the peoples they conquered, beginning with the Jews in Germany itself and ending no man can yet say where.

THE BILL THAT MARS PRESENTED

The war cost Germany approximately 4,500,000,000 marks a month the first year of the conflict. (Figures for the second year are not available as these lines are written.) This is the first installment of the bill that Mars presented. Ordinary civil expenditures probably amounted to another 500,000,000 marks a month.

Of this total of 5,000,000,000 marks the nazis raised approximately 2,700,000,000 marks by borrowings, approximately 2,000,000,000 marks by taxation and approximately 300,000,000 marks in the form of earnings of government-owned property and from other miscellaneous sources.

The nazis have been pouring money into the national economy ever since they seized power on a scale almost as large as

this. Most of this money the nazis have raised and still are raising by borrowings.

The public debt when the regime took over the country was
11,602,000,000 marks. By the outbreak of the war the disclosed
public debt had risen to 37,363,000,000 marks and there was
probably an additional undisclosed debt of at least 10,000,-
000,000 marks, making a total of between 45,000,000,000 and
50,000,000,000 marks, an increase of between 35,000,000,000
and 40,000,000,000 marks in a little more than six and one-
half years.

During the first ten months of the war, the nazis borrowed
22,810,000,000 marks more, according to the *Deutsche Allgemeine Zeitung*, and by the end of the first year of the conflict
war borrowings probably increased to 30,000,000,000 marks.
This makes a grand total of between 65,000,000,000 and 70,-
000,000,000 marks the nazis borrowed and spent from January
30, 1933, to September 1, 1940.

Nazi borrowings the first year of the war were roughly
equally divided between short-term and long-term loans. The
regime issued three kinds of short-term and two kinds of long-
term paper.

The short-term paper consisted of 3-month, 7-month and
16-month Treasury Bills. Interest on all these bills was cut the
Summer of 1940 by ⅛ of 1 per cent, to 2¼ per cent, 2⅞ per
cent and 3⅜ per cent, respectively. The government issued
a total of 13,000,000,000 marks worth of these Bills from the
outbreak of the war until June 30, 1940, the latest date during
the first 12 months of the war for which figures seem to be
available.

Long-term borrowings took the form, first, of 27-year Reich
Loans and, second, of Treasury Notes which were issued first
for 5 years, later for 10 years and still later for 20 years. The
first 27-year Loans bore 4½ per cent interest, but this was later
cut to 4 per cent. A total of 5,000,000,000 marks worth of
these bonds was issued up to the end of June, 1940. The Treasury Bills bore 4 per cent interest. The total of these notes issued approximately 4,000,000,000 marks at the end of the first
year of the war.

WAGES OF SIN POSTPONED

There has been much mystification about the "miracle" the nazis have accomplished in borrowing and spending these enormous sums without causing the kinds of disasters most people predicted would speedily result, but there is really nothing mysterious about what the nazis have done, nor how they have done it, and it certainly is no miracle. It consists essentially of nothing more esoteric and miraculous than this:

The regime stimulates production; it restricts consumption; it appropriates the margin for its own purposes. The nazis put the German national economy on a war basis. That is the "mystery." That is the "miracle."

By staggering government expenditures, financed in the first instance by borrowings, the nazis raised the value of total national production, including both industry and the handicrafts, from 38,000,000,000 marks in 1932 to 77,000,000,000 marks in 1937, an increase of 39,000,000,000 marks, or 102.6 per cent.

Employment, earnings of labor and employees and the national income all rose in this boom:

Almost 9,500,000 more persons were gainfully employed when the war broke out than had been at work at the depth of the depression in 1932, and the average number of hours worked per week increased from 41.46 to 47.04 during this same period.

Total wages and salaries paid in the Reich, which amounted to 25,700,000,000 marks in 1932, rose to 38,800,000,000 marks in 1937.

National income increased from 35,000,000,000 marks in 1932 to 76,000,000,000 marks in 1938, the last full peacetime year.

At the same time, however, the nazis managed to avoid paying, for the time being, the usual wages of economic and financial sin:

The cost of living index (1913-1914 = 100) rose only from 120.6 in 1932 to 127.3 at the outbreak of the war, and although the index has been repeatedly challenged as inaccurate, it probably is true that the cost of living for most Germans did not go up more than 20 to 25 per cent during this period.

Most of the increase in the earnings of labor, furthermore, was due to greater production rather than to higher rates of pay. The official index figure of wages per hour (1928 = 100) actually declined, in fact, from 86.2 in 1932 to 84.2 at the outbreak of the war.

Earnings of capital, too, were kept within national socialist limits. The Reichsbank discount rate was only 3.5 per cent after 12 months of war, compared with an average of 5.21 for 1932. The real yield on 4.5 per cent mortgage bonds fell from 8.38 per cent to 4.54 per cent during this same period. Surplus earnings of over 6 per cent (in some cases 8 per cent) of industry had to be invested in government paper.

Imports rose from 4,667,000,000 marks in 1932 to 6,051,-000,000 marks in 1938, but this was a small increase, under the circumstances, and it consisted to an extraordinary degree of such commodities and only such commodities as the nazis wanted to enter the country, principally production rather than consumption goods, and reserves of vital raw materials to be stored for war.

Exports fell during this period from 5,739,000,000 marks in 1932 to 5,619,000,000 marks in 1938, but the fact that the decline was no greater than this was remarkable in view of the high prices of German goods, the boycotts of them in some parts of the world, the nazis' concentration on armaments and the unsettled and unfavorable economic conditions in many markets. This achievement is primarily due to the subsidizing of exports to the extent of approximately 1,000,000,000 marks a year, or almost 18 per cent of the total value of all goods sold abroad, amounting in some cases to as much as one-half the sales price.

NO PLACE TO GO

Nazi economic and financial policy placed the average German in a predicament which was comical by old-fashioned peacetime standards of judgment but which must be an essential feature of any effective war economy:

He produced more and earned more than he had before—

but he could not spend a good deal of his increased earnings because goods on which to spend them simply were not there to buy. The citizen was all dressed up, but he had no place to go—except, of course, to war, which was the ultimate reason and purpose for the whole nazi program.

The nazis control consumption by methods of three general sorts: First, they determine what is to be produced. Second, they take as much as they possibly can of the people's earnings away from them and spend it for purposes the nazis, not the people, choose. And third, the regime rations commodities directly.

The nazis have seen to it that most of the increase in total national production since the party took over the country has been in production, not consumption, goods.

Almost 70 per cent of the increase in total national production from 1932 to 1937 was in the value of production goods, which rose from 20,000,000,000 marks to 47,000,000,000 marks during this period, an increase of 27,000,000,000 marks or 135 per cent. Only slightly more than 30 per cent of the total increase occurred in production of consumers' goods, which rose from 18,000,000,000 marks in 1932 to 30,000,000,000 marks in 1937, or by 12,000,000,000 marks or 66.6 per cent.

Prevented from spending an increasingly large proportion of what he earned, what did the citizen do with his money? He built up his savings account. He took out insurance. And, of course, he paid taxes.

He paid, in fact, exceedingly heavy taxes. The Reich's revenues from taxation rose from 6,846,000,000 marks for the fiscal year 1933-1934 to approximately 25,000,000,000 marks for 1940-1941, an increase of 18,154,000,000 marks, or 265.1 per cent.

Of the 25,000,000,000 marks tax income for 1940-1941, special war taxes brought in 5,000,000,000 marks: a 50 per cent surtax on incomes over 2,400 marks per year, and increased levies on tobacco, beer, liqueurs and sparkling wines.

But the savings banks and insurance companies did not hoard the money they got from the citizen. They used most of it to buy government securities. So the state got that money, too.

A steadily increasing proportion of the national income went to the state from the time the nazis took over the country.

In 1932 the Weimar Republic took 30.6 per cent of the national income, the Reichskreditgesellschaft estimates, whereas in 1938 the nazis took 47 per cent. A writer in the *Das Reich* in September, 1940, calculated that the state took almost exactly one-half the national income during the fiscal year 1939-1940. And Rudolf Brinkmann said in 1938 that two-thirds of the whole national income "flowed through the hands of and was redistributed by the state" in 1937, and the proportion has certainly increased since then.

According to figures published by a leading Berlin bank and cited by "Thomas Reveille," the national income of the Reich was 85,000,000,000 marks in 1940, and of this the state took 60,000,000,000 or 70 per cent, in the following forms and from the following sources:

Billions of Marks

1. Direct and indirect taxation	34
2. Released as a result of rationing and other restrictions on civilian consumption of	
a. foodstuffs	5
b. manufactured and industrial products	9
3. "Living on capital": Released as a result of	
a. increased utilization of equipment not replaced	4
b. exhaustion of raw material supplies not replaced	6
c. forced reduction in rate of private investment	2
Total	60

These are the essentials of nazi economics and financial policy —these and the methods by which the regime has looted subject peoples. This is the "secret" of the "German economic miracle."

The "miracle" is, of course, more of a political and military achievement than it is an economic or financial one: the "miracle" by which the nazis cajoled, convinced, compensated and compelled the German people into accepting the impairments of their freedom which alone made the program possible, and the military successes by which the Reich has been able to make the peoples it has conquered pay for their own destruction.

PIRATE REALM

All the borrowings and all the controlled consumption and all the other elaborate devices the nazis adopted could never have kept the regime's frenzied finances going without disaster long if it had not been for something else: for the loot the nazis seized from those they subjugated. The national socialist Reich has never been self-supporting since it was founded, except in the sense that any other pirate realm is self-supporting. It has lived throughout its history on the resources which others had accumulated by hard work and self-denial and which the nazis have taken away from the others because they have been stronger, more resolute and more unscrupulous than the others. And the Third Reich can survive only if, as and when it can go on seizing still more loot to live on.

Economically and financially (and in several other respects) the essential character of national socialism is this: by a prodigious effort that can be sustained for only a relatively short time, the nazis have first armed themselves to the teeth. Then they have used their arms to strike down others and seize the others' possessions. As long as the nazis can go on striking down others with sufficiently valuable possessions, national socialism will thrive and grow great. But whenever there is no more loot to seize, no more subject peoples to exploit, national socialism's days are numbered. Therefore the nazis will go on striking down anybody and everybody else they can who has valuable possessions. They must. There is no other way they can survive.

The nazis did not invent the slogan, "To the victors belong the spoils," nor are they the first conquerors to live on the land that they have seized. But the nazis have developed to the finest point ever achieved the art of making the defeated pay for their own ruin.

They began in Germany itself. As Douglas Miller has pointed out, they have robbed the Jews, the Catholics and other minority groups. They have taxed and have taken away by other means much of the rest of the country's accumulated wealth. They have intensively exploited mines and forests and farm land. They have consumed more and more of the liquid capital in the Reich. They have exchanged government securities for existing securities held by private persons. They have seized equities of all kinds and given nothing but their promises to pay in return.

Although it is by no means the only one of the nazis' marauding policies, the plundering of the Jews has been the most openly avowed and least inhibited of them all. The nazis "fined" German Jews 1,000,000,000 marks. They wrecked and looted all Jewish synagogues and places of business. Then they confiscated all insurance policies held by Jews covering the damage and forced the Jews to make it good themselves. They took over all Jewish businesses at a small fraction of their worth, and all Jewish medical and other professional practices without paying anything for them at all. They drove more than 3,500 Jews out of cultural occupations alone, and tens and hundreds of thousands out of other positions. They have made life insupportable for Jews—and then taxed away most of what they had left for the privilege of leaving the country alive if they could find anywhere else to go. It is probably the most barefaced and colossal looting of a defenseless minority the world has ever seen in times of so-called peace. Altogether it would be surprising if the nazis have extorted less than $1,000,000,000 from the Jews in the Reich alone.

Jews in the other countries the Reich has overrun have also paid heavy tribute to their Master People conquerors and despoilers. Jewish-owned property in Bohemia and Moravia alone was probably worth $500,000,000 when the nazis swept into the country, for example, and the nazis soon took more of this total than the Jews were allowed to retain.

But this is only the beginning of nazi looting. In Germany itself the regime has taken more from the Jews than it has from anybody else. In the countries the nazis have now conquered they make no such nice distinctions. They loot all alike.

PLUNDER

Nazi looting in the countries the Reich has conquered has taken a variety of forms limited only by the varieties of property and by the imagination of the looters, which is fertile.

The invading and occupying armies requisition enormous supplies for their own use and for shipment back to Germany. In some cases, the requisitioned goods are paid for with special army promissory notes, in others in the currency of the conquered country itself, "borrowed" from the national treasury or central bank; in still others, the nazis "pay" with "money" they themselves print especially for the purpose and in any quantity desired. This "money" may be either facsimiles of the local currency or a special form of "occupation marks" for use in conquered countries, the so-called Reichskreditkassenscheine. Citizens and banks in occupied countries must accept these "occupation marks" at rates of exchange fixed by the nazis and therefore scarcely calculated to cause the invader any grave losses.

The Reich has told the central banks in most occupied countries to hold these banknotes until the war is over and to regard them meanwhile as foreign exchange and to issue national currency against them.

Another form of booty in Germany's conquests is the local currency seized.

The nazis acquired approximately 3,000,000,000 Czech crowns when they took over the Sudeten Territories, for example, and used these funds to buy industrial, real and other property in the rest of Czechoslovakia. They also obtained approximately 600,000,000 zlotys in the parts of Poland they annexed outright to the Reich, and spent this amount in the rest of Poland. Then they suppressed the old zloty currency and issued new money in its place, thus making valueless the zloty notes held everywhere else.

State property seized in conquered countries has also helped defray the cost of the nazi program of conquest. The total value of Polish state property seized is approximately $2,400,-000,000, for example, and the loot in this form is naturally greater in more prosperous countries. Publicly owned gold the nazis have seized in conquered countries amounts to $1,500,-000,000, "Thomas Reveille" estimates.

Nor is private property secure from seizure, either. The methods and pretexts for its seizure differ, but the end result is always the same. One of the most solemn and elaborate pretexts invoked in Holland, for example, was specified in an order which provided for the confiscation of the property of all persons and organizations who (or which) "have promoted tendencies hostile to Germany in the past, are promoting such tendencies now or might be expected to promote them in future," a large enough category, in all truth, and one that doubtless is so defined and so exploited as to result in the transfer of gratifying sums from the pockets of the vanquished to those of the victors.

The levying of "punitive fines" yields further rich plunder. No comprehensive list of such fines seems to have been published, but "Thomas Reveille" cites five levied on towns and cities in Norway, Holland and France which amount to $578,000, and the total taken in this guise must be many times this amount.

Property belonging to British subjects and Jews in occupied territories is seized without any pretext at all. British-owned property on the continent has been estimated to be worth approximately $1,000,000,000.

The clearing agreements that Germany had before the war with certain of the occupied countries have afforded still another means by which the nazis have profited by their conquests. Before the war, Germany owed Denmark, for example, approximately 40,000,000 crowns under the German-Danish clearing agreement. Six months after the nazis seized Denmark, they had "bought" 360,000,000 crowns worth of Danish goods more than they had delivered to Denmark in return.

REPARATIONS IN ADVANCE

But by far the greatest racket the nazis operate in the countries they conquer is the "costs of occupation" racket. The nazis pretend that the sums they levy under this heading are designed to pay for maintaining the German forces garrisoned in each of the occupied countries. The pretense, however, is a feeble one. For the amounts the nazis extort in this guise average three to four times as much as the costs of maintaining the occupying forces, as "Thomas Reveille" points out, and are determined, not by these costs at all, but only by the question of what the traffic will bear.

The nazis have calculated that each country can be looted in this manner of approximately as much per year as the total appropriations provided for in the last budget to be voted before the nazi invasion—that is, the greatest amount the nation thought it could possibly raise to arm (and to govern) itself in order to fight for its very life—and they demand this amount for themselves as "costs of occupation." It is a form of reparations, based on capacity to pay—and to pay at the point of a bayonet, with the victorious enemy forces on hand to collect—and thus vastly superior, from the conqueror's viewpoint, to old-fashioned methods of trying to collect after the war is over and most or all of the conqueror's troops have gone home.

The nazis levy 10,480,000,000 marks per year from the conquered nations of Europe in this form. Between 2,000,000,000 and 3,000,000,000 marks of this total the nazis use to maintain the occupying forces, "Thomas Reveille" calculates. This leaves a net profit of 7,000,000,000 to 8,000,000,000 marks. The nazis use this balance to buy up property of all kinds, both in the occupied territories themselves and elsewhere: French and Belgian holdings in the Balkans, coal and iron mines in Alsace and Lorraine, steel mills and shipyards in France, Belgium and Holland, arms plants in Czechoslovakia—and American mills in the Reich itself.

The Germans' cries of anguish and moral indignation when they were called upon to pay a total of approximately 10,000,-000,000 marks in reparations throughout the entire seven-year period that the Dawes and Young Plans were in effect (and at a time when the rest of the world was pouring capital into Germany, too) still ring in every ear. This colossal sum could not be raised, and even if it could be raised it could not be transferred, without wrecking the world economy, the Germans said.

It ruined Germany and was one of the principal causes of the world depression, they said.

The nazis now collect this same amount every year in the form of "costs of occupation" alone.

The Reich paid a total of 4,000,000,000 marks in reparations to France in the years 1924-1931. The nazis now levy that much every six months on the French.

Hitler has said that the German arms program cost 90,000,-000,000 marks. He looted that much from his helpless victims the first 12 months of war.

Epilogue: World Counter-Revolution

> *I have no belief in panaceas and almost none in sudden ruin. I believe with Montesquieu that if the chances of a battle—and I may add, the passage of a law—has ruined a state, there was a general cause at work that made the state ready to perish by a single battle or a law.*
>
> MR. JUSTICE OLIVER WENDELL HOLMES,
ADDRESS BEFORE THE HARVARD LAW
SCHOOL ASSOCIATION OF NEW YORK, 1913

> *The most dangerous people on our side are those who think we can lick Hitler by force alone.*
>
> "ONE OF THE PRESIDENT'S ADVISERS,"
QUOTED BY ELIOT JANEWAY IN "LIFE"

THE NAZI REVOLUTION and the Second World War in which it reached its awful climax and culmination seemed at first to abound in mysteries:

How were such evil men as the nazis able to seize and keep control of so great a people as the Germans? How were they able to foist such a counterfeit Brave New World on them? To lead the Germans into a war the Germans hated and dreaded almost if not quite as much as any other people did? Why did the Germans yet fight so well and why did the French collapse so speedily?

There seemed, at first, to be no answers to these questions. And yet there *is* an answer—a single answer—to them all: the answer is that a world counter-revolution is under way. The war is the culmination and climax of this counter-revolution, and the war will decide whether it succeeds or not, at least for the time being, but the counter-revolution began long before and may continue long after, and the war is only a phase of something even greater and even more profound than the conflict itself.

There are, inevitably, other important aspects of what is happening, too. Most notably, there are three: there is the strength that Germany has had for generations, has been able to throw into conflicts so often before; there is Hitler himself; there are the sheer despair and exhaustion of the First World War. But none of these things, and none of the other aspects of the war, nor any or all of them together, suffices to explain the turn that events have taken, unless the talisman of counter-revolution is invoked. Taken with the others, and essential to the others, this talisman does explain it. It explains the rapidity of Germany's new rise to power (and the decline of the other nations, for both things occurred); it explains the paralysis of will and judgment among Hitler's victims both in the Reich itself and elsewhere; it explains why the war came, and why it is such a nightmare to the Germans as well as to the others, yet why the Germans go on fighting none the less, and why the French were so sure of winning and why they lost so catastrophically instead, and it explains why the Germans had such an excellent chance to win from the beginning.

There are several senses in which the war is counter-revolutionary: in the purposes for which Hitler is avowedly fighting it, in the methods by which he is fighting it, in the consequences of the fighting of it, even if Hitler loses, and, most important of all, in the fact that the whole war is possible and Hitler's purposes and methods and chances of success are possible, only because a world revolution has long been under way, a revolution which Hitler in turn rebelled against.

THE REVOLT AGAINST FREEDOM

There are duly designated victims of the counter-revolution who say, as duly designated victims often do when they have lost their faith and courage, that national socialism and the "new order" which it proclaims are riding forward on a "wave of the future," that they are part of a true revolution, a revolution striving toward the same great goal as the fundamental trend of human history, and that nothing therefore could or should be done to balk them. Surrenders like these are typical of the abject and suicidal abdications of individuals and classes in decline and decay, and this is notable in itself. But what is much more notable is that the judgment on which the surrender is based is so transparently false. For if there was ever a wave out of the past, out of the dark backward and abysm of time, a reaction and therefore a false revolution, a counter-revolution, it is the nazi assault on the West.

Because the great, main current of human affairs flows toward greater freedom, toward liberty and dignity for human individuals, toward liberty and dignity for whole societies, for working out their destinies as best they can and will. This was of the essence of Magna Carta, this was of the essence of the French and American Revolutions and of all the other countless fights of men for freedom. And is the nazi revolt riding on a wave toward this same bright hope and vision? What is happening to the Czechs and the Poles and the French and the Danes, to the Dutch and the Greeks and the Jews and a score of others—is this, then, in keeping with the destiny of man? If surrender without striking a blow is ever possible, is it possible now?

No, the signs are plain enough to anyone who has eyes and will see. This is naked reaction, naked counter-revolution, raw in tooth and claw, proud of its aims and proud of its rawness (and, as it happens, perpetually surprised at the victims who so obligingly hasten to sign their own capitulations so unnecessarily far in advance). Hitler has set out to overthrow the civilization of Western Europe. No necromancy is required to see this. Hitler says so himself, and he gives every indication that he means exactly what he says. He has come remarkably close to succeeding. Even if he fails, the consequences of his having tried will be appalling. If he should succeed, he will try to erect his "new order" on the ruins he is making of the old. But the "order" he calls "new" is neither an order nor is it new. It is the pure essence of disorder, for it knows no laws, not even its own, and it is the oldest thing in history, for it is tyranny.

THE GREAT PERHAPS

Western Europe has long been locked in the paralysis of a crisis of faith. This is perhaps the most important single fact about Hitler and the Second World War; for Hitler is a creature, the war a convulsion, of that crisis.

"A revolution that threatens the basis of society can only be explained by fundamental changes within the basis of social organization itself," says Peter Drucker. "It must be owing to a revolution of man's concept of his own nature, of the nature of his society and of his own function and place in society."

This is the secret of what has been happening to the basis of society in western Europe: not only has there been, in fact, a revolution in man's concept of his own nature, of the nature of his society and of his own function and place in society, but there has also been an even greater revolution, a revolution in man's concept of the universe and of his function and place in the universe, as well.

This two-fold revolution in men's concepts has long been under way, but it is still only partly completed: it has proceeded far enough to destroy the validity of old concepts; the faiths that men lived by earlier are dead or dying. But the revolution has not proceeded far enough to yield new faiths to take their places. Millions on millions of men in the Western world have no conceptions at all, either of their places in society or of their places in the universe. They have begun to wonder if they have any places at all. And in their hearts they are terrified by their doubts.

The first great doubt is the doubt about the universe. "I have decided to accept the universe," the young lady wrote to Carlyle, and, "By gad, you'd better," Carlyle answered. The record does not show that it occurred to either of them that the universe might not accept *her*—or him either. Yet that is precisely the awful doubt that gnaws in the breasts of millions in modern times: there is no explanation of the universe that they believe that gives to men a place and function with dignity and purpose in that universe. There have been such explanations in the past, and there may be such explanations in the future, but there certainly is none now, and men are afraid.

For much of the recorded time of man there were twin explanations of man's place, both in the universe and in society, that enjoyed a general validity and that gave dignity and purpose to men's lives: There was the religious explanation of the universe in terms of the anthropomorphic God and there was the political explanation of society in terms of the divine right of kings. The political explanation was the earthly counterpart of the religious explanation: God the Father was the King in Heaven and the reigning monarch was the king on earth, and the king on earth derived just power from the King in Heaven, and to most men, perhaps, the One must have seemed much like the other. The world stood still and men's knowledge of the world stood still, and the religious and the political explanations seemed valid because they seemed to correspond to realities as realities were then revealed, and to explain them in terms that comforted men. And deriving from these explanations and dependent upon them were values and standards and symbols which seemed also valid, in politics, in arts and sciences, in morals and in manners.

But then steam was yoked, and later electricity, and the world changed, and the microscope and the telescope were devised and men's knowledge of the world changed, and both changed very rapidly, as history measures time and men can adjust themselves to change, and both the religious explanation of the anthropomorphic God and the political explanation of the divine right of kings ceased to enjoy validity because they seemed to cease to correspond to the new realities or to explain them in terms that comforted men.

The political explanation was challenged by two new explanations, by the theory of liberalism, which later would assimilate to capitalism, and which retained a Christian faith, although a tempered one, and by Marxian socialism, which rejected the Christian faith altogether, tempered though it came to be. For a time these new political explanations satisfied men something as the discarded explanation had satisfied them. But even when they did, they circumscribed men's faith, for they had no counterpart in Heaven, as the earlier explanation had. And there was no new religious explanation at all to comfort men:

The earth is not the center of the universe, and man is not the center of the earth, the newer explanations said (this or something like it). The earth was not made in six days by a Creator who rested on the seventh, and man was not made from breathed-on dust, nor woman from his rib. The earth was a flaming clot of mud cast off, perhaps by accident, from some much greater planet, and time and warmth and water and amoebae have done the rest, assisted, in some sense, it might well be, by Cosmic Law: Creative Evolution.

The newer explanations are ingenious, each one seems highly plausible in turn (although each, too, is abandoned in turn with disconcerting swiftness as new facts are found to discredit it), and the best of them imply a Will and Purpose that partake of greater sweep and grandeur than the earlier views. (Although some, also, do not: it is all very well to think of Christ as the First Advertising Man; in some quarters this has been regarded as paying Him a compliment. But it does not greatly console a mother whose baby has died, and this is what faiths must do.)

Yet even the best of the new explanations all have a fatal flaw: the Cosmic Will and Purpose are too intellectual, remote and comfortless. They provide an explanation of the universe, if you like; they even provide a whole series of explanations. But no two explanations are alike, and no one of them provides an explanation that gives dignity and purpose to men's places in the universe. They do not give the faith that men must have to live by. Nor can they, therefore, give the sanction that values and standards and symbols must have to be respected, in politics, in arts and sciences, in morals and in manners. The more men have learned about the universe they live in, the less important have they seemed themselves—themselves and what they do and how. The more facts they have acquired, the less faith have they had. Men's belief in an explanation of the universe that gives to life a meaning has become, "like that of Rabelais, a Great Perhaps."

THE ERA OF THE DEAD DOG

In the long run, there must be some faith- and hope-inspiring explanation of the universe. Life is unbearable without it. The lack of it is like a cancer in men's souls. Even the explanation of man's place in society depends in the end for credence on it. But the lack of an explanation that gave dignity and purpose to man's place in the universe could be borne with greater or lesser fortitude as long as there was at least an explanation that gave dignity and purpose to his place in society, and for a time this was the case.

Men were divided as to which explanation was the valid one, the explanation of liberal capitalism or the explanation of Marxian socialism; neither theory had the general validity that the theory of the divine right of kings had had. But while men believed different things, at least they believed. And as long as they did not disagree irreconcilably in what they thought, they could live together and societies could exist and function— and there might, perhaps, be time enough to find a new religious explanation, too, before disaster came.

But there was not time enough, in the event. There was only the Nineteenth Century and the first generation of the Twentieth, and no new faith- and hope-inspiring explanation was found of man's place in the universe and then disaster overtook the explanations of man's place in society, too, and in this double abandonment of faiths there came the counter-revolution.

Men blamed the First World War for this abandonment of faiths, but the most the First War did, and the most the Second could do, was accelerate or retard or divert a trend already there. Both wars were at least as much effects as they were causes. And the Jazz Age that came between wars was only a latter-day incident in the Revolt against the Nineteenth Century and the Puritans; the Lost Generation that mourned itself so garrulously in that Age had no more right (and no less) to do so than every other generation since Copernicus or Galileo —none of whom had, however, thought to make of its grievances a philosophy of life. For most men, actually, the Twenties were and should have been an era of new hope and faith:

The war had been won, liberty had been saved and free enterprise had justified itself. It was hind-sighted wisdom that later saw the faults in this Utopia, but the authors of the ululations of the Twenties had no such wisdom then. A Keynes might know enough, but they did not, to have a right to be so publicly unhappy (if anybody ever has that right) about mistaken and imagined imperfections. It was, in fact, the very hope and faith of peoples in that era which, being dashed and stricken later, turned disillusionment into despair.

Disillusionment never has a fixed beginning and seldom has any end, but to the extent that dates mean anything, this was the time-table of political despair:

Men lost their faith in socialism in 1914, when all the Marxist groups of Europe threw their internationalism overboard and fought their worker-brothers on the other side; in the insurrections that came when the war had ended, when some of the parties, at least, had socialism in their times within their grasp and lacked the resolution to achieve it; in 1925 and 1926 when the Italian party yielded to Mussolini; and in 1932 and 1933 when the Germans yielded to Papen and Hitler.

Men lost their faith in old-fashioned, "horse-and-buggy" liberal capitalism in the American economic catastrophe of 1929 and the European political and moral catastrophe of 1939.

Men lost their faith in communism when the Soviets affected first to make a common cause with the democracies, affected, then, to make it with the fascists—and failed to achieve true communism at home into the bargain in the meantime.

Thus did the peoples lose their faiths in the only explanations of society they knew that gave dignity and purpose to the lives they lived. They lost faith in the forms and processes that derived from these explanations and incorporated them. They lost faith in the leaders who had made or inherited these forms and supervised these processes. And the leaders lost faith in themselves.

Having lost faith, both the peoples and their leaders lost vision and judgment and purpose and will as well. Not knowing what to believe about the past and the present, they also did not know what to believe and hope about the future. Not knowing what to believe and hope about the future, they did not know how to act with a view to shaping and securing the future. Not knowing how to act with a view to the future, they did not know how to act with continuity and purpose and resolution at all. Western Europe had something like a collective nervous breakdown, a breakdown in faith. It was stricken with a paralysis of belief.

"What direction will Quai d'Orsay policy take?" Philippe Berthelot was asked shortly after the First World War.

"The direction of a dead dog floating downstream," he replied.

It was a whole era of the dead dog and of the dead dog policy.

This was the first part of the story of the world counter-revolution; this was what made it possible.

THE FALSE ALTERNATIVES

The loss of political faith, of belief in an explanation of society, would have been dangerous enough even if men still had had religious faith, a belief in an explanation of the universe. But men had lost their religious faith even before they had lost their political faiths. The Great Perhaps corroded *all* belief. And this was fatal. It left men with little or no faith in anything whatever, either in the Kingdom of Heaven or in the kingdoms of the earth. It left a vacuum in men's souls, and men can bear a vacuum in their souls as little as nature can bear one anywhere else. Something had to fill the vacuum. Something did—several somethings did. The story of these vacuums and of the several somethings that rushed in to fill them is the second part of the story of the counter-revolution; these are the things that happened once it had become possible for them to happen:

The course and character of the First World War did much to determine where the vacuums would occur first and what would fill them and, therefore, to determine the course and character of the war that was to come. The shocks and dislocations the first war caused hastened the process of disillusion and despair among some peoples and postponed it (only, perhaps, to make it more savage and bitter when it came) among others. It hastened the process in Russia and Italy and Germany; it postponed it in England and France.

In Russia the vacuum which despair had made was filled by communism. It was filled, that is, by a reaction against, a renunciation of, the search for freedom, a reaction and renunciation that, by definition, constituted counter-revolution. (For the true revolution, the true wave of the future, is the revolution, or the wave, that strives toward greater freedom.)

The promise that communism made was a false promise, but millions of men so deeply despaired that they could not, would not, see the falseness; all they would see was the promise, and they had to have a promise—any promise. The vacuums in their souls could not be borne; the communist promise entered in to fill it.

In this sense, at least, if not otherwise, communism was an alternative to other systems that might go bankrupt elsewhere later: it was false but it existed, it was there. Wherever a sufficient number of men should despair in sufficient degree for a sufficient time, the communist alternative was bound to be considered.

But the communist promise was a promise to the disinherited workers; it was therefore equally a threat to both middle and upper classes. All the classes everywhere now looked toward Moscow, they looked about themselves at home, they looked at each other with new perspectives and they were hopeful or fearful as their interests seemed to dictate, but they were all suspicious of each other.

So long as liberal capitalism or socialism seemed to function elsewhere, the promise and alternative of Moscow failed to lure. But when they failed or seemed to fail, the promise and alternative beckoned.

In Italy and the Reich, when failure came, some of the workers looked, inevitably, for a time at least, with longing toward the Kremlin. But here it was not the workers who decided the alternative; it was the middle classes. They looked with fear and loathing toward the Kremlin; the promise and alternative they chose was fascism: a new reaction against, a new renunciation of, the search for freedom, a second form, by equal definition, of the counter-revolution.

The promise that this alternative, too, held out, was false. But here, too, millions of men so deeply despaired that they could not, would not, see its falseness; all they could see was the promise, and they, too, had to have a promise—any promise. They chose this alternative, believed this promise.

Again, in this sense, if not otherwise, fascism was an alternative to other systems that might go bankrupt later. It was false, but it existed, it was there. Given the bitter circumstances, fascism, too, was bound to be considered.

But the fascist promise was a promise to the disinherited middle classes. It was therefore equally a threat to both the workers and the upper classes. All the classes everywhere now looked, not alone to Moscow, but to Rome and Berlin, too, they looked about themselves at home as well, they looked at each other with new perspectives and they were hopeful or fearful as interests seemed to dictate, but they were all—and doubly, now—suspicious of each other.

SCHIZOPHRENIA—AND DISASTER

So faithless, fearful and suspicious had millions of men become that their wills and judgments both were paralyzed. Even the instinct to survive did not function fully. The penultimate proof was the great mistake that both the commune and the upper classes, or significant segments of both, make when they were confronted by the rising menace of the fascist middle class. (The ultimate proof was the war itself.)

By the same fatality of blinded vision, Moscow and Paris and London alike, and the Herren Clubs and Liebknecht Houses everywhere, decided that fascism was to be the last resort of capitalism. And both the commune and the upper classes wanted this last resort afforded capitalism, wanted the capitalist system enabled to make this (false) last stand. The commune willed it so because it was convinced that capitalism would be beaten, finally beaten, there, just as it had been in its previous stands. The upper classes willed it so because they were convinced that capitalism would survive in this last stand despite its having lost the others that had gone before.

The commune and the upper classes both were wrong: the commune wrong because the capitalist system certainly could survive, be saved; the upper classes wrong because it certainly was not the fascists who could or wanted to save it. But both the commune and the upper classes redoubled their zeal when they had mistaken their aim, and both ended by destroying themselves while they were trying to destroy each other, by committing suicide in the process of trying to commit murder.

First the great mistake was made within national boundaries: Did not the communist parties make their worst assaults on socialists, not nazis, and did not the Schachts and Krupps and Thyssens help the Hitlers to win power?

But even this was not enough of tragedy; the great mistake was then committed on a world-wide scale as well: workmen in France made common cause (or tried to) with the Kremlin and employers with Palazzo Venezia and the Reichskanzlei. The British ruling classes, and some of the Laborites, too, helped the Reich against the French and Soviets alike.

Men on both sides of the average income level confused what they mistook for their class interests with what they were no longer able to see were their national interests (and which were therefore in the end their true class interests, too), and ended by destroying both. They dreamed of saving everything or acquiring everything, things which were equally impossible in the world they had to live in; they lived some of the time in their worlds of dreams and felt and acted sometimes in terms of one while they were really living in the other. This was collective schizophrenia, split mind, or, perhaps better, a manic-depressive insanity. It was also collective disaster.

For weakness is a criminal provocation, as poets have pointed out and politicians have always known. "All the lambs of this world have all the sins of all the lions on their consciences," as Edmond Taylor puts it. And this was perhaps the greatest single reason why the war came and why it took the course and character it did.

Germany and Italy and Russia and Japan were the lions of

the awful fable now to be enacted: Japan had never had, apparently, a modern crisis of its faiths, and Germany and Italy and Russia had had their crises long enough before to have had their reactions, too. Both the reactions were false, the communist reaction and the fascist reaction, but for the purpose and the moment that was not important. What was important was that the reactions had brought men to the top who knew exactly what they believed and what they wanted, who were passionately and recklessly and ruthlessly determined to get what they wanted, and who had far-reaching, comprehensive plans for getting what they wanted.

France and Britain, though, were the lambs of the fable: their crises of faith had proceeded far enough to confuse and demoralize but they had not proceeded far enough to produce a reaction, either a true reaction or a false reaction, and the men still at the top were men who still did not know what they believed or what they wanted and who therefore could not be resolute because they did not know what they could or should be resolute about.

The shock of war itself produced a reaction of a sort, but it produced it disastrously late. In France the reaction came too late. In Britain only time would tell whether the reaction had come too late or not. But even if Britain survived, the reaction that would have saved her was only a temporary and, in this sense, a false reaction: It was no solution of the fundamental problem of faith. That problem remained unsolved.

THE PROBLEM OF IDEAS

The final, tragic paradox of the world-wide crisis of faith is that the German and Italian peoples, at least, whatever may be true of the Russians and Japanese, believe even less in their "new" faiths than the French and British believe in their old ones. Fascism and national socialism are false, and they are unsound in the long run, and the Italians and Germans know in their hearts that they are false and unsound in the long run. The war is a nightmare to the Germans and Italians even more than it is to the French and British.

The Italians are skeptics to begin with, they have had enough experience of fascism to learn beyond doubt how false and weak is it, Italy is feeble, Italy's grievance is feeble, and Italy began to lose the war, so Italy collapsed.

The Germans, though, are essentially believers by nature, they have had too little experience of national socialism to have to admit its falseness and weakness in full to themselves, Germany is strong, Germany's grievance is bitter and Germany has been winning the war—or at least the battles—so the Germans have gone on fighting. They have to try to believe in something and the only thing they can even try to believe in is national socialism—that and Germany and German success.

This is the lesson that has to be learned from the world-wide counter-revolution, the lesson that men's faiths must be reanimated. The problem of stopping Hitler is not only a problem of arms. It is even more a problem of faith and of ideas, and has been from the first. If either the arms or the faith and ideas fail the British, then Germany has won. If both are found in time, then Britain has won.

And even if the British do win, although most particularly, perhaps, if they do not, a true new faith and true new order will still have to be found. For until true new ones are found, there will always be false ones to deal with, because there will always be nazis everywhere to propose and propagate them and there will always be palsied leaders everywhere to abdicate before them and panic-stricken peoples everywhere to embrace them.

THE CHANCE MEN HAVE

Tempered in the holocaust, a new faith is emerging from the war. It began to emerge with the First Battle for Britain:

The battle began on August 8 and ended on October 8, 1940. The Germans lost it.

Germany might still win the war in the end. Even in this battle, and in the other battles that have followed, the Germans have inflicted much more punishment on Britain than the British have inflicted on the Reich. The nazis still have a margin of immediate military superiority.

But the Germans lost the First Battle for Britain because they failed to achieve the purpose of the battle and drew off. They failed to win control of the air. They could not land an army in Britain and they could not force Britain's capitulation by bombings.

The British, in winning that battle, won much more than just a battle. They won a chance to win the whole war. It seemed a slender chance, but it was a chance, and a chance was a very great deal that Summer and Fall.

More than that, even, the British gave new hope and courage to half a world. They proved that a people sound at the outset could not be brought down from within. They proved that man for man and ship for ship another air force was more than a match for the nazis, that there was no such thing as German invincibility. They proved that the peaceful ways of free societies could produce the leadership that is wanted for survival. They proved that free peoples could have faith and vision and be brave, that they could fight intelligently, even when they had sickeningly few arms to do the fighting with—and that they *would* fight.

If Britain should lose in the end, the chance for peace and decency and freedom is gone for decades, perhaps for generations. But after that battle, the chance will always be there.

And if Britain wins, what will men do with their chance? What will the new faith be?

It is too early yet to know the forms that it will take. But already there is a "faith in faith": a beginning of a new belief that there are such things as truths that men not only can but must believe in—must believe in, not because it might be convenient or comfortable to believe in them (actually, it will be neither), but because they *are* true.

The war is demonstrating again that there are such truths—and that men who cease to believe in them perish. It is demonstrating again truths that a whole generation of men, in an obscene and evil lapse, forgot: that freedom has to be fought for and that some things really are worse than death—that some things really are worth fighting and dying for, because life is not worth living without them.

The new faith will be faith in things that are worth, not only fighting and dying for, but also worth living for. It will be a very old faith, in a sense, because it will be a faith in the dignity and sanctity of the individual human being. But it will also be a new faith, because new means must be found to secure the dignity and sanctity of human beings—to make men really free.

This is the chance that men have—if they will fight for it.

Bibliographical Note

Thanks are hereby expressed to the authors and publishers of the following books which have been quoted and referred to by name in the text of *People Under Hitler:*

Cannon, Walter B., *Bodily Changes in Pain, Hunger, Fear and Rage.* D. Appleton-Century Company. (Second edition.) 1939.

Chakotin, Serge, *The Rape of the Masses.* Alliance Book Corporation. 1940.

D'Abernon, Viscount, *The Diary of an Ambassador.* Doubleday, Doran and Co. 1929, 1930.

Diesel, Eugen, *Germany and the Germans.* The Macmillan Company. 1931.

Drucker, Peter F., *The End of Economic Man.* The John Day Company. 1939.

Guillebaud, C. W., *The Economic Recovery of Germany.* London. Macmillan and Co., Ltd. 1939.

Harsch, Joseph C., *Pattern of Conquest.* Doubleday, Doran and Co. 1941.

Heiden, Konrad, *A History of National Socialism.* Alfred A. Knopf. 1935.

——, *Hitler.* Alfred A. Knopf. 1936.

Kirkpatrick, Clifford, *Nazi Germany: Its Women and Family Life.* The Bobbs-Merrill Company. 1938.

Lengyel, Emil, *Hitler.* Lincoln MacVeagh: The Dial Press. 1932.

Miller, Douglas, *You Can't Do Business with Hitler.* Little, Brown and Company. 1941.

Mowrer, Edgar Ansel, *Germany Puts the Clock Back.* William Morrow & Company. (Revised edition.) 1939.

Olden, Rudolf, *Hitler.* Covici, Friede. 1936.

Reimann, Guenter, *The Vampire Economy.* The Vanguard Press. 1939.

"Reveille, Thomas," *The Spoil of Europe.* W. W. Norton & Company, Inc. 1941.

Roberts, Stephen H., *The House That Hitler Built.* London. Methuen. 1938.

Schuman, Frederick L., *The Nazi Dictatorship.* Alfred A. Knopf. 1935.

Shirer, William L., *Berlin Diary.* Alfred A. Knopf. 1941.

Taylor, Edmond L., *The Strategy of Terror.* Houghton Mifflin Company. 1940.

Wilson, Hugh R., *Diplomat Between Wars.* Longmans, Green and Co. 1941.

Index